Publisher's Note

Science and Health with Key to the Scriptures has a proven, century-long heritage of improving the health and changing the lives of millions of readers around the world. Today, it remains one of the most effective and enduring books on spirituality and healing.

This is a book for thinkers. Whatever your occupation, education, race, or religion, you may have many reasons for reading this book. Perhaps you are exploring the power of prayer. Maybe you are seeking health and well-being. Or perhaps you are questioning the deeper purpose of your existence. Regardless of the reason, you will be rewarded with answers that will enrich your life. To begin to think and live from a spiritual standpoint is to change and improve everything — health, ethics, relationships.

First published in 1875, the message is as relevant now as it was over a century ago — maybe even more so, considering the increased globalization and pace of life today. Its logic and presentation of ideas may startle you momentarily and perhaps present a concept of man entirely new to you. You will also notice some unusual capitalization. These are synonyms for God that you may not have considered before. The open-minded, thoughtful reader will soon discover that the ideas and insights of this book are vitally important.

The column of line numbers in the right margin of each page serves a unique purpose. As you study this book you may find it useful to refer to your favorite passages quickly by page and line number. An additional study aid available from the publisher, *A Complete Concordance to Science and Health with Key to the Scriptures*, also uses the page and line number system to help readers find specific passages.

Since *Science and Health* was first published, science, economics, theology, communication, global relations, and medicine — nearly all facets of our world — have changed. These changes have brought new views and opportunities into our lives with ever-increasing speed and frequency. It is no wonder that more and more people are looking for meaningful answers. This book provides these spiritual answers.

Science and Health comes from Mary Baker Eddy's own searching and finding. The daughter of staunch New England Calvinist parents, she protested against the idea that suffering and pain are God's will. She knew intuitively that God's will was only good, and she turned to the Bible for answers. The insights she gained from her Bible study replaced hopelessness with hope, and fear with love. As she discovered these spiritual laws of God, she explained them in this book *Science and Health*.

Mary Baker Eddy dedicated her life to finding permanent solutions to mankind's struggles. And it is to all humanity that this book is offered. While this book is co-pastor (with the Bible) of the Christian Science church she founded, Mrs. Eddy's intent and hope was that the book would reach beyond denominational boundaries.

Read *Science and Health with Key to the Scriptures* on its own terms. Let it talk to you. Let it reason with you. You will be enriched, transformed, and healed as thousands of others have been for more than a century.

SCIENCE AND HEALTH

WITH KEY TO THE SCRIPTURES

Works of Mary Baker Eddy

SCIENCE AND HEALTH

WITH KEY TO THE SCRIPTURES

BY MARY BAKER EDDY

Marcas Registradas

®

President of Massachusetts Metaphysical College and
Pastor Emeritus of The First Church of Christ, Scientist
Boston, Massachusetts

Published by The First Church of Christ, Scientist, in Boston, Massachusetts, U.S.A.

ISBN 0-87952-038-8
Library of Congress Catalog Card Number 94-72340

Entered according to Act of Congress, in the year 1875, by
Mary Baker Glover
In the Office of the Librarian of Congress, at Washington
Copyright renewed 1903, by Mary Baker G. Eddy
Copyright extended, 1917
Copyright 1890, by Mary Baker G. Eddy
Copyright renewed, 1918
Copyright 1894, by Mary Baker G. Eddy
Copyright renewed, 1922
Copyright 1901, by Mary Baker G. Eddy
Copyright renewed, 1929
Copyright 1906, by Mary Baker G. Eddy
Copyright renewed, 1934

Printed in the United States of America

Ye shall know the truth,
and the truth shall make you free. — JOHN viii. 32

There is nothing either good or bad,
but thinking makes it so. — SHAKESPEARE

Oh! Thou hast heard my prayer;
And I am blest!
This is Thy high behest:—
Thou here, and **everywhere**. — MARY BAKER G. EDDY

Contents

Preface

To those leaning on the sustaining infinite, to-day is   1
big with blessings. The wakeful shepherd beholds
the first faint morning beams, ere cometh the full radiance   3
of a risen day. So shone the pale star to the prophet-
shepherds; yet it traversed the night, and came where, in
cradled obscurity, lay the Bethlehem babe, the human   6
herald of Christ, Truth, who would make plain to be-
nighted understanding the way of salvation through Christ
Jesus, till across a night of error should dawn the morn-   9
ing beams and shine the guiding star of being. The Wisemen were led to behold and to follow this daystar of
divine Science, lighting the way to eternal harmony.   12

The time for thinkers has come. Truth, independent
of doctrines and time-honored systems, knocks at the
portal of humanity. Contentment with the past and   15
the cold conventionality of materialism are crumbling
away. Ignorance of God is no longer the stepping-
stone to faith. The only guarantee of obedience is a   18
right apprehension of Him whom to know aright is
Life eternal. Though empires fall, "the Lord shall
reign forever."   21

A book introduces new thoughts, but it cannot make
them speedily understood. It is the task of the sturdy
pioneer to hew the tall oak and to cut the rough   24
granite. Future ages must declare what the pioneer
has accomplished.

Since the author's discovery of the might of Truth in   27

the treatment of disease as well as of sin, her system has   1
been fully tested and has not been found wanting; but
to reach the heights of Christian Science, man must live   3
in obedience to its divine Principle. To develop the full
might of this Science, the discords of corporeal sense
must yield to the harmony of spiritual sense, even as the   6
science of music corrects false tones and gives sweet concord to sound.

Theology and physics teach that both Spirit and   9
matter are real and good, whereas the fact is that
Spirit is good and real, and matter is Spirit's opposite. The question, What is Truth, is answered by   12
demonstration, — by healing both disease and sin; and
this demonstration shows that Christian healing confers the most health and makes the best men. On this   15
basis Christian Science will have a fair fight. Sickness
has been combated for centuries by doctors using material remedies; but the question arises, Is there less   18
sickness because of these practitioners? A vigorous
"No" is the response deducible from two connate
facts, — the reputed longevity of the Antediluvians,   21
and the rapid multiplication and increased violence of
diseases since the flood.

In the author's work, RETROSPECTION AND INTROSPEC-   24
TION, may be found a biographical sketch, narrating
experiences which led her, in the year 1866, to the discovery of the system that she denominated Christian   27
Science. As early as 1862 she began to write down and
give to friends the results of her Scriptural study, for
the Bible was her sole teacher; but these compositions   30
were crude, — the first steps of a child in the newly discovered world of Spirit.

She also began to jot down her thoughts on the   1
main subject, but these jottings were only infantile
lispings of Truth. A child drinks in the outward world   3
through the eyes and rejoices in the draught. He is
as sure of the world's existence as he is of his own; yet
he cannot describe the world. He finds a few words,   6
and with these he stammeringly attempts to convey his
feeling. Later, the tongue voices the more definite
thought, though still imperfectly.   9

So was it with the author. As a certain poet says of
himself, she "lisped in numbers, for the numbers
came." Certain essays written at that early date are   12
still in circulation among her first pupils; but they are
feeble attempts to state the Principle and practice of
Christian healing, and are not complete nor satisfac-   15
tory expositions of Truth. To-day, though rejoicing
in some progress, she still finds herself a willing disciple at the heavenly gate, waiting for the Mind of   18
Christ.

Her first pamphlet on Christian Science was copy-
righted in 1870; but it did not appear in print until   21
1876, as she had learned that this Science must be
demonstrated by healing, before a work on the subject
could be profitably studied. From 1867 until 1875,   24
copies were, however, in friendly circulation.

Before writing this work, SCIENCE AND HEALTH, she
made copious notes of Scriptural exposition, which   27
have never been published. This was during the years
1867 and 1868. These efforts show her comparative
ignorance of the stupendous Life-problem up to that   30
time, and the degrees by which she came at length
to its solution; but she values them as a parent

may treasure the memorials of a child's growth, and   1
she would not have them changed.

The first edition of SCIENCE AND HEALTH was pub-   3
lished in 1875. Various books on mental healing have
since been issued, most of them incorrect in theory
and filled with plagiarisms from SCIENCE AND HEALTH.   6
They regard the human mind as a healing agent,
whereas this mind is not a factor in the Principle of
Christian Science. A few books, however, which are   9
based on this book, are useful.

The author has not compromised conscience to suit
the general drift of thought, but has bluntly and hon-   12
estly given the text of Truth. She has made no effort
to embellish, elaborate, or treat in full detail so infinite a theme. By thousands of well-authenticated   15
cases of healing, she and her students have proved the
worth of her teachings. These cases for the most part
have been abandoned as hopeless by regular medical   18
attendants. Few invalids will turn to God till all
physical supports have failed, because there is so little
faith in His disposition and power to heal disease.   21

The divine Principle of healing is proved in the
personal experience of any sincere seeker of Truth. Its
purpose is good, and its practice is safer and more po-   24
tent than that of any other sanitary method. The un-
biased Christian thought is soonest touched by Truth,
and convinced of it. Only those quarrel with her   27
method who do not understand her meaning, or discerning the truth, come not to the light lest their
works be reproved. No intellectual proficiency is req-   30
uisite in the learner, but sound morals are most desirable.

Many imagine that the phenomena of physical heal- 1
ing in Christian Science present only a phase of the
action of the human mind, which action in some unex- 3
plained way results in the cure of disease. On the contrary, Christian Science rationally explains that all
other pathological methods are the fruits of human 6
faith in matter, — faith in the workings, not of Spirit,
but of the fleshly mind which must yield to Science.

The physical healing of Christian Science results 9
now, as in Jesus' time, from the operation of divine
Principle, before which sin and disease lose their reality in human consciousness and disappear as naturally 12
and as necessarily as darkness gives place to light and
sin to reformation. Now, as then, these mighty works
are not supernatural, but supremely natural. They are 15
the sign of Immanuel, or "God with us," — a divine
influence ever present in human consciousness and repeating itself, coming now as was promised aforetime, 18

> To preach deliverance to the captives [of sense],
> And recovering of sight to the blind,
> To set at liberty them that are bruised. 21

When God called the author to proclaim His Gospel
to this age, there came also the charge to plant and
water His vineyard. 24

The first school of Christian Science Mind-healing
was started by the author with only one student in
Lynn, Massachusetts, about the year 1867. In 1881, 27
she opened the Massachusetts Metaphysical College in
Boston, under the seal of the Commonwealth, a law
relative to colleges having been passed, which enabled 30
her to get this institution chartered for medical pur-

poses. No charters were granted to Christian Scien- 1
tists for such institutions after 1883, and up to that
date, hers was the only College of this character which 3
had been established in the United States, where
Christian Science was first introduced.

During seven years over four thousand students 6
were taught by the author in this College. Meanwhile
she was pastor of the first established Church of
Christ, Scientist; President of the first Christian Sci- 9
entist Association, convening monthly; publisher of
her own works; and (for a portion of this time) sole
editor and publisher of the Christian Science Journal, 12
the first periodical issued by Christian Scientists. She
closed her College, October 29, 1889, in the height of
its prosperity with a deep-lying conviction that the 15
next two years of her life should be given to the preparation of the revision of SCIENCE AND HEALTH, which
was published in 1891. She retained her charter, and 18
as its President, reopened the College in 1899 as auxil-
iary to her church. Until June 10, 1907, she had never
read this book throughout consecutively in order to elu- 21
cidate her idealism.

In the spirit of Christ's charity, — as one who "hopeth
all things, endureth all things," and is joyful to bear 24
consolation to the sorrowing and healing to the sick, —
she commits these pages to honest seekers for Truth.

MARY BAKER EDDY

SCIENCE AND HEALTH

Chapter 1

Prayer

For verily I say unto you,
That whosoever shall say unto this mountain,
Be thou removed, and be thou cast into the sea;
and shall not doubt in his heart, but shall believe that
those things which he saith shall come to pass;
he shall have whatsoever he saith.
Therefore I say unto you, What things soever ye desire
when ye pray, believe that ye receive them,
and ye shall have them.

Your Father knoweth what things ye have need of,
before ye ask Him. — CHRIST JESUS.

---

he prayer that reforms the sinner and heals the
sick is an absolute faith that all things are
possible to God, — a spiritual understanding of Him, 3
an unselfed love. Regardless of what another may say
or think on this subject, I speak from experience.
Prayer, watching, and working, combined with self-im- 6
molation, are God's gracious means for accomplishing
whatever has been successfully done for the Christianization and health of mankind. 9
    Thoughts unspoken are not unknown to the divine
Mind. Desire is prayer; and no loss can occur from
trusting God with our desires, that they may be 12
moulded and exalted before they take form in words
and in deeds.

What are the motives for prayer? Do we pray to   1
make ourselves better or to benefit those who hear us,

Right motives to enlighten the infinite or to be heard of   3
men? Are we benefited by praying? Yes,
the desire which goes forth hungering after righteousness is blessed of our Father, and it does not return   6
unto us void.

God is not moved by the breath of praise to do more
than He has already done, nor can the infinite do less   9

Deity unchangeable than bestow all good, since He is unchanging wisdom and Love. We can do more for
ourselves by humble fervent petitions, but the All-lov-   12
ing does not grant them simply on the ground of lip-
service, for He already knows all.

Prayer cannot change the Science of being, but it   15
tends to bring us into harmony with it. Goodness at-
tains the demonstration of Truth. A request that
God will save us is not all that is required. The mere   18
habit of pleading with the divine Mind, as one pleads
with a human being, perpetuates the belief in God as
humanly circumscribed, — an error which impedes spirit-   21
ual growth.

God is Love. Can we ask Him to be more? God is
intelligence. Can we inform the infinite Mind of any-   24

God's standard thing He does not already comprehend?
Do we expect to change perfection? Shall
we plead for more at the open fount, which is pour-   27
ing forth more than we accept? The unspoken desire
does bring us nearer the source of all existence and
blessedness.   30

Asking God to *be* God is a vain repetition. God is
"the same yesterday, and to-day, and forever;" and

He who is immutably right will do right without being   1
reminded of His province. The wisdom of man is not
sufficient to warrant him in advising God.   3

Who would stand before a blackboard, and pray the
principle of mathematics to solve the problem? The

The spiritual   rule is already established, and it is our   6
mathematics
task to work out the solution. Shall we
ask the divine Principle of all goodness to do His own
work? His work is done, and we have only to avail   9
ourselves of God's rule in order to receive His blessing, which enables us to work out our own salvation.

The Divine Being must be reflected by man, — else   12
man is not the image and likeness of the patient,
tender, and true, the One "altogether lovely;" but to
understand God is the work of eternity, and demands   15
absolute consecration of thought, energy, and desire.

How empty are our conceptions of Deity! We admit
theoretically that God is good, omnipotent, omni-   18

Prayerful   present, infinite, and then we try to give
ingratitude
information to this infinite Mind. We plead
for unmerited pardon and for a liberal outpouring of   21
benefactions. Are we really grateful for the good
already received? Then we shall avail ourselves of the
blessings we have, and thus be fitted to receive more.   24
Gratitude is much more than a verbal expression of
thanks. Action expresses more gratitude than speech.

If we are ungrateful for Life, Truth, and Love, and   27
yet return thanks to God for all blessings, we are insincere and incur the sharp censure our Master pro-
nounces on hypocrites. In such a case, the only   30
acceptable prayer is to put the finger on the lips and
remember our blessings. While the heart is far from

divine Truth and Love, we cannot conceal the ingrati- 1
tude of barren lives.

What we most need is the prayer of fervent desire 3
for growth in grace, expressed in patience, meekness,

Efficacious
petitions
love, and good deeds. To keep the commandments of our Master and follow his 6
example, is our proper debt to him and the only
worthy evidence of our gratitude for all that he has
done. Outward worship is not of itself sufficient to 9
express loyal and heartfelt gratitude, since he has
said: "If ye love me, keep my commandments."

The habitual struggle to be always good is unceas- 12
ing prayer. Its motives are made manifest in the
blessings they bring, — blessings which, even if not
acknowledged in audible words, attest our worthiness 15
to be partakers of Love.

Simply asking that we may love God will never
make us love Him; but the longing to be better 18

Watchfulness
requisite
and holier, expressed in daily watchfulness and in striving to assimilate more of
the divine character, will mould and fashion us 21
anew, until we awake in His likeness. We reach the
Science of Christianity through demonstration of the
divine nature; but in this wicked world goodness 24
will "be evil spoken of," and patience must bring
experience.

Audible prayer can never do the works of spiritual 27
understanding, which regenerates; but silent prayer,

Veritable
devotion
watchfulness, and devout obedience enable
us to follow Jesus' example. Long prayers, 30
superstition, and creeds clip the strong pinions of love,
and clothe religion in human forms. Whatever mate-

rializes worship hinders man's spiritual growth and keeps 1
him from demonstrating his power over error.

Sorrow for wrong-doing is but one step towards reform 3
and the very easiest step. The next and great step re-
Sorrow and reformation quired by wisdom is the test of our sincerity,
— namely, reformation. To this end we are 6
placed under the stress of circumstances. Temptation
bids us repeat the offence, and woe comes in return for
what is done. So it will ever be, till we learn that there 9
is no discount in the law of justice and that we must pay
"the uttermost farthing." The measure ye mete "shall
be measured to you again," and it will be full "and run- 12
ning over."

Saints and sinners get their full award, but not always
in this world. The followers of Christ drank his cup. 15
Ingratitude and persecution filled it to the brim; but God
pours the riches of His love into the understanding and
affections, giving us strength according to our day. Sin- 18
ners flourish "like a green bay tree;" but, looking farther,
the Psalmist could see their end, — the destruction of sin
through suffering. 21

Prayer is not to be used as a confessional to cancel sin.
Such an error would impede true religion. Sin is forgiven
Cancellation of human sin only as it is destroyed by Christ, — Truth and 24
Life. If prayer nourishes the belief that sin is
cancelled, and that man is made better merely by praying,
prayer is an evil. He grows worse who continues in sin 27
because he fancies himself forgiven.

An apostle says that the Son of God [Christ] came to
Diabolism destroyed "destroy the *works* of the devil." We should 30
follow our divine Exemplar, and seek the de-
struction of all evil works, error and disease included.

We cannot escape the penalty due for sin. The Scrip- 1
tures say, that if we deny Christ, "he also will deny us."

Divine Love corrects and governs man. Men may 3
pardon, but this divine Principle alone reforms the

Pardon and amendment sinner. God is not separate from the wisdom He bestows. The talents He gives we 6
must improve. Calling on Him to forgive our work
badly done or left undone, implies the vain supposition
that we have nothing to do but to ask pardon, and 9
that afterwards we shall be free to repeat the offence.

To cause suffering as the result of sin, is the means
of destroying sin. Every supposed pleasure in sin 12
will furnish more than its equivalent of pain, until belief in material life and sin is destroyed. To reach
heaven, the harmony of being, we must understand 15
the divine Principle of being.

"God is Love." More than this we cannot ask,
higher we cannot look, farther we cannot go. To 18

Mercy without partiality suppose that God forgives or punishes sin
according as His mercy is sought or un-
sought, is to misunderstand Love and to make prayer 21
the safety-valve for wrong-doing.

Jesus uncovered and rebuked sin before he cast it
out. Of a sick woman he said that Satan had bound 24

Divine severity her, and to Peter he said, "Thou art an offence unto me." He came teaching and
showing men how to destroy sin, sickness, and death. 27
He said of the fruitless tree, "[It] is hewn down."

It is believed by many that a certain magistrate,
who lived in the time of Jesus, left this record: "His 30
rebuke is fearful." The strong language of our Master confirms this description.

The only civil sentence which he had for error was, 1
"Get thee behind me, Satan." Still stronger evidence
that Jesus' reproof was pointed and pungent is found 3
in his own words, — showing the necessity for such
forcible utterance, when he cast out devils and healed
the sick and sinning. The relinquishment of error de- 6
prives material sense of its false claims.

Audible prayer is impressive; it gives momentary
solemnity and elevation to thought. But does it pro- 9

Audible
praying

duce any lasting benefit? Looking deeply
into these things, we find that "a zeal . . .
not according to knowledge" gives occasion for reac- 12
tion unfavorable to spiritual growth, sober resolve, and
wholesome perception of God's requirements. The motives for verbal prayer may embrace too much love of 15
applause to induce or encourage Christian sentiment.

Physical sensation, not Soul, produces material ecstasy and emotion. If spiritual sense always guided 18

Emotional
utterances

men, there would grow out of ecstatic moments a higher experience and a better life
with more devout self-abnegation and purity. A self- 21
satisfied ventilation of fervent sentiments never makes
a Christian. God is not influenced by man. The "divine ear" is not an auditory nerve. It is the all-hearing 24
and all-knowing Mind, to whom each need of man is
always known and by whom it will be supplied.

The danger from prayer is that it may lead us into temp- 27
tation. By it we may become involuntary hypocrites, ut-

Danger
from audible
prayer

tering desires which are not real and consoling
ourselves in the midst of sin with the recollection 30
that we have prayed over it or mean to ask forgiveness at some later day. Hypocrisy is fatal to religion.

A wordy prayer may afford a quiet sense of self-   1
justification, though it makes the sinner a hypocrite.
We never need to despair of an honest heart; but   3
there is little hope for those who come only spasmodi-
cally face to face with their wickedness and then seek to
hide it. Their prayers are indexes which do not correspond   6
with their character. They hold secret fellowship with
sin, and such externals are spoken of by Jesus as "like
unto whited sepulchres . . . full . . . of all uncleanness."   9

If a man, though apparently fervent and prayerful,
is impure and therefore insincere, what must be the
Aspiration comment upon him? If he reached the   12
and love loftiness of his prayer, there would be no
occasion for comment. If we feel the aspiration, humility, gratitude, and love which our words express, —   15
this God accepts; and it is wise not to try to deceive
ourselves or others, for "there is nothing covered that
shall not be revealed." Professions and audible pray-   18
ers are like charity in one respect, — they "cover the
multitude of sins." Praying for humility with whatever fervency of expression does not always mean a   21
desire for it. If we turn away from the poor, we are
not ready to receive the reward of Him who blesses
the poor. We confess to having a very wicked heart   24
and ask that it may be laid bare before us, but do
we not already know more of this heart than we are
willing to have our neighbor see?   27

We should examine ourselves and learn what is the
affection and purpose of the heart, for in this way
Searching only can we learn what we honestly are. If a   30
the heart friend informs us of a fault, do we listen patiently to the rebuke and credit what is said? Do we not

rather give thanks that we are "not as other men"? 1
During many years the author has been most grateful
for merited rebuke. The wrong lies in unmerited cen- 3
sure, — in the falsehood which does no one any good.

The test of all prayer lies in the answer to these
questions: Do we love our neighbor better because of 6

Summit of aspiration

this asking? Do we pursue the old selfishness, satisfied with having prayed for something better, though we give no evidence of the sin- 9
cerity of our requests by living consistently with our
prayer? If selfishness has given place to kindness,
we shall regard our neighbor unselfishly, and bless 12
them that curse us; but we shall never meet this great
duty simply by asking that it may be done. There is
a cross to be taken up before we can enjoy the fruition 15
of our hope and faith.

Dost thou "love the Lord thy God with all thy
heart, and with all thy soul, and with all thy mind"? 18

Practical religion

This command includes much, even the sur-
render of all merely material sensation, affection, and worship. This is the El Dorado of Christianity. 21
It involves the Science of Life, and recognizes only the
divine control of Spirit, in which Soul is our master,
and material sense and human will have no place. 24

Are you willing to leave all for Christ, for Truth, and
so be counted among sinners? No! Do you really desire

The chalice sacrificial

to attain this point? No! Then why make long 27
prayers about it and ask to be Christians,
since you do not care to tread in the footsteps of our
dear Master? If unwilling to follow his example, why 30
pray with the lips that you may be partakers of his
nature? Consistent prayer is the desire to do right.

Prayer means that we desire to walk and will walk in   1
the light so far as we receive it, even though with bleeding footsteps, and that waiting patiently on the Lord,   3
we will leave our real desires to be rewarded by Him.

The world must grow to the spiritual understanding
of prayer. If good enough to profit by Jesus' cup of   6
earthly sorrows, God will sustain us under these sorrows. Until we are thus divinely qualified and are
willing to drink his cup, millions of vain repetitions   9
will never pour into prayer the unction of Spirit in
demonstration of power and "with signs following."
Christian Science reveals a necessity for overcoming the   12
world, the flesh, and evil, and thus destroying all error.

Seeking is not sufficient. It is striving that enables
us to enter. Spiritual attainments open the door to a   15
higher understanding of the divine Life.

One of the forms of worship in Thibet is to carry a
praying-machine through the streets, and stop at the   18

Perfunctory prayers

doors to earn a penny by grinding out a
prayer. But the advance guard of progress has
paid for the privilege of prayer the price of persecution.   21

Experience teaches us that we do not always receive
the blessings we ask for in prayer. There is some mis-

Asking amiss

apprehension of the source and means of   24
all goodness and blessedness, or we should
certainly receive that for which we ask. The Scriptures say: "Ye ask, and receive not, because ye ask   27
amiss, that ye may consume it upon your lusts." That
which we desire and for which we ask, it is not always
best for us to receive. In this case infinite Love will   30
not grant the request. Do you ask wisdom to be mer-
ciful and not to punish sin? Then "ye ask amiss."

Without punishment, sin would multiply. Jesus' prayer, 1
"Forgive us our debts," specified also the terms of
forgiveness. When forgiving the adulterous woman he 3
said, "Go, and sin no more."

A magistrate sometimes remits the penalty, but this
may be no moral benefit to the criminal, and at best, it 6

Remission of penalty only saves the criminal from one form of
punishment. The moral law, which has the
right to acquit or condemn, always demands restitu- 9
tion before mortals can "go up higher." Broken law
brings penalty in order to compel this progress.

Mere legal pardon (and there is no other, for divine 12
Principle never pardons our sins or mistakes till they

Truth annihilates error are corrected) leaves the offender free to repeat the offence, if indeed, he has not already 15
suffered sufficiently from vice to make him turn from it
with loathing. Truth bestows no pardon upon error, but
wipes it out in the most effectual manner. Jesus suffered 18
for our sins, not to annul the divine sentence for an individual's sin, but because sin brings inevitable suffering.

Petitions bring to mortals only the results of mor- 21
tals' own faith. We know that a desire for holiness is

Desire for holiness requisite in order to gain holiness; but if we
desire holiness above all else, we shall sac- 24
rifice everything for it. We must be willing to do this,
that we may walk securely in the only practical road
to holiness. Prayer cannot change the unalterable 27
Truth, nor can prayer alone give us an understanding
of Truth; but prayer, coupled with a fervent habitual
desire to know and do the will of God, will bring us 30
into all Truth. Such a desire has little need of audible
expression. It is best expressed in thought and in life.

"The prayer of faith shall save the sick," says the   1
Scripture. What is this healing prayer? A mere request that God will heal the sick has no   3

Prayer for
the sick

power to gain more of the divine presence
than is always at hand. The beneficial effect of
such prayer for the sick is on the human mind, mak-   6
ing it act more powerfully on the body through a blind
faith in God. This, however, is one belief casting out
another, — a belief in the unknown casting out a belief   9
in sickness. It is neither Science nor Truth which
acts through blind belief, nor is it the human understanding of the divine healing Principle as manifested   12
in Jesus, whose humble prayers were deep and conscientious protests of Truth, — of man's likeness to
God and of man's unity with Truth and Love.   15

Prayer to a corporeal God affects the sick like a
drug, which has no efficacy of its own but borrows its
power from human faith and belief. The drug does   18
nothing, because it has no intelligence. It is a mortal
belief, not divine Principle or Love, which causes a
drug to be apparently either poisonous or sanative.   21

The common custom of praying for the recovery of the
sick finds help in blind belief, whereas help should come
from the enlightened understanding. Changes in belief   24
may go on indefinitely, but they are the merchandise of
human thought and not the outgrowth of divine Science.

Does Deity interpose in behalf of one worshipper,   27
and not help another who offers the same measure of

Love impartial
and universal

prayer? If the sick recover because they
pray or are prayed for audibly, only peti-   30
tioners (*per se* or by proxy) should get well. In divine
Science, where prayers are mental, *all* may avail them-

selves of God as "a very present help in trouble." 1
Love is impartial and universal in its adaptation and
bestowals. It is the open fount which cries, "Ho, 3
every one that thirsteth, come ye to the waters."

In public prayer we often go beyond our convictions,
beyond the honest standpoint of fervent desire. If we 6

Public exaggerations are not secretly yearning and openly striving for the accomplishment of all we ask,
our prayers are "vain repetitions," such as the heathen 9
use. If our petitions are sincere, we labor for what we
ask; and our Father, who seeth in secret, will reward
us openly. Can the mere public expression of our de- 12
sires increase them? Do we gain the omnipotent ear
sooner by words than by thoughts? Even if prayer is
sincere, God knows our need before we tell Him or our 15
fellow-beings about it. If we cherish the desire honestly and silently and humbly, God will bless it, and
we shall incur less risk of overwhelming our real 18
wishes with a torrent of words.

If we pray to God as a corporeal person, this will
prevent us from relinquishing the human doubts and 21

Corporeal ignorance fears which attend such a belief, and so we
cannot grasp the wonders wrought by infi-
nite, incorporeal Love, to whom all things are possible. 24
Because of human ignorance of the divine Principle,
Love, the Father of all is represented as a corporeal
creator; hence men recognize themselves as merely 27
physical, and are ignorant of man as God's image or reflection and of man's eternal incorporeal existence. The
world of error is ignorant of the world of Truth, — blind 30
to the reality of man's existence, — for the world of sensation is not cognizant of life in Soul, not in body.

If we are sensibly with the body and regard omnipo-   1
tence as a corporeal, material person, whose ear we

Bodily
presence
would gain, we are not "absent from the   3
body" and "present with the Lord" in the
demonstration of Spirit. We cannot "serve two masters." To be "present with the Lord" is to have, not   6
mere emotional ecstasy or faith, but the actual demonstration and understanding of Life as revealed in
Christian Science. To be "with the Lord" is to be in   9
obedience to the law of God, to be absolutely governed
by divine Love, — by Spirit, not by matter.

Become conscious for a single moment that Life and   12
intelligence are purely spiritual, — neither in nor of

Spiritualized
consciousness
matter, — and the body will then utter no
complaints. If suffering from a belief in   15
sickness, you will find yourself suddenly well. Sorrow
is turned into joy when the body is controlled by spiritual Life, Truth, and Love. Hence the hope of the   18
promise Jesus bestows: "He that believeth on me,
the works that I do shall he do also; . . . because I
go unto my Father," — [because the Ego is absent from   21
the body, and present with Truth and Love.] The
Lord's Prayer is the prayer of Soul, not of material
sense.   24

Entirely separate from the belief and dream of material living, is the Life divine, revealing spiritual understanding and the consciousness of man's dominion   27
over the whole earth. This understanding casts out
error and heals the sick, and with it you can speak
"as one having authority."   30

"When thou prayest, enter into thy closet, and,
when thou hast shut thy door, pray to thy Father

which is in secret; and thy Father, which seeth in 1
secret, shall reward thee openly."

So spake Jesus. The closet typifies the sanctuary of 3
Spirit, the door of which shuts out sinful sense but
Spiritual sanctuary lets in Truth, Life, and Love. Closed to
error, it is open to Truth, and *vice versa.* 6
The Father in secret is unseen to the physical senses,
but He knows all things and rewards according to
motives, not according to speech. To enter into the 9
heart of prayer, the door of the erring senses must be
closed. Lips must be mute and materialism silent,
that man may have audience with Spirit, the divine 12
Principle, Love, which destroys all error.

In order to pray aright, we must enter into the
closet and shut the door. We must close the lips and 15
Effectual invocation silence the material senses. In the quiet
sanctuary of earnest longings, we must
deny sin and plead God's allness. We must resolve to 18
take up the cross, and go forth with honest hearts to
work and watch for wisdom, Truth, and Love. We
must "pray without ceasing." Such prayer is an- 21
swered, in so far as we put our desires into practice.
The Master's injunction is, that we pray in secret and
let our lives attest our sincerity. 24

Christians rejoice in secret beauty and bounty, hidden
from the world, but known to God. Self-forgetfulness,
Trustworthy beneficence purity, and affection are constant prayers. 27
Practice not profession, understanding not
belief, gain the ear and right hand of omnipotence and
they assuredly call down infinite blessings. Trustworthi- 30
ness is the foundation of enlightened faith. Without a
fitness for holiness, we cannot receive holiness.

A great sacrifice of material things must precede this   1
advanced spiritual understanding. The highest prayer

Loftiest
adoration
is not one of faith merely; it is demonstra-   3
tion. Such prayer heals sickness, and must
destroy sin and death. It distinguishes between Truth
that is sinless and the falsity of sinful sense.   6

Our Master taught his disciples one brief prayer,
which we name after him the Lord's Prayer. Our Mas-

The prayer of
Jesus Christ
ter said, "After this manner therefore pray   9
ye," and then he gave that prayer which
covers all human needs. There is indeed some doubt
among Bible scholars, whether the last line is not an   12
addition to the prayer by a later copyist; but this does
not affect the meaning of the prayer itself.

In the phrase, "Deliver us from evil," the original   15
properly reads, "Deliver us from the evil one." This
reading strengthens our scientific apprehension of the peti-
tion, for Christian Science teaches us that "the evil one," or   18
one evil, is but another name for the first lie and all liars.

Only as we rise above all material sensuousness and
sin, can we reach the heaven-born aspiration and spir-   21
itual consciousness, which is indicated in the Lord's
Prayer and which instantaneously heals the sick.

Here let me give what I understand to be the spir-   24
itual sense of the Lord's Prayer:

Our Father which art in heaven,
   Our Father-Mother God, all-harmonious,   27

Hallowed be Thy name.
   Adorable One.

Thy kingdom come.   30
   Thy kingdom is come; Thou art ever-present.

Thy will be done in earth, as it is in heaven. 1
Enable us to know, — as in heaven, so on earth, — God is
omnipotent, supreme. 3

Give us this day our daily bread;
Give us grace for to-day; feed the famished affections;

And forgive us our debts, as we forgive our debtors. 6
And Love is reflected in love;

And lead us not into temptation, but deliver us from
evil; 9
And God leadeth us not into temptation, but delivereth
us from sin, disease, and death.

For Thine is the kingdom, and the power, and the 12
glory, forever.
For God is infinite, all-power, all Life, Truth, Love, over
all, and All. 15

Chapter 2

Atonement and Eucharist

And they that are Christ's have crucified the flesh
with the affections and lusts. — PAUL.

For Christ sent me not to baptize,
but to preach the gospel. — PAUL.

For I say unto you,
I will not drink of the fruit of the vine,
until the kingdom of God shall come. — JESUS.

A tonement is the exemplification of man's unity 1
with God, whereby man reflects divine Truth, Life,
and Love. Jesus of Nazareth taught and demonstrated 3
man's oneness with the Father, and for this we owe him
Divine endless homage. His mission was both in-
oneness dividual and collective. He did life's work 6
aright not only in justice to himself, but in mercy to
mortals, — to show them how to do theirs, but not to do
it for them nor to relieve them of a single responsibility. 9
Jesus acted boldly, against the accredited evidence of the
senses, against Pharisaical creeds and practices, and he
refuted all opponents with his healing power. 12

The atonement of Christ reconciles man to God, not
God to man; for the divine Principle of Christ is God,
Human and how can God propitiate Himself? Christ 15
reconciliation is Truth, which reaches no higher than itself.
The fountain can rise no higher than its source. Christ,
Truth, could conciliate no nature above his own, derived 18

from the eternal Love. It was therefore Christ's purpose   1
to reconcile man to God, not God to man. Love and
Truth are not at war with God's image and likeness.   3
Man cannot exceed divine Love, and so atone for himself. Even Christ cannot reconcile Truth to error, for
Truth and error are irreconcilable. Jesus aided in recon-   6
ciling man to God by giving man a truer sense of Love,
the divine Principle of Jesus' teachings, and this truer
sense of Love redeems man from the law of matter,   9
sin, and death by the law of Spirit, — the law of divine
Love.

The Master forbore not to speak the whole truth, de-   12
claring precisely what would destroy sickness, sin, and
death, although his teaching set households at variance,
and brought to material beliefs not peace, but a   15
sword.

Every pang of repentance and suffering, every effort
for reform, every good thought and deed, will help us to   18

Efficacious repentance understand Jesus' atonement for sin and aid
its efficacy; but if the sinner continues to pray
and repent, sin and be sorry, he has little part in the atone-   21
ment, — in the *at-one-ment* with God, — for he lacks the
practical repentance, which reforms the heart and enables
man to do the will of wisdom. Those who cannot dem-   24
onstrate, at least in part, the divine Principle of the teachings and practice of our Master have no part in God. If
living in disobedience to Him, we ought to feel no secur-   27
ity, although God is good.

Jesus urged the commandment, "Thou shalt have no
Jesus' sinless career other gods before me," which may be ren-   30
dered: Thou shalt have no belief of Life as
mortal; thou shalt not know evil, for there is one Life, —

even God, good. He rendered "unto Caesar the things   1
which are Caesar's; and unto God the things that are
God's." He at last paid no homage to forms of doctrine   3
or to theories of man, but acted and spake as he was moved,
not by spirits but by Spirit.

To the ritualistic priest and hypocritical Pharisee   6
Jesus said, "The publicans and the harlots go into the
kingdom of God before you." Jesus' history made a
new calendar, which we call the Christian era; but he   9
established no ritualistic worship. He knew that men
can be baptized, partake of the Eucharist, support the
clergy, observe the Sabbath, make long prayers, and yet   12
be sensual and sinful.

Jesus bore our infirmities; he knew the error of mortal
belief, and "with his stripes [the rejection of error] we are   15

Perfect example

healed." "Despised and rejected of men,"
returning blessing for cursing, he taught mor-
tals the opposite of themselves, even the nature of God;   18
and when error felt the power of Truth, the scourge and
the cross awaited the great Teacher. Yet he swerved not,
well knowing that to obey the divine order and trust God,   21
saves retracing and traversing anew the path from sin to
holiness.

Material belief is slow to acknowledge what the   24
spiritual fact implies. The truth is the centre of all

Behest of the cross

religion. It commands sure entrance into
the realm of Love. St. Paul wrote, "Let us   27
lay aside every weight, and the sin which doth so
easily beset us, and let us run with patience the race that
is set before us;" that is, let us put aside material self   30
and sense, and seek the divine Principle and Science of
all healing.

Moral victory

If Truth is overcoming error in your daily walk and 1
conversation, you can finally say, "I have fought a
good fight . . . I have kept the faith," be- 3
cause you are a better man. This is having
our part in the at-one-ment with Truth and Love.
Christians do not continue to labor and pray, expecting 6
because of another's goodness, suffering, and triumph,
that they shall reach his harmony and reward.

If the disciple is advancing spiritually, he is striv- 9
ing to enter in. He constantly turns away from material sense, and looks towards the imperishable things
of Spirit. If honest, he will be in earnest from the 12
start, and gain a little each day in the right direction,
till at last he finishes his course with joy.

If my friends are going to Europe, while I am *en* 15
route for California, we are not journeying together.

Inharmonious travellers

We have separate time-tables to consult,
different routes to pursue. Our paths have 18
diverged at the very outset, and we have little opportunity to help each other. On the contrary, if my
friends pursue my course, we have the same railroad 21
guides, and our mutual interests are identical; or, if I
take up their line of travel, they help me on, and our
companionship may continue. 24

Being in sympathy with matter, the worldly man is at
the beck and call of error, and will be attracted thither-

Zigzag course

ward. He is like a traveller going westward 27
for a pleasure-trip. The company is alluring
and the pleasures exciting. After following the sun for
six days, he turns east on the seventh, satisfied if he can 30
only imagine himself drifting in the right direction. By-
and-by, ashamed of his zigzag course, he would borrow

the passport of some wiser pilgrim, thinking with the aid   1
of this to find and follow the right road.

Vibrating like a pendulum between sin and the hope   3
of forgiveness, — selfishness and sensuality causing con-

Moral retrogression   stant retrogression, — our moral progress will
be slow. Waking to Christ's demand, mortals   6
experience suffering. This causes them, even as drowning men, to make vigorous efforts to save themselves; and
through Christ's precious love these efforts are crowned   9
with success.

"Work out your own salvation," is the demand of
Life and Love, for to this end God worketh with you.   12

Wait for reward   "Occupy till I come!" Wait for your reward, and "be not weary in well doing." If
your endeavors are beset by fearful odds, and you receive   15
no present reward, go not back to error, nor become a
sluggard in the race.

When the smoke of battle clears away, you will dis-   18
cern the good you have done, and receive according to
your deserving. Love is not hasty to deliver us from
temptation, for Love means that we shall be tried and   21
purified.

Final deliverance from error, whereby we rejoice in
immortality, boundless freedom, and sinless sense, is not   24

Deliverance not vicarious   reached through paths of flowers nor by pinning
one's faith without works to another's vicarious
effort. Whosoever believeth that wrath is righteous or   27
that divinity is appeased by human suffering, does not
understand God.

Justice requires reformation of the sinner. Mercy   30
cancels the debt only when justice approves. Revenge
is inadmissible. Wrath which is only appeased is not

destroyed, but partially indulged. Wisdom and Love   1
may require many sacrifices of self to save us from sin.

Justice and substitution   One sacrifice, however great, is insufficient to   3
pay the debt of sin. The atonement requires
constant self-immolation on the sinner's part. That
God's wrath should be vented upon His beloved Son, is   6
divinely unnatural. Such a theory is man-made. The
atonement is a hard problem in theology, but its scientific explanation is, that suffering is an error of sinful sense   9
which Truth destroys, and that eventually both sin and suffering will fall at the feet of everlasting Love.

Rabbinical lore said: "He that taketh one doctrine,   12
firm in faith, has the Holy Ghost dwelling in him."

Doctrines and faith   This preaching receives a strong rebuke in
the Scripture, "Faith without works is dead."   15
Faith, if it be mere belief, is as a pendulum swinging between nothing and something, having no fixity. Faith,
advanced to spiritual understanding, is the evidence gained   18
from Spirit, which rebukes sin of every kind and estab-
lishes the claims of God.

In Hebrew, Greek, Latin, and English, *faith* and the   21
words corresponding thereto have these two defini-

Self-reliance and confidence   tions, *trustfulness* and *trustworthiness*. One
kind of faith trusts one's welfare to others.   24
Another kind of faith understands divine Love and how
to work out one's "own salvation, with fear and trembling." "Lord, I believe; help thou mine unbelief!"   27
expresses the helplessness of a blind faith; whereas the
injunction, "Believe . . . and thou shalt be saved!"
demands self-reliant trustworthiness, which includes spir-   30
itual understanding and confides all to God.

The Hebrew verb *to believe* means also *to be firm* or

to be constant. This certainly applies to Truth and Love 1
understood and practised. Firmness in error will never
save from sin, disease, and death. 3

Acquaintance with the original texts, and willingness
to give up human beliefs (established by hierarchies, and
Life's healing instigated sometimes by the worst passions of 6
currents
men), open the way for Christian Science to be
understood, and make the Bible the chart of life, where
the buoys and healing currents of Truth are pointed 9
out.

He to whom "the arm of the Lord" is revealed will
believe our report, and rise into newness of life with re- 12
Radical generation. This is having part in the atone-
changes
ment; this is the understanding, in which
Jesus suffered and triumphed. The time is not distant 15
when the ordinary theological views of atonement will
undergo a great change, — a change as radical as that
which has come over popular opinions in regard to pre- 18
destination and future punishment.

Does erudite theology regard the crucifixion of Jesus
chiefly as providing a ready pardon for all sinners who 21
Purpose of ask for it and are willing to be forgiven?
crucifixion
Does spiritualism find Jesus' death necessary
only for the presentation, after death, of the material 24
Jesus, as a proof that spirits can return to earth? Then
we must differ from them both.

The efficacy of the crucifixion lay in the practical af- 27
fection and goodness it demonstrated for mankind. The
truth had been lived among men; but until they saw that
it enabled their Master to triumph over the grave, his own 30
disciples could not admit such an event to be possible.
After the resurrection, even the unbelieving Thomas was

forced to acknowledge how complete was the great proof of   1
Truth and Love.

The spiritual essence of blood is sacrifice. The effi-   3
cacy of Jesus' spiritual offering is infinitely greater than

True flesh and blood can be expressed by our sense of human
blood. The material blood of Jesus was no   6
more efficacious to cleanse from sin when it was shed
upon "the accursed tree," than when it was flowing in
his veins as he went daily about his Father's business.   9
His true flesh and blood were his Life; and they truly eat
his flesh and drink his blood, who partake of that divine
Life.   12

Jesus taught the way of Life by demonstration, that
we may understand how this divine Principle heals

Effective triumph the sick, casts out error, and triumphs over   15
death. Jesus presented the ideal of God better
than could any man whose origin was less spiritual. By
his obedience to God, he demonstrated more spiritu-   18
ally than all others the Principle of being. Hence the
force of his admonition, "If ye love me, keep my commandments."   21

Though demonstrating his control over sin and disease,
the great Teacher by no means relieved others from giving
the requisite proofs of their own piety. He worked for   24
their guidance, that they might demonstrate this power as
he did and understand its divine Principle. Implicit faith
in the Teacher and all the emotional love we can bestow   27
on him, will never alone make us imitators of him. We
must go and do likewise, else we are not improving the
great blessings which our Master worked and suffered to   30
bestow upon us. The divinity of the Christ was made
manifest in the humanity of Jesus.

While we adore Jesus, and the heart overflows with   1
gratitude for what he did for mortals, — treading alone
his loving pathway up to the throne of   3
glory, in speechless agony exploring the way
for us, — yet Jesus spares us not one individual experience, if we follow his commands faithfully; and all   6
have the cup of sorrowful effort to drink in proportion
to their demonstration of his love, till all are redeemed
through divine Love.   9

The Christ was the Spirit which Jesus implied in his
own statements: "I am the way, the truth, and the life;"
"I and my Father are one." This Christ,   12
or divinity of the man Jesus, was his divine
nature, the godliness which animated him. Divine Truth,
Life, and Love gave Jesus authority over sin, sickness,   15
and death. His mission was to reveal the Science of
celestial being, to prove what God is and what He does
for man.   18

A musician demonstrates the beauty of the music he
teaches in order to show the learner the way by practice as well as precept. Jesus' teaching and   21
practice of Truth involved such a sacrifice
as makes us admit its Principle to be Love. This was
the precious import of our Master's sinless career and   24
of his demonstration of power over death. He proved
by his deeds that Christian Science destroys sickness, sin,
and death.   27

Our Master taught no mere theory, doctrine, or belief.
It was the divine Principle of all real being which he
taught and practised. His proof of Christianity was no   30
form or system of religion and worship, but Christian
Science, working out the harmony of Life and Love.

Jesus sent a message to John the Baptist, which was in-   1
tended to prove beyond a question that the Christ had
come: "Go your way, and tell John what things ye have   3
seen and heard; how that the blind see, the lame walk,
the lepers are cleansed, the deaf hear, the dead are raised,
to the poor the gospel is preached." In other words: 6
Tell John what the demonstration of divine power is,
and he will at once perceive that God is the power in
the Messianic work.   9

That Life is God, Jesus proved by his reappearance
after the crucifixion in strict accordance with his scien-
Living   tific statement: "Destroy this temple [body],   12
temple   and in three days I [Spirit] will raise it up."
It is as if he had said: The I — the Life, substance,
and intelligence of the universe — is not in matter to   15
be destroyed.

Jesus' parables explain Life as never mingling with
sin and death. He laid the axe of Science at the root   18
of material knowledge, that it might be ready to cut
down the false doctrine of pantheism, — that God, or
Life, is in or of matter.   21

Jesus sent forth seventy students at one time, but only
eleven left a desirable historic record. Tradition credits
Recreant   him with two or three hundred other disciples   24
disciples   who have left no name. "Many are called,
but few are chosen." They fell away from grace because
they never truly understood their Master's instruction.   27

Why do those who profess to follow Christ reject the
essential religion he came to establish? Jesus' persecutors made their strongest attack upon this very point.   30
They endeavored to hold him at the mercy of matter and
to kill him according to certain assumed material laws.

The Pharisees claimed to know and to teach the di- 1
vine will, but they only hindered the success of Jesus'

Help and hindrance mission. Even many of his students stood 3
in his way. If the Master had not taken a
student and taught the unseen verities of God, he would
not have been crucified. The determination to hold Spirit 6
in the grasp of matter is the persecutor of Truth and
Love.

While respecting all that is good in the Church or out 9
of it, one's consecration to Christ is more on the ground
of demonstration than of profession. In conscience, we
cannot hold to beliefs outgrown; and by understanding 12
more of the divine Principle of the deathless Christ, we
are enabled to heal the sick and to triumph over sin.

Neither the origin, the character, nor the work of 15
Jesus was generally understood. Not a single compo-

Misleading conceptions nent part of his nature did the material
world measure aright. Even his righteous- 18
ness and purity did not hinder men from saying: He
is a glutton and a friend of the impure, and Beelzebub is
his patron. 21

Remember, thou Christian martyr, it is enough if
thou art found worthy to unloose the sandals of thy

Persecution prolonged Master's feet! To suppose that persecution 24
for righteousness' sake belongs to the past,
and that Christianity to-day is at peace with the world
because it is honored by sects and societies, is to mis- 27
take the very nature of religion. Error repeats itself.
The trials encountered by prophet, disciple, and apostle,
"of whom the world was not worthy," await, in some 30
form, every pioneer of truth.

There is too much animal courage in society and not

sufficient moral courage. Christians must take up arms 1
against error at home and abroad. They must grapple

Christian warfare

with sin in themselves and in others, and 3
continue this warfare until they have finished
their course. If they keep the faith, they will have the
crown of rejoicing. 6

Christian experience teaches faith in the right and dis-
belief in the wrong. It bids us work the more earnestly
in times of persecution, because then our labor is more 9
needed. Great is the reward of self-sacrifice, though we
may never receive it in this world.

There is a tradition that Publius Lentulus wrote to 12
the authorities at Rome: "The disciples of Jesus be-

The Father-hood of God

lieve him the Son of God." Those instructed
in Christian Science have reached the glori- 15
ous perception that God is the only author of man.
The Virgin-mother conceived this idea of God, and
gave to her ideal the name of Jesus — that is, Joshua, 18
or Saviour.

The illumination of Mary's spiritual sense put to
silence material law and its order of generation, and 21

Spiritual conception

brought forth her child by the revelation of
Truth, demonstrating God as the Father of
men. The Holy Ghost, or divine Spirit, overshadowed 24
the pure sense of the Virgin-mother with the full recog-
nition that being is Spirit. The Christ dwelt forever
an idea in the bosom of God, the divine Principle of the 27
man Jesus, and woman perceived this spiritual idea,
though at first faintly developed.

Man as the offspring of God, as the idea of Spirit, 30
is the immortal evidence that Spirit is harmonious and
man eternal. Jesus was the offspring of Mary's self-

conscious communion with God. Hence he could give   1
a more spiritual idea of life than other men, and could
demonstrate the Science of Love — his Father or divine   3
Principle.

Born of a woman, Jesus' advent in the flesh partook
partly of Mary's earthly condition, although he was en-   6

Jesus the
way-shower

dowed with the Christ, the divine Spirit, without measure. This accounts for his struggles
in Gethsemane and on Calvary, and this enabled him to   9
be the mediator, or *way-shower*, between God and men.
Had his origin and birth been wholly apart from mortal
usage, Jesus would not have been appreciable to mortal   12
mind as "the way."

Rabbi and priest taught the Mosaic law, which said:
"An eye for an eye," and "Whoso sheddeth man's blood,   15
by man shall his blood be shed." Not so did Jesus, the
new executor for God, present the divine law of Love,
which blesses even those that curse it.   18

As the individual ideal of Truth, Christ Jesus came to
rebuke rabbinical error and all sin, sickness, and death, —

Rebukes
helpful

to point out the way of Truth and Life. This   21
ideal was demonstrated throughout the whole
earthly career of Jesus, showing the difference between
the offspring of Soul and of material sense, of Truth and   24
of error.

If we have triumphed sufficiently over the errors of
material sense to allow Soul to hold the control, we   27
shall loathe sin and rebuke it under every mask. Only
in this way can we bless our enemies, though they
may not so construe our words. We cannot choose for   30
ourselves, but must work out our salvation in the way
Jesus taught. In meekness and might, he was found

preaching the gospel to the poor. Pride and fear are unfit
to bear the standard of Truth, and God will never place
it in such hands.

Jesus acknowledged no ties of the flesh. He said: "Call
no man your father upon the earth: for one is your Father,
which is in heaven." Again he asked: "Who
is my mother, and who are my brethren," im-
plying that it is they who do the will of his Father. We
have no record of his calling any man by the name of
father. He recognized Spirit, God, as the only creator, and
therefore as the Father of all.

First in the list of Christian duties, he taught his followers the healing power of Truth and Love. He attached
no importance to dead ceremonies. It is the
living Christ, the practical Truth, which makes
Jesus "the resurrection and the life" to all who follow him
in deed. Obeying his precious precepts, — following his
demonstration so far as we apprehend it, — we drink of
his cup, partake of his bread, are baptized with his purity; and at last we shall rest, sit down with him, in a full
understanding of the divine Principle which triumphs
over death. For what says Paul? "As often as ye eat
this bread, and drink this cup, ye do show the Lord's
death till he come."

Referring to the materiality of the age, Jesus said:
"The hour cometh, and now is, when the true wor-
shippers shall worship the Father in spirit
and in truth." Again, foreseeing the persecution which would attend the Science of Spirit, Jesus
said: "They shall put you out of the synagogues; yea,
the time cometh, that whosoever killeth you will think
that he doeth God service; and these things will they

Fleshly ties temporal

Healing primary

Painful prospect

do unto you, because they have not known the Father   1
nor me."

In ancient Rome a soldier was required to swear   3
allegiance to his general. The Latin word for this oath

was *sacramentum,* and our English word
sacrament is derived from it. Among the   6
Jews it was an ancient custom for the master of a
feast to pass each guest a cup of wine. But the
Eucharist does not commemorate a Roman soldier's   9
oath, nor was the wine, used on convivial occasions and
in Jewish rites, the cup of our Lord. The cup shows
forth his bitter experience, — the cup which he prayed   12
might pass from him, though he bowed in holy submission to the divine decree.

"As they were eating, Jesus took bread, and blessed   15
it and brake it, and gave it to the disciples, and said,
Take, eat; this is my body. And he took the cup, and
gave thanks, and gave it to them saying, Drink ye all   18
of it."

The true sense is spiritually lost, if the sacrament is
confined to the use of bread and wine. The disciples   21

had eaten, yet Jesus prayed and gave them
bread. This would have been foolish in a
literal sense; but in its spiritual signification, it was nat-   24
ural and beautiful. Jesus prayed; he withdrew from the
material senses to refresh his heart with brighter, with
spiritual views.   27

The Passover, which Jesus ate with his disciples in
the month Nisan on the night before his crucifixion,

was a mournful occasion, a sad supper taken   30
at the close of day, in the twilight of a
glorious career with shadows fast falling around; and

this supper closed forever Jesus' ritualism or concessions 1
to matter.

His followers, sorrowful and silent, anticipating the hour 3
of their Master's betrayal, partook of the heavenly manna,

Heavenly supplies which of old had fed in the wilderness the
persecuted followers of Truth. Their bread 6
indeed came down from heaven. It was the great truth
of spiritual being, healing the sick and casting out error.
Their Master had explained it all before, and now this 9
bread was feeding and sustaining them. They had borne
this bread from house to house, *breaking* (explaining) it to
others, and now it comforted themselves. 12

For this truth of spiritual being, their Master was about
to suffer violence and drain to the dregs his cup of sorrow.
He must leave them. With the great glory of an everlast- 15
ing victory overshadowing him, he gave thanks and said,
"Drink ye all of it."

When the human element in him struggled with the 18
divine, our great Teacher said: "Not my will, but

The holy struggle Thine, be done!" — that is, Let not the flesh,
but the Spirit, be represented in me. This 21
is the new understanding of spiritual Love. It gives all
for Christ, or Truth. It blesses its enemies, heals the
sick, casts out error, raises the dead from trespasses 24
and sins, and preaches the gospel to the poor, the meek
in heart.

Christians, are you drinking his cup? Have you 27
shared the blood of the New Covenant, the persecutions

Incisive questions which attend a new and higher understanding of God? If not, can you then say that 30
you have commemorated Jesus in his cup? Are all
who eat bread and drink wine in memory of Jesus willing

truly to drink his cup, take his cross, and leave all for   1
the Christ-principle? Then why ascribe this inspiration to a dead rite, instead of showing, by casting out   3
error and making the body "holy, acceptable unto God,"
that Truth has come to the understanding? If Christ,
Truth, has come to us in demonstration, no other com-   6
memoration is requisite, for demonstration is Immanuel,
or *God with us;* and if a friend be with us, why need we
memorials of that friend?   9

If all who ever partook of the sacrament had really
commemorated the sufferings of Jesus and drunk of

Millennial
glory
his cup, they would have revolutionized the   12
world. If all who seek his commemoration
through material symbols will take up the cross, heal
the sick, cast out evils, and preach Christ, or Truth,   15
to the poor, — the receptive thought, — they will bring
in the millennium.

Through all the disciples experienced, they became more   18
spiritual and understood better what the Master had

Fellowship
with Christ
taught. His resurrection was also their resurrection. It helped them to raise themselves and   21
others from spiritual dulness and blind belief in God into
the perception of infinite possibilities. They needed this
quickening, for soon their dear Master would rise again   24
in the spiritual realm of reality, and ascend far above
their apprehension. As the reward for his faithfulness,
he would disappear to material sense in that change which   27
has since been called the ascension.

What a contrast between our Lord's last supper and

The last
breakfast
his last spiritual breakfast with his disciples   30
in the bright morning hours at the joyful
meeting on the shore of the Galilean Sea! His gloom

had passed into glory, and his disciples' grief into repent- 1
ance, — hearts chastened and pride rebuked. Convinced
of the fruitlessness of their toil in the dark and wakened 3
by their Master's voice, they changed their methods, turned
away from material things, and cast their net on the right
side. Discerning Christ, Truth, anew on the shore of 6
time, they were enabled to rise somewhat from mortal
sensuousness, or the burial of mind in matter, into newness of life as Spirit. 9

This spiritual meeting with our Lord in the dawn of a
new light is the morning meal which Christian Scientists
commemorate. They bow before Christ, Truth, to re- 12
ceive more of his reappearing and silently to commune
with the divine Principle, Love. They celebrate their
Lord's victory over death, his probation in the flesh 15
after death, its exemplification of human probation, and
his spiritual and final ascension above matter, or the flesh,
when he rose out of material sight. 18

Our baptism is a purification from all error. Our
church is built on the divine Principle, Love. We can
Spiritual unite with this church only as we are new- 21
Eucharist born of Spirit, as we reach the Life which
is Truth and the Truth which is Life by bringing forth
the fruits of Love, — casting out error and healing the 24
sick. Our Eucharist is spiritual communion with the one
God. Our bread, "which cometh down from heaven,"
is Truth. Our cup is the cross. Our wine the inspira- 27
tion of Love, the draught our Master drank and com-
mended to his followers.

The design of Love is to reform the sinner. If the 30
sinner's punishment here has been insufficient to reform him, the good man's heaven would be a hell to

the sinner. They, who know not purity and affection by 1
experience, can never find bliss in the blessed company of

Final
purpose

Truth and Love simply through translation 3
into another sphere. Divine Science reveals
the necessity of sufficient suffering, either before or after
death, to quench the love of sin. To remit the penalty 6
due for sin, would be for Truth to pardon error. Escape
from punishment is not in accordance with God's government, since justice is the handmaid of mercy. 9

Jesus endured the shame, that he might pour his
dear-bought bounty into barren lives. What was his
earthly reward? He was forsaken by all save John, 12
the beloved disciple, and a few women who bowed in
silent woe beneath the shadow of his cross. The earthly
price of spirituality in a material age and the great moral 15
distance between Christianity and sensualism preclude
Christian Science from finding favor with the worldly-
minded. 18

A selfish and limited mind may be unjust, but the unlimited and divine Mind is the immortal law of justice as

Righteous
retribution

well as of mercy. It is quite as impossible for 21
sinners to receive their full punishment this
side of the grave as for this world to bestow on the righteous their full reward. It is useless to suppose that the 24
wicked can gloat over their offences to the last moment
and then be suddenly pardoned and pushed into heaven,
or that the hand of Love is satisfied with giving us only 27
toil, sacrifice, cross-bearing, multiplied trials, and mockery of our motives in return for our efforts at well doing.

Vicarious
suffering

Religious history repeats itself in the suf- 30
fering of the just for the unjust. Can God
therefore overlook the law of righteousness which de-

stroys the belief called sin? Does not Science show that 1
sin brings suffering as much to-day as yesterday? They
who sin must suffer. "With what measure ye mete, it 3
shall be measured to you again."

History is full of records of suffering. "The blood of
the martyrs is the seed of the Church." Mortals try in 6

Martyrs inevitable

vain to slay Truth with the steel or the stake,
but error falls only before the sword of Spirit.
Martyrs are the human links which connect one stage with 9
another in the history of religion. They are earth's lumi-
naries, which serve to cleanse and rarefy the atmosphere of
material sense and to permeate humanity with purer ideals. 12
Consciousness of right-doing brings its own reward; but
not amid the smoke of battle is merit seen and appreciated
by lookers-on. 15

When will Jesus' professed followers learn to emulate
him in *all* his ways and to imitate his mighty works?

Complete emulation

Those who procured the martyrdom of that 18
righteous man would gladly have turned his
sacred career into a mutilated doctrinal platform. May
the Christians of to-day take up the more practical im- 21
port of that career! It is possible, — yea, it is the duty
and privilege of every child, man, and woman, — to follow
in some degree the example of the Master by the demon- 24
stration of Truth and Life, of health and holiness. Christians claim to be his followers, but do they follow him in
the way that he commanded? Hear these imperative com- 27
mands: "Be ye therefore perfect, even as your Father
which is in heaven is perfect!" "Go ye into all the world,
and preach the gospel to every creature!" *"Heal the* 30
sick!"

Why has this Christian demand so little inspiration

to stir mankind to Christian effort? Because men are   1
assured that this command was intended only for a par-

Jesus' teaching ticular period and for a select number of fol-   3
belittled   lowers. This teaching is even more pernicious
than the old doctrine of foreordination, — the election of a
few to be saved, while the rest are damned; and so it will   6
be considered, when the lethargy of mortals, produced
by man-made doctrines, is broken by the demands of
divine Science.   9

Jesus said: "These signs shall follow them that believe; . . . they shall lay hands on the sick, and they
shall recover." Who believes him? He was addressing   12
his disciples, yet he did not say, "These signs shall follow
you," but *them* — "them that believe" in all time to come.
Here the word *hands* is used metaphorically, as in the text,   15
"The right hand of the Lord is exalted." It expresses
spiritual power; otherwise the healing could not have
been done spiritually. At another time Jesus prayed, not   18
for the twelve only, but for as many as should believe
"through their word."

Jesus experienced few of the pleasures of the physical   21
senses, but his sufferings were the fruits of other peo-

Material   ple's sins, not of his own. The eternal Christ,
pleasures   his spiritual selfhood, never suffered. Jesus   24
mapped out the path for others. He unveiled the Christ,
the spiritual idea of divine Love. To those buried in the
belief of sin and self, living only for pleasure or the grati-   27
fication of the senses, he said in substance: Having eyes
ye see not, and having ears ye hear not; lest ye should understand and be converted, and I might heal you. He   30
taught that the material senses shut out Truth and its
healing power.

Mockery
of truth

Meekly our Master met the mockery of his unrecog- 1
nized grandeur. Such indignities as he received, his followers will endure until Christianity's last 3
triumph. He won eternal honors. He over-
came the world, the flesh, and all error, thus proving
their nothingness. He wrought a full salvation from sin, 6
sickness, and death. We need "Christ, and him crucified." We must have trials and self-denials, as well as
joys and victories, until all error is destroyed. 9

A belief
suicidal

The educated belief that Soul is in the body causes
mortals to regard death as a friend, as a stepping-stone
out of mortality into immortality and bliss. 12
The Bible calls death an enemy, and Jesus
overcame death and the grave instead of yielding to them.
He was "the way." To him, therefore, death was not 15
the threshold over which he must pass into living
glory.

Present
salvation

"*Now,*" cried the apostle, "is the accepted time; be- 18
hold, *now* is the day of salvation," — meaning, not that
now men must prepare for a future-world salvation, or safety, but that now is the time in which 21
to experience that salvation in spirit and in life. Now is
the time for so-called material pains and material pleasures to pass away, for both are unreal, because impossible 24
in Science. To break this earthly spell, mortals must get
the true idea and divine Principle of all that really exists
and governs the universe harmoniously. This thought is 27
apprehended slowly, and the interval before its attainment is attended with doubts and defeats as well as
triumphs. 30

Who will stop the practice of sin so long as he believes
in the pleasures of sin? When mortals once admit that

evil confers no pleasure, they turn from it. Remove error   1
from thought, and it will not appear in effect. The ad-

Sin and vanced thinker and devout Christian, perceiv-   3
penalty ing the scope and tendency of Christian healing
and its Science, will support them. Another will say:
"Go thy way for this time; when I have a convenient   6
season I will call for thee."

Divine Science adjusts the balance as Jesus adjusted
it. Science removes the penalty only by first removing   9
the sin which incurs the penalty. This is my sense of
divine pardon, which I understand to mean God's method
of destroying sin. If the saying is true, "While there's   12
life there's hope," its opposite is also true, While there's
sin there's doom. Another's suffering cannot lessen our
own liability. Did the martyrdom of Savonarola make   15
the crimes of his implacable enemies less criminal?

Was it just for Jesus to suffer? No; but it was
inevitable, for not otherwise could he show us the way   18
Suffering and the power of Truth. If a career so great
inevitable and good as that of Jesus could not avert a
felon's fate, lesser apostles of Truth may endure human   21
brutality without murmuring, rejoicing to enter into
fellowship with him through the triumphal arch of
Truth and Love.   24

Our heavenly Father, divine Love, demands that all
men should follow the example of our Master and his
Service and apostles and not merely worship his personal-   27
worship ity. It is sad that the phrase *divine service*
has come so generally to mean public worship instead of
daily deeds.   30

The nature of Christianity is peaceful and blessed,
but in order to enter into the kingdom, the anchor of

Key to the kingdom

not physical but metaphysical, not material but scien-   1
tifically spiritual. Human philosophy, ethics, and superstition afford no demonstrable divine Principle   3
by which mortals can escape from sin; yet
to escape from sin, is what the Bible demands. "Work
out your own salvation with fear and trembling," says   6
the apostle, and he straightway adds: "for it is God
which worketh in you both to will and to do of His good
pleasure" (Philippians ii. 12, 13). Truth has furnished   9
the key to the kingdom, and with this key Christian Science has opened the door of the human understanding.
None may pick the lock nor enter by some other door.   12
The ordinary teachings are material and not spiritual.
Christian Science teaches only that which is spiritual and
divine, and not human. Christian Science is unerring   15
and Divine; the human sense of things errs because it
is human.

Those individuals, who adopt theosophy, spiritualism,   18
or hypnotism, may possess natures above some others
who eschew their false beliefs. Therefore my contest is
not with the individual, but with the false system. I   21
love mankind, and shall continue to labor and to endure.

The calm, strong currents of true spirituality, the
manifestations of which are health, purity, and self-   24
immolation, must deepen human experience, until the
beliefs of material existence are seen to be a bald imposi-
tion, and sin, disease, and death give everlasting place   27
to the scientific demonstration of divine Spirit and to
God's spiritual, perfect man.

Chapter 5

Animal Magnetism Unmasked

For out of the heart proceed evil thoughts,
murders, adulteries, fornications,
thefts, false witness, blasphemies:
these are the things which defile a man. — JESUS.

esmerism or animal magnetism was first brought   1
into notice by Mesmer in Germany in 1775. According to the American Cyclopædia, he regarded this   3
so-called force, which he said could be ex-
erted by one living organism over another, as
a means of alleviating disease. His propositions were   6
as follows:

Earliest investigations

"There exists a mutual influence between the celestial
bodies, the earth, and animated things. Animal bodies   9
are susceptible to the influence of this agent, disseminat-
ing itself through the substance of the nerves."

In 1784, the French government ordered the medical   12
faculty of Paris to investigate Mesmer's theory and to
report upon it. Under this order a commission was
appointed, and Benjamin Franklin was one of the com-   15
missioners. This commission reported to the government as follows:

"In regard to the existence and utility of animal mag-   18
netism, we have come to the unanimous conclusions that
there is no proof of the existence of the animal magnetic

fluid; that the violent effects, which are observed in 1
the public practice of magnetism, are due to manipula-
tions, or to the excitement of the imagination and the 3
impressions made upon the senses; and that there is one
more fact to be recorded in the history of the errors of
the human mind, and an important experiment upon 6
the power of the imagination."

In 1837, a committee of nine persons was appointed,
among whom were Roux, Bouillaud, and Clo- 9
quet, which tested during several sessions the
phenomena exhibited by a reputed clairvoyant. Their
report stated the results as follows: 12

"The facts which had been promised by Monsieur
Berna [the magnetizer] as conclusive, and as adapted to
throw light on physiological and therapeutical questions, 15
are certainly not conclusive in favor of the doctrine of
animal magnetism, and have nothing in common with
either physiology or therapeutics." 18

This report was adopted by the Royal Academy of
Medicine in Paris.

The author's own observations of the workings of 21
animal magnetism convince her that it is not
a remedial agent, and that its effects upon
those who practise it, and upon their subjects who do 24
not resist it, lead to moral and to physical death.

If animal magnetism seems to alleviate or to cure disease, this appearance is deceptive, since error cannot 27
remove the effects of error. Discomfort under error is
preferable to comfort. In no instance is the effect of
animal magnetism, recently called hypnotism, other 30
than the effect of illusion. Any seeming benefit derived
from it is proportional to one's faith in esoteric magic.

Marginal headings:

Clairvoyance, magnetism

Personal conclusions

Animal magnetism has no scientific foundation, for   1
God governs all that is real, harmonious, and eternal, and

Mere negation   His power is neither animal nor human. Its   3
basis being a belief and this belief animal, in
Science animal magnetism, mesmerism, or hypnotism is
a mere negation, possessing neither intelligence, power,   6
nor reality, and in sense it is an unreal concept of the so-
called mortal mind.

There is but one real attraction, that of Spirit. The   9
pointing of the needle to the pole symbolizes this all-
embracing power or the attraction of God, divine Mind.

The planets have no more power over man than over   12
his Maker, since God governs the universe; but man,
reflecting God's power, has dominion over all the earth
and its hosts.   15

The mild forms of animal magnetism are disappearing, and its aggressive features are coming to the front.

Hidden agents   The looms of crime, hidden in the dark re-   18
cesses of mortal thought, are every hour weav-
ing webs more complicated and subtle. So secret are the
present methods of animal magnetism that they ensnare   21
the age into indolence, and produce the very apathy on
the subject which the criminal desires. The following
is an extract from the Boston Herald: 24

"Mesmerism is a problem not lending itself to an easy
explanation and development. It implies the exercise
of despotic control, and is much more likely to be abused   27
by its possessor, than otherwise employed, for the individual or society."

Mankind must learn that evil is not power. Its so-   30
called despotism is but a phase of nothingness. Christian
Science despoils the kingdom of evil, and pre-eminently

promotes affection and virtue in families and therefore 1
in the community. The Apostle Paul refers to the

Mental despotism personification of evil as "the god of this 3
world," and further defines it as dishonesty
and craftiness. Sin was the Assyrian moon-god.

The destruction of the claims of mortal mind through 6

Liberation of mental powers Science, by which man can escape from sin
and mortality, blesses the whole human fam-
ily. As in the beginning, however, this libera- 9
tion does not scientifically show itself in a knowledge of
both good and evil, for the latter is unreal.

On the other hand, Mind-science is wholly separate 12
from any half-way impertinent knowledge, because Mind-
science is of God and demonstrates the divine Principle,
working out the purposes of good only. The maximum 15
of good is the infinite God and His idea, the All-in-all.
Evil is a suppositional lie.

As named in Christian Science, animal magnetism or 18
hypnotism is the specific term for error, or mortal mind.

The genus of error It is the false belief that mind is in matter, and
is both evil and good; that evil is as real as 21
good and more powerful. This belief has not one quality of Truth. It is either ignorant or malicious. The
malicious form of hypnotism ultimates in moral idiocy. 24
The truths of immortal Mind sustain man, and they annihilate the fables of mortal mind, whose flimsy and gaudy
pretensions, like silly moths, singe their own wings and 27
fall into dust.

In reality there is no *mortal* mind, and conse-

Thought-transference quently no transference of mortal thought 30
and will-power. Life and being are of
God. In Christian Science, man can do no harm, for

scientific thoughts are true thoughts, passing from God   1
to man.

When Christian Science and animal magnetism are   3
both comprehended, as they will be at no distant date,
it will be seen why the author of this book has been
so unjustly persecuted and belied by wolves in sheep's   6
clothing.

Agassiz, the celebrated naturalist and author, has
wisely said: "Every great scientific truth goes through   9
three stages. First, people say it conflicts with the Bible.
Next, they say it has been discovered before. Lastly,
they say they have always believed it."   12

Christian Science goes to the bottom of mental action,
and reveals the theodicy which indicates the rightness of

**Perfection
of divine
government**

all divine action, as the emanation of divine   15
Mind, and the consequent wrongness of the
opposite so-called action, — evil, occultism,
necromancy, mesmerism, animal magnetism, hypnotism.   18

The medicine of Science is divine Mind; and dishonesty,
sensuality, falsehood, revenge, malice, are animal pro-

**Adulteration
of Truth**

pensities and by no means the mental quali-   21
ties which heal the sick. The hypnotizer
employs one error to destroy another. If he heals sickness through a belief, and a belief originally caused the   24
sickness, it is a case of the greater error overcoming the
lesser. This greater error thereafter occupies the ground,
leaving the case worse than before it was grasped by the   27
stronger error.

Our courts recognize evidence to prove the motive as

**Motives
considered**

well as the commission of a crime. Is it not   30
clear that the human mind must move the
body to a wicked act? Is not mortal mind the mur-

derer? The hands, without mortal mind to direct them, could not commit a murder.

Courts and juries judge and sentence mortals in order to restrain crime, to prevent deeds of violence or to punish them. To say that these tribunals have no jurisdiction over the carnal or mortal mind, would be to contradict precedent and to admit that the power of human law is restricted to matter, while mortal mind, evil, which is the real outlaw, defies justice and is recommended to mercy. Can matter commit a crime? Can matter be punished? Can you separate the mentality from the body over which courts hold jurisdiction? Mortal mind, not matter, is the criminal in every case; and human law rightly estimates crime, and courts reasonably pass sentence, according to the motive.

When our laws eventually take cognizance of mental crime and no longer apply legal rulings wholly to physical offences, these words of Judge Parmenter of Boston will become historic: "I see no reason why metaphysics is not as important to medicine as to mechanics or mathematics."

Whoever uses his developed mental powers like an escaped felon to commit fresh atrocities as opportunity occurs is never safe. God will arrest him. Divine justice will manacle him. His sins will be millstones about his neck, weighing him down to the depths of ignominy and death. The aggravation of error foretells its doom, and confirms the ancient axiom: "Whom the gods would destroy, they first make mad."

The distance from ordinary medical practice to Christian Science is full many a league in the line of light; but to go in healing from the use of

Marginal notes:
Mental crimes

Important decision

Evil let loose

The misuse of mental power

Line numbers: 1, 3, 6, 9, 12, 15, 18, 21, 24, 27, 30

inanimate drugs to the criminal misuse of human will-   1
power, is to drop from the platform of common manhood
into the very mire of iniquity, to work against the free   3
course of honesty and justice, and to push vainly against
the current running heavenward.

Like our nation, Christian Science has its Declaration   6
of Independence. God has endowed man with inalien-

**Proper self-
government**

able rights, among which are self-government,
reason, and conscience. Man is properly self-   9
governed only when he is guided rightly and governed by
his Maker, divine Truth and Love.

Man's rights are invaded when the divine order is in-   12
terfered with, and the mental trespasser incurs the divine
penalty due this crime.

Let this age, which sits in judgment on Christian   15
Science, sanction only such methods as are demonstrable

**Right
methods**

in Truth and known by their fruit, and classify
all others as did St. Paul in his great epistle   18
to the Galatians, when he wrote as follows:

"Now the works of the flesh are manifest, which are
these; Adultery, fornication, uncleanness, lasciviousness,   21
idolatry, *witchcraft*, hatred, variance, emulations, wrath,
strife, seditions, heresies, envyings, murders, drunkenness,
revellings and such like: of the which I tell you before,   24
as I have also told you in time past, that they which do
such things shall not inherit the kingdom of God. But
the fruit of the Spirit is love, joy, peace, longsuffering,   27
gentleness, goodness, faith, meekness, temperance: against
such there is no law."

Chapter 6

Science, Theology, Medicine

But I certify you, brethren,
that the gospel which was preached of me is not after man.
For I neither received it of man, neither was I taught it,
but by the revelation of Jesus Christ. — PAUL.

The kingdom of heaven is like unto leaven, which a woman took,
and hid in three measures of meal, till the whole was leavened. — JESUS.

Christian Science discovered

In the year 1866, I discovered the Christ Science or divine laws of Life, Truth, and Love, and named my discovery Christian Science. God had been graciously preparing me during many years for the reception of this final revelation of the absolute divine Principle of scientific mental healing. 1

3

6

Mission of Christian Science

This apodictical Principle points to the revelation of Immanuel, "God with us," — the sovereign ever-presence, delivering the children of men from every ill "that flesh is heir to." Through Christian Science, religion and medicine are inspired with a diviner nature and essence; fresh pinions are given to faith and understanding, and thoughts acquaint themselves intelligently with God. 9

12

Discontent with life

Feeling so perpetually the false consciousness that life inheres in the body, yet remembering that in reality God is our Life, we may well tremble in the prospect of those days in which we must say, "I have no pleasure in them." 15

18

Whence came to me this heavenly conviction, — a con- 1
viction antagonistic to the testimony of the physical senses?
According to St. Paul, it was "the gift of the grace of 3
God given unto me by the effectual working of His power."
It was the divine law of Life and Love, unfolding to me
the demonstrable fact that matter possesses neither sen- 6
sation nor life; that human experiences show the falsity
of all material things; and that immortal cravings, "the
price of learning love," establish the truism that the 9
only sufferer is mortal mind, for the divine Mind cannot
suffer.

My conclusions were reached by allowing the evidence 12
of this revelation to multiply with mathematical certainty

Demonstrable evidence   and the lesser demonstration to prove the
greater, as the product of three multiplied by 15
three, equalling nine, proves conclusively that three times
three duodecillions must be nine duodecillions, — not
a fraction more, not a unit less. 18

When apparently near the confines of mortal existence,
standing already within the shadow of the death-valley,

Light shining in darkness   I learned these truths in divine Science: that 21
all real being is in God, the divine Mind, and
that Life, Truth, and Love are all-powerful and ever-
present; that the opposite of Truth, — called error, sin, 24
sickness, disease, death, — is the false testimony of false
material sense, of mind in matter; that this false sense
evolves, in belief, a subjective state of mortal mind which 27
this same so-called mind names *matter*, thereby shutting
out the true sense of Spirit.

New lines of thought   My discovery, that erring, mortal, misnamed 30
mind produces all the organism and action of
the mortal body, set my thoughts to work in new channels,

and led up to my demonstration of the proposition that   1
Mind is All and matter is naught as the leading factor in
Mind-science.   3

Christian Science reveals incontrovertibly that Mind
is All-in-all, that the only realities are the divine Mind
Scientific   and idea. This great fact is not, however, seen   6
evidence   to be supported by sensible evidence, until its
divine Principle is demonstrated by healing the sick and
thus proved absolute and divine. This proof once seen,   9
no other conclusion can be reached.

For three years after my discovery, I sought the solution of this problem of Mind-healing, searched the Scrip-   12
Solitary   tures and read little else, kept aloof from so-
research   ciety, and devoted time and energies to dis-
covering a positive rule. The search was sweet, calm, and   15
buoyant with hope, not selfish nor depressing. I knew
the Principle of all harmonious Mind-action to be God,
and that cures were produced in primitive Christian   18
healing by holy, uplifting faith; but I must know the
Science of this healing, and I won my way to absolute
conclusions through divine revelation, reason, and dem-   21
onstration. The revelation of Truth in the understanding came to me gradually and apparently through divine
power. When a new spiritual idea is borne to earth, the   24
prophetic Scripture of Isaiah is renewedly fulfilled:
"Unto us a child is born, . . . and his name shall be
called Wonderful."   27

Jesus once said of his lessons: "My doctrine is not
mine, but His that sent me. If any man will do His will,
he shall know of the doctrine, whether it be of God, or   30
whether I speak of myself." (John vii. 16, 17.)

The three great verities of Spirit, omnipotence, omni-

presence, omniscience, — Spirit possessing all power, 1
filling all space, constituting all Science, — contradict

God's allness learned

forever the belief that matter can be actual. 3
These eternal verities reveal primeval existence as the radiant reality of God's creation,
in which all that He has made is pronounced by His wis- 6
dom good.

Thus it was that I beheld, as never before, the awful
unreality called evil. The equipollence of God brought 9
to light another glorious proposition, — man's perfecti-
bility and the establishment of the kingdom of heaven on
earth. 12

In following these leadings of scientific revelation,
the Bible was my only textbook. The Scriptures were

Scriptural foundations

illumined; reason and revelation were recon- 15
ciled, and afterwards the truth of Christian
Science was demonstrated. No human pen nor tongue
taught me the Science contained in this book, SCIENCE 18
AND HEALTH; and neither tongue nor pen can overthrow it. This book may be distorted by shallow criticism or by careless or malicious students, and its ideas 21
may be temporarily abused and misrepresented; but the
Science and truth therein will forever remain to be discerned and demonstrated. 24

Jesus demonstrated the power of Christian Science to
heal mortal minds and bodies. But this power was lost

The demonstration lost and found

sight of, and must again be spiritually dis- 27
cerned, taught, and demonstrated according
to Christ's command, with "signs following."
Its Science must be apprehended by as many as believe 30
on Christ and spiritually understand Truth.

No analogy exists between the vague hypotheses of

agnosticism, pantheism, theosophy, spiritualism, or   1
millenarianism and the demonstrable truths of Chris-

Mystical antagonists

tian Science; and I find the will, or sensuous   3
reason of the human mind, to be opposed to
the divine Mind as expressed through divine Science.

Christian Science is natural, but not physical. The   6
Science of God and man is no more supernatural than

Optical illustration of Science

is the science of numbers, though departing
from the realm of the physical, as the Science   9
of God, Spirit, must, some may deny its right to
the name of Science. The Principle of divine metaphysics
is God; the practice of divine metaphysics is the utiliza-   12
tion of the power of Truth over error; its rules demonstrate its Science. Divine metaphysics reverses perverted
and physical hypotheses as to Deity, even as the ex-   15
planation of optics rejects the incidental or inverted
image and shows what this inverted image is meant to
represent.   18

A prize of one hundred pounds, offered in Oxford University, England, for the best essay on Natural Science,

Pertinent proposal

— an essay calculated to offset the tendency of   21
the age to attribute physical effects to physical
causes rather than to a final spiritual cause, — is one of
many incidents which show that Christian Science meets   24
a yearning of the human race for spirituality.

After a lengthy examination of my discovery and its
demonstration in healing the sick, this fact became evi-   27

Confirmatory tests

dent to me, — that Mind governs the body,
not partially but wholly. I submitted my
metaphysical system of treating disease to the broad-   30
est practical tests. Since then this system has gradually
gained ground, and has proved itself, whenever scien-

tifically employed, to be the most effective curative agent   1
in medical practice.

Is there more than one school of Christian Science?   3
Christian Science is demonstrable. There can, therefore, be but one method in its teaching. Those who de-

**One school
of Truth**
part from this method forfeit their claims to   6
belong to its school, and they become adher-
ents of the Socratic, the Platonic, the Spencerian, or some
other school. By this is meant that they adopt and ad-   9
here to some particular system of human opinions. Although these opinions may have occasional gleams of
divinity, borrowed from that truly divine Science which   12
eschews man-made systems, they nevertheless remain
wholly human in their origin and tendency and are not
scientifically Christian.   15

From the infinite One in Christian Science comes one
Principle and its infinite idea, and with this infinitude

**Unchanging
Principle**
come spiritual rules, laws, and their demon-   18
stration, which, like the great Giver, are "the
same yesterday, and to-day, and forever;" for thus are
the divine Principle of healing and the Christ-idea charac-   21
terized in the epistle to the Hebrews.

Any theory of Christian Science, which departs from
what has already been stated and proved to be true, af-   24

**On sandy
foundations**
fords no foundation upon which to establish
a genuine school of this Science. Also, if any
so-called new school claims to be Christian Science, and   27
yet uses another author's discoveries without giving that
author proper credit, such a school is erroneous, for it
inculcates a breach of that divine commandment in the   30
Hebrew Decalogue, "Thou shalt not steal."

God is the Principle of divine metaphysics. As there

is but one God, there can be but one divine Principle of   1
all Science; and there must be fixed rules for the demon-

Principle and practice   stration of this divine Principle. The letter   3
of Science plentifully reaches humanity to-day,
but its spirit comes only in small degrees. The vital part,
the heart and soul of Christian Science, is Love. With-   6
out this, the letter is but the dead body of Science, —
pulseless, cold, inanimate.

The fundamental propositions of divine metaphysics   9
are summarized in the four following, to me, *self-evident*

Reversible propositions   propositions. Even if reversed, these propositions will be found to agree in statement and   12
proof, showing mathematically their exact relation to
Truth. De Quincey says mathematics has not a foot to
stand upon which is not purely metaphysical.   15

1. God is All-in-all.

2. God is good. Good is Mind.

3. God, Spirit, being all, nothing is matter.   18

4. Life, God, omnipotent good, deny death, evil, sin,
disease. — Disease, sin, evil, death, deny good, omnipotent God, Life.   21

Which of the denials in proposition four is true? Both
are not, cannot be, true. According to the Scripture,
I find that God is true, "but every [mortal] man a   24
liar."

The divine metaphysics of Christian Science, like the
method in mathematics, proves the rule by inversion.   27

Metaphysical inversions   For example: There is no pain in Truth, and
no truth in pain; no nerve in Mind, and no
mind in nerve; no matter in Mind, and no mind in mat-   30
ter; no matter in Life, and no life in matter; no matter
in good, and no good in matter.

Usage classes both evil and good together as *mind;*   1
therefore, to be understood, the author calls sick and sin-

Definition of ful humanity *mortal mind,* — meaning by this   3
mortal mind term the flesh opposed to Spirit, the human
mind and evil in contradistinction to the divine Mind, or
Truth and good. The spiritually unscientific definition   6
of mind is based on the evidence of the physical senses,
which makes minds many and calls *mind* both human and
divine.   9

In Science, Mind is *one,* including noumenon and phenomena, God and His thoughts.

Mortal mind is a solecism in language, and involves an   12
improper use of the word *mind.* As Mind is immortal,

Imperfect the phrase *mortal mind* implies something un-
terminology true and therefore unreal; and as the phrase   15
is used in teaching Christian Science, it is meant to
designate that which has no real existence. Indeed, if
a better word or phrase could be suggested, it would   18
be used; but in expressing the new tongue we must
sometimes recur to the old and imperfect, and the new
wine of the Spirit has to be poured into the old bottles of   21
the letter.

Christian Science explains all cause and effect as mental, not physical. It lifts the veil of mystery from Soul and   24

Causation body. It shows the scientific relation of man
mental to God, disentangles the interlaced ambiguities
of being, and sets free the imprisoned thought. In divine   27
Science, the universe, including man, is spiritual, harmonious, and eternal. Science shows that what is termed *mat-*
ter is but the subjective state of what is termed by the   30
author *mortal mind.*

Apart from the usual opposition to everything new,

the one great obstacle to the reception of that spiritual- 1
ity, through which the understanding of Mind-science

Philological inadequacy comes, is the inadequacy of material terms for 3
metaphysical statements, and the consequent
difficulty of so expressing metaphysical ideas as to make
them comprehensible to any reader, who has not person- 6
ally demonstrated Christian Science as brought forth in
my discovery. Job says: "The ear trieth words, as the
mouth tasteth meat." The great difficulty is to give the 9
right impression, when translating material terms back
into the original spiritual tongue.

SCIENTIFIC TRANSLATION OF IMMORTAL MIND 12

Divine synonyms GOD: Divine Principle, Life, Truth, Love,
Soul, Spirit, Mind.

Divine image MAN: God's spiritual idea, individual, per- 15
fect, eternal.

Divine reflection IDEA: An image in Mind; the immediate
object of understanding. — *Webster.* 18

SCIENTIFIC TRANSLATION OF MORTAL MIND

First Degree: Depravity.

PHYSICAL. Evil beliefs, passions and appetites, fear, 21
Unreality depraved will, self-justification, pride, envy, de-
ceit, hatred, revenge, sin, sickness, disease,
death. 24

Second Degree: Evil beliefs disappearing.

Transitional qualities MORAL. Humanity, honesty, affection, com-
passion, hope, faith, meekness, temperance. 27

Third Degree: Understanding.   1

SPIRITUAL. Wisdom, purity, spiritual understanding,

Reality   spiritual power, love, health, holiness.   3

In the third degree mortal mind disappears, and man as
God's image appears. Science so reverses the evidence
Spiritual   before the corporeal human senses, as to make   6
universe
this Scriptural testimony true in our hearts,
"The last shall be first, and the first last," so that God
and His idea may be to us what divinity really is and   9
must of necessity be, — all-inclusive.

A correct view of Christian Science and of its adaptation to healing includes vastly more than is at first seen.   12
Aim of   Works on metaphysics leave the grand point
Science
untouched. They never crown the power of
Mind as the Messiah, nor do they carry the day against   15
physical enemies, — even to the extinction of all belief in
matter, evil, disease, and death, — nor insist upon the fact
that God is all, therefore that matter is nothing beyond an   18
image in mortal mind.

Christian Science strongly emphasizes the thought that
Divine   God is not *corporeal*, but *incorporeal*, — that is,   21
personality
bodiless. Mortals are corporeal, but God is
incorporeal.

As the words *person* and *personal* are commonly and   24
ignorantly employed, they often lead, when applied to
Deity, to confused and erroneous conceptions of divinity
and its distinction from humanity. If the term personality,   27
as applied to God, means infinite personality, then God *is*
infinite *Person,* — in the sense of infinite personality, but
not in the lower sense. An infinite Mind in a finite form   30
is an absolute impossibility.

The term *individuality* is also open to objections, be-   1
cause an individual may be one of a series, one of many,
as an individual man, an individual horse; whereas God   3
is *One*, — not one of a series, but one alone and without
an equal.

God is Spirit; therefore the language of Spirit must   6
be, and is, spiritual. Christian Science attaches no physi-
Spiritual   cal nature and significance to the Supreme
language   Being or His manifestation; mortals alone do   9
this. God's essential language is spoken of in the last
chapter of Mark's Gospel as the new tongue, the spiritual meaning of which is attained through "signs   12
following."

Ear hath not heard, nor hath lip spoken, the pure language of Spirit. Our Master taught spirituality by simili-   15
The miracles   tudes and parables. As a divine student he
of Jesus   unfolded God to man, illustrating and demonstrating Life and Truth in himself and by his power over   18
the sick and sinning. Human theories are inadequate to
interpret the divine Principle involved in the miracles
(marvels) wrought by Jesus and especially in his mighty,   21
crowning, unparalleled, and triumphant exit from the
flesh.

Evidence drawn from the five physical senses relates   24
Opacity of   solely to human reason; and because of opaci-
the senses   ty to the true light, human reason dimly reflects and feebly transmits Jesus' works and words. Truth   27
is a revelation.

Jesus bade his disciples beware of the leaven of the
Leaven   Pharisees and of the Sadducees, which he de-   30
of Truth   fined as human doctrines. His parable of the
"leaven, which a woman took, and hid in three measures

of meal, till the whole was leavened," impels the infer-   1
ence that the spiritual leaven signifies the Science of Christ
and its spiritual interpretation, — an inference far above   3
the merely ecclesiastical and formal applications of the
illustration.

Did not this parable point a moral with a prophecy,   6
foretelling the second appearing in the flesh of the
Christ, Truth, hidden in sacred secrecy from the visible world?   9

Ages pass, but this leaven of Truth is ever at work. It
must destroy the entire mass of error, and so be eternally
glorified in man's spiritual freedom.   12

In their spiritual significance, Science, Theology, and
Medicine are means of divine thought, which include spirit-

The divine and human contrasted

ual laws emanating from the invisible and in-   15
finite power and grace. The parable may
import that these spiritual laws, perverted by
a perverse material sense of law, are metaphysically pre-   18
sented as three measures of meal, — that is, three modes
of mortal thought. In all mortal forms of thought, dust
is dignified as the natural status of men and things, and   21
modes of material motion are honored with the name of
laws. This continues until the leaven of Spirit changes
the whole of mortal thought, as yeast changes the chemical   24
properties of meal.

The definitions of material law, as given by natural
science, represent a kingdom necessarily divided against   27

Certain contradictions

itself, because these definitions portray law as
physical, not spiritual. Therefore they con-
tradict the divine decrees and violate the law of Love, in   30
which nature and God are one and the natural order of
heaven comes down to earth.

When we endow matter with vague spiritual power, — that is, when we do so in our theories, for of course we

Unescapable dilemma

cannot really endow matter with what it does not and cannot possess, — we disown the Almighty, for such theories lead to one of two things. They either presuppose the self-evolution and self-government of matter, or else they assume that matter is the product of Spirit. To seize the first horn of this dilemma and consider matter as a power in and of itself, is to leave the creator out of His own universe; while to grasp the other horn of the dilemma and regard God as the creator of matter, is not only to make Him responsible for all disasters, physical and moral, but to announce Him as their source, thereby making Him guilty of maintaining perpetual misrule in the form and under the name of natural law.

In one sense God is identical with nature, but this nature is spiritual and is not expressed in matter. The law-

God and nature

giver, whose lightning palsies or prostrates in death the child at prayer, is not the divine ideal of omnipresent Love. God is natural good, and is represented only by the idea of goodness; while evil should be regarded as unnatural, because it is opposed to the nature of Spirit, God.

In viewing the sunrise, one finds that it contradicts the evidence before the senses to believe that the earth

The sun and Soul

is in motion and the sun at rest. As astronomy reverses the human perception of the movement of the solar system, so Christian Science reverses the seeming relation of Soul and body and makes body tributary to Mind. Thus it is with man, who is but the humble servant of the restful Mind, though it

seems otherwise to finite sense. But we shall never under- 1
stand this while we admit that soul is in body or mind in
matter, and that man is included in non-intelligence. 3
Soul, or Spirit, is God, unchangeable and eternal; and
man coexists with and reflects Soul, God, for man is God's
image. 6

Science reverses the false testimony of the physical
senses, and by this reversal mortals arrive at the funda-

Reversal of mental facts of being. Then the question in- 9
testimony evitably arises: Is a man sick if the material
senses indicate that he is in good health? No! for matter
can make no conditions for man. And is he well if the 12
senses say he is sick? Yes, he is well in Science in which
health is normal and disease is abnormal.

Health is not a condition of matter, but of Mind; nor 15
can the material senses bear reliable testimony on the sub-

Health and ject of health. The Science of Mind-healing
the senses shows it to be impossible for aught but Mind 18
to testify truly or to exhibit the real status of man. Therefore the divine Principle of Science, reversing the testimony of the physical senses, reveals man as harmoniously 21
existent in Truth, which is the only basis of health; and
thus Science denies all disease, heals the sick, overthrows
false evidence, and refutes materialistic logic. 24

Any conclusion *pro* or *con*, deduced from supposed sensation in matter or from matter's supposed consciousness
of health or disease, instead of reversing the testimony of 27
the physical senses, confirms that testimony as legitimate
and so leads to disease.

Historic When Columbus gave freer breath to the 30
illustrations globe, ignorance and superstition chained the
limbs of the brave old navigator, and disgrace and star-

vation stared him in the face; but sterner still would have   1
been his fate, if his discovery had undermined the favorite inclinations of a sensuous philosophy.   3

Copernicus mapped out the stellar system, and before
he spake, astrography was chaotic, and the heavenly fields
were incorrectly explored.   6

The Chaldean Wisemen read in the stars the fate of
empires and the fortunes of men. Though no higher

Perennial
beauty

revelation than the horoscope was to them dis-   9
played upon the empyrean, earth and heaven
were bright, and bird and blossom were glad in God's
perennial and happy sunshine, golden with Truth. So   12
we have goodness and beauty to gladden the heart; but
man, left to the hypotheses of material sense unexplained
by Science, is as the wandering comet or the desolate   15
star — "a weary searcher for a viewless home."

The earth's diurnal rotation is invisible to the physical
eye, and the sun seems to move from east to west, instead   18

Astronomic
unfoldings

of the earth from west to east. Until rebuked
by clearer views of the everlasting facts, this
false testimony of the eye deluded the judgment and in-   21
duced false conclusions. Science shows appearances often
to be erroneous, and corrects these errors by the simple
rule that the greater controls the lesser. The sun is the   24
central stillness, so far as our solar system is concerned,
and the earth revolves about the sun once a year, besides
turning daily on its own axis.   27

As thus indicated, astronomical order imitates the
action of divine Principle; and the universe, the reflection of God, is thus brought nearer the spiritual fact, and   30
is allied to divine Science as displayed in the everlasting
government of the universe.

The evidence of the physical senses often reverses the   1
real Science of being, and so creates a reign of discord, —
assigning seeming power to sin, sickness, and   3
death; but the great facts of Life, rightly understood, defeat this triad of errors, contradict their false
witnesses, and reveal the kingdom of heaven, — the actual   6
reign of harmony on earth. The material senses' reversal of the Science of Soul was practically exposed nine-
teen hundred years ago by the demonstrations of Jesus;   9
yet these so-called senses still make mortal mind tributary
to mortal body, and ordain certain sections of matter, such
as brain and nerves, as the seats of pain and pleasure,   12
from which matter reports to this so-called mind its status
of happiness or misery.

The optical focus is another proof of the illusion of   15
material sense. On the eye's retina, sky and tree-tops

apparently join hands, clouds and ocean meet
and mingle. The barometer, — that little   18
prophet of storm and sunshine, denying the testimony of
the senses, — points to fair weather in the midst of murky
clouds and drenching rain. Experience is full of instances   21
of similar illusions, which every thinker can recall for
himself.

To material sense, the severance of the jugular vein   24

takes away life; but to spiritual sense and
in Science, Life goes on unchanged and
being is eternal. Temporal life is a false sense of   27
existence.

Our theories make the same mistake regarding Soul
and body that Ptolemy made regarding the solar system.   30
They insist that soul is in body and mind therefore tributary to matter. Astronomical science has destroyed the

false theory as to the relations of the celestial bodies, and   1
Christian Science will surely destroy the greater error as
Ptolemaic and psychical error to our terrestrial bodies. The true idea and   3
Principle of man will then appear. The Ptole-
maic blunder could not affect the harmony of
being as does the error relating to soul and body, which   6
reverses the order of Science and assigns to matter the
power and prerogative of Spirit, so that man becomes
the most absolutely weak and inharmonious creature in   9
the universe.

The verity of Mind shows conclusively how it is that
Seeming and being matter seems to be, but is not. Divine Science,   12
rising above physical theories, excludes matter,
resolves *things* into *thoughts*, and replaces the objects of
material sense with spiritual ideas.   15

The term CHRISTIAN SCIENCE was introduced by
the author to designate the scientific system of divine
healing.   18

The revelation consists of two parts:

1. The discovery of this divine Science of Mind-
healing, through a spiritual sense of the Scriptures and   21
through the teachings of the Comforter, as promised by
the Master.

2. The proof, by present demonstration, that the so-   24
called miracles of Jesus did not specially belong to a
dispensation now ended, but that they illustrated an
ever-operative divine Principle. The operation of this   27
Principle indicates the eternality of the scientific order
and continuity of being.

Scientific basis Christian Science differs from material sci-   30
ence, but not on that account is it less scien-
tific. On the contrary, Christian Science is pre-emi-

nently scientific, being based on Truth, the Principle of all science. 1

Physical science (so-called) is human knowledge, — a law of mortal mind, a blind belief, a Samson shorn of his strength. When this human belief lacks organ- izations to support it, its foundations are gone. Having neither moral might, spiritual basis, nor holy Principle of its own, this belief mistakes effect for cause and seeks to find life and intelligence in matter, thus limiting Life and holding fast to discord and death. In a word, human belief is a blind conclusion from material reasoning. This is a mortal, finite sense of things, which immortal Spirit silences forever. 3

Physical science a blind belief 6

9

12

The universe, like man, is to be interpreted by Science from its divine Principle, God, and then it can be under- stood; but when explained on the basis of physical sense and represented as subject to growth, maturity, and decay, the universe, like man, is, and must continue to be, an enigma. 15

Right interpretation 18

Adhesion, cohesion, and attraction are properties of Mind. They belong to divine Principle, and support the equipoise of that thought-force, which launched the earth in its orbit and said to the proud wave, "Thus far and no farther." 21

All force mental 24

Spirit is the life, substance, and continuity of all things. We tread on forces. Withdraw them, and creation must collapse. Human knowledge calls them forces of matter; but divine Science declares that they belong wholly to divine Mind, are inherent in this Mind, and so restores them to their rightful home and classification. 27

30

The elements and functions of the physical body and

Master demonstrated that Truth could save from sickness   1
as well as from sin.

Mind as far outweighs drugs in the cure of disease as   3
in the cure of sin. The more excellent way is divine

Blunders and blunderers Science in every case. Is *materia medica* a
science or a bundle of speculative human   6
theories? The prescription which succeeds in one instance fails in another, and this is owing to the different
mental states of the patient. These states are not com-   9
prehended, and they are left without explanation except
in Christian Science. The rule and its perfection of operation never vary in Science. If you fail to succeed in any   12
case, it is because you have not demonstrated the life of
Christ, Truth, more in your own life, — because you have
not obeyed the rule and proved the Principle of divine   15
Science.

A physician of the old school remarked with great
gravity: "We know that mind affects the body some-   18
Old-school physician what, and advise our patients to be hopeful
and cheerful and to take as little medicine as
possible; but mind can never cure organic difficulties."   21
The logic is lame, and facts contradict it. The author
has cured what is termed organic disease as readily as she
has cured purely functional disease, and with no power   24
but the divine Mind.

Since God, divine Mind, governs all, not partially but
supremely, predicting disease does not dignify therapeutics.   27
Tests in our day Whatever guides thought spiritually benefits
mind and body. We need to understand the
affirmations of divine Science, dismiss superstition, and   30
demonstrate truth according to Christ. To-day there
is hardly a city, village, or hamlet, in which are not to

be found living witnesses and monuments to the virtue 1
and power of Truth, as applied through this Christian
system of healing disease. 3

To-day the healing power of Truth is widely demonstrated as an immanent, eternal Science, instead of a

The main purpose phenomenal exhibition. Its appearing is the 6
coming anew of the gospel of "on earth peace,
good-will toward men." This coming, as was promised
by the Master, is for its establishment as a permanent 9
dispensation among men; but the mission of Christian
Science now, as in the time of its earlier demonstration,
is not primarily one of physical healing. Now, as then, 12
signs and wonders are wrought in the metaphysical healing of physical disease; but these signs are only to demonstrate its divine origin, — to attest the reality of the higher 15
mission of the Christ-power to take away the sins of the
world.

The science (so-called) of physics would have one be- 18
lieve that both matter and mind are subject to disease,
Exploded doctrine and that, too, in spite of the individual's protest and contrary to the law of divine Mind. 21
This human view infringes man's free moral agency; and
it is as evidently erroneous to the author, and will be to
all others at some future day, as the practically rejected 24
doctrine of the predestination of souls to damnation or
salvation. The doctrine that man's harmony is governed by physical conditions all his earthly days, and that 27
he is then thrust out of his own body by the operation of
matter, — even the doctrine of the superiority of matter
over Mind, — is fading out. 30

The hosts of Æsculapius are flooding the world with
diseases, because they are ignorant that the human mind

and body are myths. To be sure, they sometimes treat   1
the sick as if there was but one factor in the case; but

Disease mental this one factor they represent to be body, not   3
mind. Infinite Mind could not possibly create
a remedy outside of itself, but erring, finite, human mind
has an absolute need of something beyond itself for its   6
redemption and healing.

Great respect is due the motives and philanthropy of
the higher class of physicians. We know that if they un-   9

Intentions respected derstood the Science of Mind-healing, and were
in possession of the enlarged power it confers
to benefit the race physically and spiritually, they would   12
rejoice with us. Even this one reform in medicine would
ultimately deliver mankind from the awful and oppressive bondage now enforced by false theories, from which   15
multitudes would gladly escape.

Mortal belief says that death has been occasioned by
fright. Fear never stopped being and its action. The   18

Man governed by Mind blood, heart, lungs, brain, etc., have nothing
to do with Life, God. Every function of the
real man is governed by the divine Mind. The human   21
mind has no power to kill or to cure, and it has no control over God's man. The divine Mind that made man
maintains His own image and likeness. The human   24
mind is opposed to God and must be put off, as St. Paul
declares. All that really exists is the divine Mind and
its idea, and in this Mind the entire being is found har-   27
monious and eternal. The straight and narrow way is to
see and acknowledge this fact, yield to this power, and
follow the leadings of truth.   30

That mortal mind claims to govern every organ of the
mortal body, we have overwhelming proof. But this so-

called mind is a myth, and must by its own consent yield 1
to Truth. It would wield the sceptre of a monarch, but

Mortal mind
dethroned

it is powerless. The immortal divine Mind 3
takes away all its supposed sovereignty, and
saves mortal mind from itself. The author has endeavored
to make this book the Æsculapius of mind as well as of 6
body, that it may give hope to the sick and heal them,
although they know not how the work is done. Truth
has a healing effect, even when not fully understood. 9

Anatomy describes muscular action as produced by
mind in one instance and not in another. Such errors

All activity
from thought

beset every material theory, in which one 12
statement contradicts another over and over
again. It is related that Sir Humphry Davy once apparently cured a case of paralysis simply by introducing 15
a thermometer into the patient's mouth. This he did
merely to ascertain the temperature of the patient's body;
but the sick man supposed this ceremony was intended 18
to heal him, and he recovered accordingly. Such a fact
illustrates our theories.

The author's medical researches and experiments had 21
prepared her thought for the metaphysics of Christian

The author's
experiments
in medicine

Science. Every material dependence had
failed her in her search for truth; and she can 24
now understand why, and can see the means
by which mortals are divinely driven to a spiritual source
for health and happiness. 27

Her experiments in homœopathy had made her skep-
tical as to material curative methods. Jahr, from

Homœopathic
attenuations

Aconitum to *Zincum oxydatum*, enumerates 30
the general symptoms, the characteristic
signs, which demand different remedies; but the drug

is frequently attenuated to such a degree that not a ves- 1
tige of it remains. Thus we learn that it is not the drug
which expels the disease or changes one of the symptoms 3
of disease.

The author has attenuated *Natrum muriaticum* (common table-salt) until there was not a single saline property 6

Only salt and water

left. The salt had "lost his savour;" and yet,
with one drop of that attenuation in a goblet of
water, and a teaspoonful of the water administered at in- 9
tervals of three hours, she has cured a patient sinking in
the last stage of typhoid fever. The highest attenuation
of homœopathy and the most potent rises above matter into 12
mind. This discovery leads to more light. From it may
be learned that either human faith or the divine Mind is
the healer and that there is no efficacy in a drug. 15

You say a boil is painful; but that is impossible, for
matter without mind is not painful. The boil simply

Origin of pain

manifests, through inflammation and swell- 18
ing, a belief in pain, and this belief is called a
boil. Now administer mentally to your patient a high
attenuation of truth, and it will soon cure the boil. The 21
fact that pain cannot exist where there is no mortal mind
to feel it is a proof that this so-called mind makes its
own pain — that is, its own *belief* in pain. 24

We weep because others weep, we yawn because they
yawn, and we have smallpox because others have it; but

Source of contagion

mortal mind, not matter, contains and carries 27
the infection. When this mental contagion is
understood, we shall be more careful of our mental conditions, and we shall avoid loquacious tattling about 30
disease, as we would avoid advocating crime. Neither
sympathy nor society should ever tempt us to cherish

error in any form, and certainly we should not be error's   1
advocate.

Disease arises, like other mental conditions, from as-   3
sociation. Since it is a law of mortal mind that certain
diseases should be regarded as contagious, this law ob-
tains credit through association, — calling up the fear that   6
creates the image of disease and its consequent manifestation in the body.

This fact in metaphysics is illustrated by the following   9
incident: A man was made to believe that he occupied a

Imaginary cholera bed where a cholera patient had died. Immediately the symptoms of this disease appeared,   12
and the man died. The fact was, that he had not caught
the cholera by material contact, because no cholera patient
had been in that bed.   15

If a child is exposed to contagion or infection, the
mother is frightened and says, "My child will be sick."

Children's ailments The law of mortal mind and her own fears gov-   18
ern her child more than the child's mind gov-
erns itself, and they produce the very results which might
have been prevented through the opposite understanding.   21
Then it is believed that exposure to the contagion wrought
the mischief.

That mother is not a Christian Scientist, and her affec-   24
tions need better guidance, who says to her child: "You
look sick," "You look tired," "You need rest," or "You
need medicine."   27

Such a mother runs to her little one, who thinks she has
hurt her face by falling on the carpet, and says, moaning
more childishly than her child, "Mamma knows you are   30
hurt." The better and more successful method for any
mother to adopt is to say: "Oh, never mind! You're not

hurt, so don't think you are." Presently the child forgets 1
all about the accident, and is at play.

When the sick recover by the use of drugs, it is the law 3
of a general belief, culminating in individual faith, which
Drug-power mental heals; and according to this faith will the effect
be. Even when you take away the individual 6
confidence in the drug, you have not yet divorced the drug
from the general faith. The chemist, the botanist, the
druggist, the doctor, and the nurse equip the medicine 9
with their faith, and the beliefs which are in the majority
rule. When the general belief endorses the inanimate
drug as doing this or that, individual dissent or faith, un- 12
less it rests on Science, is but a belief held by a minority,
and such a belief is governed by the majority.

The universal belief in physics weighs against the high 15
and mighty truths of Christian metaphysics. This errone-
Belief in physics ous general belief, which sustains medicine and
produces all medical results, works against 18
Christian Science; and the percentage of power on the
side of this Science must mightily outweigh the power of
popular belief in order to heal a single case of disease. The 21
human mind acts more powerfully to offset the discords
of matter and the ills of flesh, in proportion as it puts less
weight into the material or fleshly scale and more weight 24
into the spiritual scale. Homœopathy diminishes the
drug, but the potency of the medicine increases as the
drug disappears. 27

Vegetarianism, homœopathy, and hydropathy have
diminished drugging; but if drugs are an antidote to
Nature of drugs disease, why lessen the antidote? If drugs 30
are good things, is it safe to say that the
less in quantity you have of them the better? If drugs

possess intrinsic virtues or intelligent curative qualities,   1
these qualities must be mental. Who named drugs, and
what made them good or bad for mortals, beneficial or   3
injurious?

A case of dropsy, given up by the faculty, fell into
my hands. It was a terrible case. Tapping had been   6

employed, and yet, as she lay in her bed, the
patient looked like a barrel. I prescribed
the fourth attenuation of *Argentum nitratum* with occa-   9
sional doses of a high attenuation of *Sulphuris.* She improved perceptibly. Believing then somewhat in the
ordinary theories of medical practice, and learning that   12
her former physician had prescribed these remedies, I
began to fear an aggravation of symptoms from their
prolonged use, and told the patient so; but she was   15
unwilling to give up the medicine while she was re-
covering. It then occurred to me to give her unmedicated pellets and watch the result. I did so, and   18
she continued to gain. Finally she said that she would
give up her medicine for one day, and risk the
effects. After trying this, she informed me that she   21
could get along two days without globules; but on
the third day she again suffered, and was relieved by
taking them. She went on in this way, taking the   24
unmedicated pellets, — and receiving occasional visits
from me, — but employing no other means, and she was
cured.   27

Metaphysics, as taught in Christian Science, is the
next stately step beyond homœopathy. In metaphysics,

matter disappears from the remedy entirely,   30
and Mind takes its rightful and supreme
place. Homœopathy takes mental symptoms largely

into consideration in its diagnosis of disease. Christian 1
Science deals wholly with the mental cause in judging and
destroying disease. It succeeds where homœopathy fails, 3
solely because its one recognized Principle of healing is
Mind, and the whole force of the mental element is employed through the Science of Mind, which never shares 6
its rights with inanimate matter.

Christian Science exterminates the drug, and rests on
Mind alone as the curative Principle, acknowledging that 9

The modus of homœopathy the divine Mind has all power. Homœopathy
mentalizes a drug with such repetition of
thought-attenuations, that the drug becomes 12
more like the human mind than the substratum of this so-
called mind, which we call matter; and the drug's power
of action is proportionately increased. 15

If drugs are part of God's creation, which (according
to the narrative in Genesis) He pronounced *good*, then

Drugging unchristian drugs cannot be poisonous. If He could cre- 18
ate drugs intrinsically bad, then they should
never be used. If He creates drugs at all and designs
them for medical use, why did Jesus not employ them 21
and recommend them for the treatment of disease?
Matter is not self-creative, for it is unintelligent. Erring
mortal mind confers the power which the drug seems to 24
possess.

Narcotics quiet mortal mind, and so relieve the body;
but they leave both mind and body worse for this sub- 27
mission. Christian Science impresses the entire corporeality, — namely, mind and body, — and brings out the
proof that Life is continuous and harmonious. Science 30
both neutralizes error and destroys it. Mankind is the
better for this spiritual and profound pathology.

It is recorded that the profession of medicine originated   1
in idolatry with pagan priests, who besought the gods to

Mythology
and materia
medica
heal the sick and designated Apollo as "the god   3
of medicine." He was supposed to have dic-
tated the first prescription, according to the
"History of Four Thousand Years of Medicine." It is   6
here noticeable that Apollo was also regarded as the sender
of disease, "the god of pestilence." Hippocrates turned
from image-gods to vegetable and mineral drugs for heal-   9
ing. This was deemed progress in medicine; but
what we need is the truth which heals both mind and
body. The future history of material medicine may   12
correspond with that of its material god, Apollo, who was
banished from heaven and endured great sufferings
upon earth.   15

Drugs, cataplasms, and whiskey are stupid substitutes
for the dignity and potency of divine Mind and its effi-

Footsteps to
intemperance
cacy to heal. It is pitiful to lead men into   18
temptation through the byways of this wilderness world, — to victimize the race with intoxicating
prescriptions for the sick, until mortal mind acquires an   21
educated appetite for strong drink, and men and women
become loathsome sots.

Evidences of progress and of spiritualization greet us   24
on every hand. Drug-systems are quitting their hold on

Advancing
degrees
matter and so letting in matter's higher stratum, mortal mind. Homœopathy, a step in   27
advance of allopathy, is doing this. Matter is going out
of medicine; and mortal mind, of a higher attenuation
than the drug, is governing the pellet.   30

A woman in the city of Lynn, Massachusetts, was
etherized and died in consequence, although her physi-

cians insisted that it would be unsafe to perform a needed 1
surgical operation without the ether. After the autopsy,

Effects of fear

her sister testified that the deceased protested 3
against inhaling the ether and said it would kill
her, but that she was compelled by her physicians to take
it. Her hands were held, and she was forced into sub- 6
mission. The case was brought to trial. The evidence
was found to be conclusive, and a verdict was returned that
death was occasioned, not by the ether, but by fear of 9
inhaling it.

Is it skilful or scientific surgery to take no heed of mental conditions and to treat the patient as if she were so 12

Mental conditions to be heeded

much mindless matter, and as if matter were
the only factor to be consulted? Had these
unscientific surgeons understood metaphysics, 15
they would have considered the woman's state of mind,
and not have risked such treatment. They would either
have allayed her fear or would have performed the opera- 18
tion without ether.

The sequel proved that this Lynn woman died from
effects produced by mortal mind, and not from the disease 21
or the operation.

The medical schools would learn the state of man
from matter instead of from Mind. They examine the 24

False source of knowledge

lungs, tongue, and pulse to ascertain how
much harmony, or health, matter is permit-
ting to matter, — how much pain or pleasure, action or 27
stagnation, one form of matter is allowing another form
of matter.

Ignorant of the fact that a man's belief produces dis- 30
ease and all its symptoms, the ordinary physician is
liable to increase disease with his own mind, when he

should address himself to the work of destroying it through   1
the power of the divine Mind.

The systems of physics act against metaphysics, and   3
vice versa. When mortals forsake the material for the
spiritual basis of action, drugs lose their healing force,
for they have no innate power. Unsupported by the   6
faith reposed in it, the inanimate drug becomes
powerless.

The motion of the arm is no more dependent upon the   9
direction of mortal mind, than are the organic action and

Obedient
muscles
secretion of the viscera. When this so-called
mind quits the body, the heart becomes as tor-   12
pid as the hand.

Anatomy finds a necessity for nerves to convey the mandate of mind to muscle and so cause action; but what does   15

Anatomy
and mind
anatomy say when the cords contract and become immovable? Has mortal mind ceased
speaking to them, or has it bidden them to be impotent?   18
Can muscles, bones, blood, and nerves rebel against mind
in one instance and not in another, and become cramped
despite the mental protest?   21

Unless muscles are self-acting at all times, they are
never so, — never capable of acting contrary to mental
direction. If muscles can cease to act and become rigid   24
of their own preference, — be deformed or symmetrical,
as they please or as disease directs, — they must be self-
directing. Why then consult anatomy to learn how mor-   27
tal mind governs muscle, if we are only to learn from
anatomy that muscle is not so governed?

Mind over
matter
Is man a material fungus without Mind   30
to help him? Is a stiff joint or a contracted
muscle as much a result of law as the supple and

elastic condition of the healthy limb, and is God the 1
lawgiver?

You say, "*I* have burned my finger." This is an 3
exact statement, more exact than you suppose; for mortal mind, and not matter, burns it. Holy inspiration
has created states of mind which have been able to nullify 6
the action of the flames, as in the Bible case of the three
young Hebrew captives, cast into the Babylonian furnace;
while an opposite mental state might produce spontaneous 9
combustion.

In 1880, Massachusetts put her foot on a proposed
tyrannical law, restricting the practice of medicine. If 12

Restrictive
regulations
her sister States follow this example in harmony with our Constitution and Bill of Rights,
they will do less violence to that immortal sentiment of the 15
Declaration, "Man is endowed by his Maker with certain
inalienable rights, among which are life, liberty, and the
pursuit of happiness." 18

The oppressive state statutes touching medicine re-
mind one of the words of the famous Madame Roland,
as she knelt before a statue of Liberty, erected near the 21
guillotine: "Liberty, what crimes are committed in thy
name!"

The ordinary practitioner, examining bodily symptoms, 24
telling the patient that he is sick, and treating the case ac-

Metaphysics
challenges
physics
cording to his physical diagnosis, would naturally induce the very disease he is trying to cure, 27
even if it were not already determined by mortal mind. Such unconscious mistakes would not occur, if
this old class of philanthropists looked as deeply for cause 30
and effect into mind as into matter. The physician agrees
with his "adversary quickly," but upon different terms

than does the metaphysician; for the matter-physician   1
agrees with the disease, while the metaphysician agrees
only with health and challenges disease.   3

    Christian Science brings to the body the sunlight of
Truth, which invigorates and purifies. Christian Science

Truth an alterative   acts as an alterative, neutralizing error with   6
Truth. It changes the secretions, expels hu-
mors, dissolves tumors, relaxes rigid muscles, restores
carious bones to soundness. The effect of this Science is   9
to stir the human mind to a change of base, on which it
may yield to the harmony of the divine Mind.

    Experiments have favored the fact that Mind governs   12
the body, not in one instance, but in every instance. The

Practical success   indestructible faculties of Spirit exist without
the conditions of matter and also without the   15
false beliefs of a so-called material existence. Working
out the rules of Science in practice, the author has restored health in cases of both acute and chronic disease in   18
their severest forms. Secretions have been changed, the
structure has been renewed, shortened limbs have been
elongated, ankylosed joints have been made supple, and   21
carious bones have been restored to healthy conditions. I
have restored what is called the lost substance of lungs, and
healthy organizations have been established where disease   24
was organic. Christian Science heals organic disease as
surely as it heals what is called functional, for it requires
only a fuller understanding of the divine Principle of   27
Christian Science to demonstrate the higher rule.

Testimony of medical teachers   With due respect for the faculty, I kindly
quote from Dr. Benjamin Rush, the famous   30
Philadelphia teacher of medical practice. He
declared that "it is impossible to calculate the mischief

which Hippocrates has done, by first marking Nature   1
with his name, and afterward letting her loose upon sick
people."   3

Dr. Benjamin Waterhouse, Professor in Harvard University, declared himself "sick of learned quackery."

Dr. James Johnson, Surgeon to William IV, King of   6
England, said:

"I declare my conscientious opinion, founded on long
observation and reflection, that if there were not a single   9
physician, surgeon, apothecary, man-midwife, chemist,
druggist, or drug on the face of the earth, there would be
less sickness and less mortality."   12

Dr. Mason Good, a learned Professor in London,
said:

"The effects of medicine on the human system are in   15
the highest degree uncertain; except, indeed, that it has
already destroyed more lives than war, pestilence, and
famine, all combined."   18

Dr. Chapman, Professor of the Institutes and Practice
of Physic in the University of Pennsylvania, in a published
essay said: 21

"Consulting the records of our science, we cannot
help being disgusted with the multitude of hypotheses
obtruded upon us at different times. Nowhere is the   24
imagination displayed to a greater extent; and perhaps
so ample an exhibition of human invention might gratify
our vanity, if it were not more than compensated by the   27
humiliating view of so much absurdity, contradiction,
and falsehood. To harmonize the contrarieties of medical doctrines is indeed a task as impracticable as to   30
arrange the fleeting vapors around us, or to reconcile the
fixed and repulsive antipathies of nature. Dark and

perplexed, our devious career resembles the groping of   1
Homer's Cyclops around his cave."

Sir John Forbes, M.D., F.R.S., Fellow of the Royal   3
College of Physicians, London, said:

"No systematic or theoretical classification of diseases
or of therapeutic agents, ever yet promulgated, is true, or   6
anything like the truth, and none can be adopted as a safe
guidance in practice."

It is just to say that generally the cultured class of medi-   9
cal practitioners are grand men and women, therefore
they are more scientific than are false claimants to Christian Science. But all human systems based on material   12
premises are minus the unction of divine Science. Much
yet remains to be said and done before all mankind is
saved and all the mental microbes of sin and all diseased   15
thought-germs are exterminated.

If you or I should appear to die, we should not be
dead. The seeming decease, caused by a majority of   18
human beliefs that man must die, or produced by mental
assassins, does not in the least disprove Christian Science;
rather does it evidence the truth of its basic proposition   21
that mortal thoughts in belief rule the materiality mis-
called life in the body or in matter. But the forever fact
remains paramount that Life, Truth, and Love save from   24
sin, disease, and death. "When this corruptible shall have
put on incorruption, and this mortal shall have put on
immortality [divine Science], then shall be brought to pass   27
the saying that is written, Death is swallowed up in
victory" (St. Paul).

confined to his bed six months with hip-disease, caused by 1
a fall upon a wooden spike when quite a boy. On enter-
Mind cures ing the house I met his physician, who said that 3
hip-disease
the patient was dying. The physician had just
probed the ulcer on the hip, and said the bone was carious
for several inches. He even showed me the probe, which 6
had on it the evidence of this condition of the bone. The
doctor went out. Mr. Clark lay with his eyes fixed and
sightless. The dew of death was on his brow. I went to 9
his bedside. In a few moments his face changed; its
death-pallor gave place to a natural hue. The eyelids
closed gently and the breathing became natural; he was 12
asleep. In about ten minutes he opened his eyes and
said: "I feel like a new man. My suffering is all gone."
It was between three and four o'clock in the afternoon 15
when this took place.

I told him to rise, dress himself, and take supper with
his family. He did so. The next day I saw him in the 18
yard. Since then I have not seen him, but am informed
that he went to work in two weeks. The discharge from
the sore stopped, and the sore was healed. The diseased 21
condition had continued there ever since the injury was
received in boyhood.

Since his recovery I have been informed that his physi- 24
cian claims to have cured him, and that his mother has
been threatened with incarceration in an insane asylum
for saying: "It was none other than God and that woman 27
who healed him." I cannot attest the truth of that
report, but what I saw and did for that man, and what
his physician said of the case, occurred just as I have 30
narrated.

It has been demonstrated to me that Life is God

and that the might of omnipotent Spirit shares not its   1
strength with matter or with human will. Review-
ing this brief experience, I cannot fail to discern the   3
coincidence of the spiritual idea of man with the divine
Mind.

A change in human belief changes all the physical symp-   6
toms, and determines a case for better or for
worse. When one's false belief is corrected,
Truth sends a report of health over the body.   9

Change of belief

Destruction of the auditory nerve and paralysis of the
optic nerve are not necessary to ensure deafness and blindness; for if mortal mind says, "I am deaf and blind," it   12
will be so without an injured nerve. Every theory opposed to this fact (as I learned in metaphysics) would
presuppose man, who is immortal in spiritual under-   15
standing, a mortal in material belief.

The authentic history of Kaspar Hauser is a useful hint
as to the frailty and inadequacy of mortal mind. It   18
proves beyond a doubt that education constitutes this so-called mind, and that, in turn,
mortal mind manifests itself in the body by the false   21
sense it imparts. Incarcerated in a dungeon, where
neither sight nor sound could reach him, at the age of
seventeen Kaspar was still a mental infant, crying and   24
chattering with no more intelligence than a babe, and
realizing Tennyson's description:

Power of habit

> An infant crying in the night,   27
> An infant crying for the light,
> And with no language but a cry.

His case proves material sense to be but a belief formed   30
by education alone. The light which affords us joy gave

him a belief of intense pain. His eyes were inflamed by ¹
the light. After the babbling boy had been taught to
speak a few words, he asked to be taken back to his dun- ³
geon, and said that he should never be happy elsewhere.
Outside of dismal darkness and cold silence he found no
peace. Every sound convulsed him with anguish. All ⁶
that he ate, except his black crust, produced violent
retchings. All that gives pleasure to our educated senses
gave him pain through those very senses, trained in an ⁹
opposite direction.

The point for each one to decide is, whether it is mortal

Useful
knowledge

mind or immortal Mind that is causative. We ¹²
should forsake the basis of matter for metaphysical Science and its divine Principle.

Whatever furnishes the semblance of an idea governed ¹⁵
by its Principle, furnishes food for thought. Through astronomy, natural history, chemistry, music, mathematics,
thought passes naturally from effect back to cause. ¹⁸

Academics of the right sort are requisite. Observation, invention, study, and original thought are expansive
and should promote the growth of mortal mind out of it- ²¹
self, out of all that is mortal.

It is the tangled barbarisms of learning which we
deplore, — the mere dogma, the speculative theory, the ²⁴
nauseous fiction. Novels, remarkable only for their
exaggerated pictures, impossible ideals, and specimens
of depravity, fill our young readers with wrong tastes ²⁷
and sentiments. Literary commercialism is lowering the
intellectual standard to accommodate the purse and to
meet a frivolous demand for amusement instead of for ³⁰
improvement. Incorrect views lower the standard of
truth.

If materialistic knowledge is power, it is not wisdom.   1
It is but a blind force. Man has "sought out many inventions," but he has not yet found it true that knowledge can   3
save him from the dire effects of knowledge. The power
of mortal mind over its own body is little understood.

Better the suffering which awakens mortal mind from   6

Sin destroyed through suffering

its fleshly dream, than the false pleasures
which tend to perpetuate this dream. Sin
alone brings death, for sin is the only element   9
of destruction.

"Fear him which is able to destroy both soul and body
in hell," said Jesus. A careful study of this text shows   12
that here the word *soul* means a false sense or material
consciousness. The command was a warning to beware,
not of Rome, Satan, nor of God, but of sin. Sickness,   15
sin, and death are not concomitants of Life or Truth.
No law supports them. They have no relation to God
wherewith to establish their power. Sin makes its own   18
hell, and goodness its own heaven.

Such books as will rule disease out of mortal mind, —

Dangerous shoals avoided

and so efface the images and thoughts of dis-   21
ease, instead of impressing them with forcible
descriptions and medical details, — will help
to abate sickness and to destroy it.   24

Many a hopeless case of disease is induced by a single
post mortem examination, — not from infection nor from
contact with material virus, but from the fear of the   27
disease and from the image brought before the mind; it
is a mental state, which is afterwards outlined on the
body.   30

The press unwittingly sends forth many sorrows and
diseases among the human family. It does this by giv-

ing names to diseases and by printing long descriptions 1
which mirror images of disease distinctly in thought. A

Pangs caused by the press

new name for an ailment affects people like a 3
Parisian name for a novel garment. Every one
hastens to get it. A minutely described disease costs many a man his earthly days of comfort. What 6
a price for human knowledge! But the price does not exceed the original cost. God said of the tree of knowledge,
which bears the fruit of sin, disease, and death, "In the 9
day that thou eatest thereof thou shalt surely die."

The less that is said of physical structure and laws, and

Higher standard for mortals

the more that is thought and said about moral 12
and spiritual law, the higher will be the standard of living and the farther mortals will be removed from imbecility or disease. 15

We should master fear, instead of cultivating it. It
was the ignorance of our forefathers in the departments
of knowledge now broadcast in the earth, that made them 18
hardier than our trained physiologists, more honest than
our sleek politicians.

We are told that the simple food our forefathers ate 21
helped to make them healthy, but that is a mistake.

Diet and dyspepsia

Their diet would not cure dyspepsia at this
period. With rules of health in the head 24
and the most digestible food in the stomach, there would
still be dyspeptics. Many of the effeminate constitutions
of our time will never grow robust until individual opin- 27
ions improve and mortal belief loses some portion of its
error.

The doctor's mind reaches that of his patient. The 30
doctor should suppress his fear of disease, else his belief
in its reality and fatality will harm his patients even more

than his calomel and morphine, for the higher stratum of   1
mortal mind has in belief more power to harm man than
the substratum, matter. A patient hears the   3
doctor's verdict as a criminal hears his death-
sentence. The patient may seem calm under it, but he is
not. His fortitude may sustain him, but his fear, which   6
has already developed the disease that is gaining the
mastery, is increased by the physician's words.

The materialistic doctor, though humane, is an art-   9
ist who outlines his thought relative to disease, and then
fills in his delineations with sketches from text-
books. It is better to prevent disease from   12
forming in mortal mind afterwards to appear on the
body; but to do this requires attention. The thought of
disease is formed before one sees a doctor and before   15
the doctor undertakes to dispel it by a counter-irritant,
— perhaps by a blister, by the application of caustic or
croton oil, or by a surgical operation. Again, giving an-   18
other direction to faith, the physician prescribes drugs,
until the elasticity of mortal thought haply causes a
vigorous reaction upon itself, and reproduces a picture   21
of healthy and harmonious formations.

A patient's belief is more or less moulded and formed
by his doctor's belief in the case, even though the doctor   24
says nothing to support his theory. His thoughts and his
patient's commingle, and the stronger thoughts rule the
weaker. Hence the importance that doctors be Christian   27
Scientists.

Because the muscles of the blacksmith's arm are

strongly developed, it does not follow that   30
exercise has produced this result or that a
less used arm must be weak. If matter were the cause

of action, and if muscles, without volition of mortal   1
mind, could lift the hammer and strike the anvil, it
might be thought true that hammering would enlarge   3
the muscles. The trip-hammer is not increased in size
by exercise. Why not, since muscles are as material as
wood and iron? Because nobody believes that mind is   6
producing such a result on the hammer.

Muscles are not self-acting. If mind does not move
them, they are motionless. Hence the great fact that   9
Mind alone enlarges and empowers man through its
mandate, — by reason of its demand for and supply of
power. Not because of muscular exercise, but by rea-   12
son of the blacksmith's faith in exercise, his arm becomes
stronger.

Mortals develop their own bodies or make them sick,   15
according as they influence them through mortal mind.

Latent fear
subdued

To know whether this development is produced
consciously or unconsciously, is of less impor-   18
tance than a knowledge of the fact. The feats of the gym-
nast prove that latent mental fears are subdued by him.
The devotion of thought to an honest achievement makes   21
the achievement possible. Exceptions only confirm this
rule, proving that failure is occasioned by a too feeble
faith.   24

Had Blondin believed it impossible to walk the rope
over Niagara's abyss of waters, he could never have
done it. His belief that he could do it gave his thought- 27
forces, called muscles, their flexibility and power which
the unscientific might attribute to a lubricating oil. His
fear must have disappeared before his power of putting   30
resolve into action could appear.

When Homer sang of the Grecian gods, Olympus was

dark, but through his verse the gods became alive in a   1
nation's belief. Pagan worship began with muscularity,

Homer and
Moses

but the law of Sinai lifted thought into the   3
song of David. Moses advanced a nation to
the worship of God in Spirit instead of matter, and illustrated the grand human capacities of being bestowed   6
by immortal Mind.

Whoever is incompetent to explain Soul would be wise
not to undertake the explanation of body. Life is, always   9

A mortal
not man

has been, and ever will be independent of
matter; for Life is God, and man is the idea
of God, not formed materially but spiritually, and not   12
subject to decay and dust. The Psalmist said: "Thou
madest him to have dominion over the works of Thy
hands. Thou hast put all things under his feet."   15

The great truth in the Science of being, that the real
man was, is, and ever shall be perfect, is incontrovertible;
for if man is the image, reflection, of God, he is neither   18
inverted nor subverted, but upright and Godlike.

The suppositional antipode of divine infinite Spirit
is the so-called human soul or spirit, in other words   21
the five senses, — the flesh that warreth against Spirit.
These so-called material senses must yield to the infinite
Spirit, named God.   24

St. Paul said: "For I determined not to know anything among you, save Jesus Christ, and him crucified."
(I Cor. ii. 2.) Christian Science says: I am determined   27
not to know anything among you, save Jesus Christ, and
him glorified.

Chapter 8

Footsteps of Truth

Remember, Lord, the reproach of Thy servants;
how I do bear in my bosom the reproach of all the mighty people;
wherewith Thine enemies have reproached, O Lord;
wherewith they have reproached the footsteps of Thine anointed. — PSALMS.

The best sermon ever preached is Truth practised   1
and demonstrated by the destruction of sin, sickness,

Practical preaching and death. Knowing this and knowing too   3
that one affection would be supreme in us and
take the lead in our lives, Jesus said, "No man can serve
two masters."   6

We cannot build safely on false foundations. Truth
makes a new creature, in whom old things pass away
and "all things are become new." Passions, selfishness,   9
false appetites, hatred, fear, all sensuality, yield to spirituality, and the superabundance of being is on the side
of God, good.   12

We cannot fill vessels already full. They must first be
The uses of truth emptied. Let us disrobe error. Then, when
the winds of God blow, we shall not hug our   15
tatters close about us.

The way to extract error from mortal mind is to pour
in truth through flood-tides of Love. Christian perfec-   18
tion is won on no other basis.

Grafting holiness upon unholiness, supposing that sin

can be forgiven when it is not forsaken, is as foolish as 1
straining out gnats and swallowing camels.

The scientific unity which exists between God and man 3
must be wrought out in life-practice, and God's will must
be universally done.

If men would bring to bear upon the study of the 6
Science of Mind half the faith they bestow upon the so-

Divine study called pains and pleasures of material sense,
they would not go on from bad to worse, 9
until disciplined by the prison and the scaffold; but
the whole human family would be redeemed through
the merits of Christ, — through the perception and ac- 12
ceptance of Truth. For this glorious result Christian
Science lights the torch of spiritual understanding.

Outside of this Science all is mutable; but immortal 15
man, in accord with the divine Principle of his being,

Harmonious life-work God, neither sins, suffers, nor dies. The days
of our pilgrimage will multiply instead of di- 18
minish, when God's kingdom comes on earth; for the
true way leads to Life instead of to death, and earthly
experience discloses the finity of error and the infinite 21
capacities of Truth, in which God gives man dominion
over all the earth.

Our beliefs about a Supreme Being contradict the 24
practice growing out of them. Error abounds where

Belief and practice Truth should "much more abound." We
admit that God has almighty power, is "a 27
very present help in trouble;" and yet we rely on a drug
or hypnotism to heal disease, as if senseless matter or erring mortal mind had more power than omnipotent Spirit. 30

Common opinion admits that a man may take cold in
the act of doing good, and that this cold may produce

fatal pulmonary disease; as though evil could overbear 1

Sure reward of righteousness the law of Love, and check the reward for doing good. In the Science of Christianity, Mind 3
— omnipotence — has all-power, assigns sure
rewards to righteousness, and shows that matter can
neither heal nor make sick, create nor destroy. 6

If God were understood instead of being merely believed, this understanding would establish health. The
Our belief and understanding accusation of the rabbis, "He made himself 9
the Son of God," was really the justification
of Jesus, for to the Christian the only true
spirit is Godlike. This thought incites to a more exalted 12
worship and self-abnegation. Spiritual perception brings
out the possibilities of being, destroys reliance on aught
but God, and so makes man the image of his Maker in 15
deed and in truth.

We are prone to believe either in more than one Supreme Ruler or in some power less than God. We im- 18
agine that Mind can be imprisoned in a sensuous body.
When the material body has gone to ruin, when evil has
overtaxed the belief of life in matter and destroyed it, 21
then mortals believe that the deathless Principle, or
Soul, escapes from matter and lives on; but this is not
true. Death is not a stepping-stone to Life, immortality, 24
Suicide and sin and bliss. The so-called sinner is a suicide.
Sin kills the sinner and will continue to kill
him so long as he sins. The foam and fury of illegiti- 27
mate living and of fearful and doleful dying should
disappear on the shore of time; then the waves of sin,
sorrow, and death beat in vain. 30

God, divine good, does not kill a man in order to give
him eternal Life, for God alone is man's life. God is at

once the centre and circumference of being. It is evil   1
that dies; good dies not.

All forms of error support the false conclusions that   3
there is more than one Life; that material history is as

Spirit the only   real and living as spiritual history; that mortal
intelligence
and substance   error is as conclusively mental as immortal   6
Truth; and that there are two separate, an-
tagonistic entities and beings, two powers, — namely,
Spirit and matter, — resulting in a third person (mortal   9
man) who carries out the delusions of sin, sickness, and
death.

The first power is admitted to be good, an intelligence or 12
Mind called God. The so-called second power, evil, is the
unlikeness of good. It cannot therefore be mind, though
so called. The third power, mortal man, is a supposed   15
mixture of the first and second antagonistic powers, intelligence and non-intelligence, of Spirit and matter.

Such theories are evidently erroneous. They can never 18
stand the test of Science. Judging them by their fruits,

Unscientific   they are corrupt. When will the ages under-
theories   stand the Ego, and realize only one God, one   21
Mind or intelligence?

False and self-assertive theories have given sinners the
notion that they can create what God cannot, — namely,   24
sinful mortals in God's image, thus usurping the name
without the nature of the image or reflection of divine
Mind; but in Science it can never be said that man   27
has a mind of his own, distinct from God, the *all*
Mind.

The belief that God lives in matter is pantheistic. The 30
error, which says that Soul is in body, Mind is in matter,
and good is in evil, must unsay it and cease from such

utterances; else God will continue to be hidden from hu-   1
manity, and mortals will sin without knowing that they
are sinning, will lean on matter instead of Spirit, stumble   3
with lameness, drop with drunkenness, consume with disease, — all because of their blindness, their false sense
concerning God and man.   6

When will the error of believing that there is life in
matter, and that sin, sickness, and death are creations of

Creation
perfect
God, be unmasked? When will it be under-   9
stood that matter has neither intelligence, life,
nor sensation, and that the opposite belief is the prolific
source of all suffering? God created all through Mind,   12
and made all perfect and eternal. Where then is the
necessity for recreation or procreation?

Befogged in error (the error of believing that matter   15
can be intelligent for good or evil), we can catch clear

Perceiving
the divine
image
glimpses of God only as the mists disperse,
or as they melt into such thinness that we per-   18
ceive the divine image in some word or deed
which indicates the true idea, — the supremacy and reality of good, the nothingness and unreality of evil.   21

When we realize that there is one Mind, the divine law

Redemption
from
selfishness
of loving our neighbor as ourselves is unfolded;
whereas a belief in many ruling minds hinders   24
man's normal drift towards the one Mind, one
God, and leads human thought into opposite channels
where selfishness reigns.   27

Selfishness tips the beam of human existence towards
the side of error, not towards Truth. Denial of the oneness of Mind throws our weight into the scale, not of   30
Spirit, God, good, but of matter.

When we fully understand our relation to the Divine,

we can have no other Mind but His, — no other Love,   1
wisdom, or Truth, no other sense of Life, and no consciousness of the existence of matter or error.   3

    The power of the human will should be exercised only
in subordination to Truth; else it will misguide the judg-

**Will-power
unrighteous**

ment and free the lower propensities. It is the   6
province of spiritual sense to govern man.
Material, erring, human thought acts injuriously both
upon the body and through it.   9

    Will-power is capable of all evil. It can never heal
the sick, for it is the prayer of the unrighteous; while
the exercise of the sentiments — hope, faith, love — is the 12
prayer of the righteous. This prayer, governed by Science
instead of the senses, heals the sick.

    In the scientific relation of God to man, we find that   15
whatever blesses one blesses all, as Jesus showed with
the loaves and the fishes, — Spirit, not matter, being the
source of supply.   18

    Does God send sickness, giving the mother her child
for the brief space of a few years and then taking it away

**Birth and
death unreal**

by death? Is God creating anew what He   21
has already created? The Scriptures are defi-
nite on this point, declaring that His work was *finished*,
nothing is new to God, and that it was *good*.   24

    Can there be any birth or death for man, the spiritual
image and likeness of God? Instead of God sending
sickness and death, He destroys them, and brings to light   27
immortality. Omnipotent and infinite Mind made all
and includes all. This Mind does not make mistakes
and subsequently correct them. God does not cause man   30
to sin, to be sick, or to die.

    There are evil beliefs, often called evil spirits; but

these evils are not Spirit, for there is no evil in Spirit. 1
Because God is Spirit, evil becomes more apparent and

No evil in Spirit

obnoxious proportionately as we advance spir- 3
itually, until it disappears from our lives.

This fact proves our position, for every scientific statement in Christianity has its proof. Error of statement 6
leads to error in action.

God is not the creator of an evil mind. Indeed, evil
is not Mind. We must learn that evil is the awful decep- 9

Subordination of evil

tion and unreality of existence. Evil is not
supreme; good is not helpless; nor are the
so-called laws of matter primary, and the law of Spirit 12
secondary. Without this lesson, we lose sight of the perfect Father, or the divine Principle of man.

Body is not first and Soul last, nor is evil mightier than 15

Evident impossibilities

good. The Science of being repudiates self-
evident impossibilities, such as the amalgama-
tion of Truth and error in cause or effect. Science sepa- 18
rates the tares and wheat in time of harvest.

There is but one primal cause. Therefore there can
be no effect from any other cause, and there can be no 21

One primal cause

reality in aught which does not proceed from
this great and only cause. Sin, sickness, disease, and death belong not to the Science of being. They 24
are the errors, which presuppose the absence of Truth,
Life, or Love.

The spiritual reality is the scientific fact in all things. 27
The spiritual fact, repeated in the action of man and the
whole universe, is harmonious and is the ideal of Truth.
Spiritual facts are not inverted; the opposite discord, 30
which bears no resemblance to spirituality, is not real.
The only evidence of this inversion is obtained from

suppositional error, which affords no proof of God, 1
Spirit, or of the spiritual creation. Material sense defines all things materially, and has a finite sense of the 3
infinite.

The Scriptures say, "In Him we live, and move, and
have our being." What then is this seeming power, in- 6

Seemingly
independent
authority
dependent of God, which causes disease and
cures it? What is it but an error of belief, —
a law of mortal mind, wrong in every sense, 9
embracing sin, sickness, and death? It is the very antipode of immortal Mind, of Truth, and of spiritual law.
It is not in accordance with the goodness of God's char- 12
acter that He should make man sick, then leave man to
heal himself; it is absurd to suppose that matter can both
cause and cure disease, or that Spirit, God, produces 15
disease and leaves the remedy to matter.

John Young of Edinburgh writes: "God is the father
of mind, and of nothing else." Such an utterance is 18
"the voice of one crying in the wilderness" of human
beliefs and preparing the way of Science. Let us learn
of the real and eternal, and prepare for the reign of 21
Spirit, the kingdom of heaven, — the reign and rule of
universal harmony, which cannot be lost nor remain
forever unseen. 24

Mind, not matter, is causation. A material body
only expresses a material and mortal mind. A mortal

Sickness as
only thought
man possesses this body, and he makes it 27
harmonious or discordant according to the
images of thought impressed upon it. You embrace
your body in your thought, and you should delineate 30
upon it thoughts of health, not of sickness. You should
banish all thoughts of disease and sin and of other beliefs

included in matter. Man, being immortal, has a perfect 1
indestructible life. It is the mortal belief which makes
the body discordant and diseased in proportion as igno- 3
rance, *fear,* or human will governs mortals.

Mind, supreme over all its formations and governing
them all, is the central sun of its own systems of ideas, 6

**Allness of
Truth**

the life and light of all its own vast creation;
and man is tributary to divine Mind. The
material and mortal body or mind is not the man. 9

The world would collapse without Mind, without the intelligence which holds the winds in its grasp. Neither
philosophy nor skepticism can hinder the march of the 12
Science which reveals the supremacy of Mind. The immanent sense of Mind-power enhances the glory of Mind.
Nearness, not distance, lends enchantment to this view. 15

The compounded minerals or aggregated substances
composing the earth, the relations which constituent

**Spiritual
translation**

masses hold to each other, the magnitudes, 18
distances, and revolutions of the celestial
bodies, are of no real importance, when we remember
that they all must give place to the spiritual fact by the 21
translation of man and the universe back into Spirit. In
proportion as this is done, man and the universe will be
found harmonious and eternal. 24

Material substances or mundane formations, astronomical calculations, and all the paraphernalia of speculative theories, based on the hypothesis of material law 27
or life and intelligence resident in matter, will ultimately vanish, swallowed up in the infinite calculus of
Spirit. 30

Spiritual sense is a conscious, constant capacity to understand God. It shows the superiority of faith by works

over faith in words. Its ideas are expressed only in "new   1
tongues;" and these are interpreted by the translation of
the spiritual original into the language which human   3
thought can comprehend.

The Principle and proof of Christianity are discerned
by spiritual sense. They are set forth in Jesus' demon-   6

**Jesus'
disregard
of matter**

strations, which show — by his healing the
sick, casting out evils, and destroying death,
"the last enemy that shall be destroyed," —   9
his disregard of matter and its so-called laws.

Knowing that Soul and its attributes were forever
manifested through man, the Master healed the sick,   12
gave sight to the blind, hearing to the deaf, feet to the
lame, thus bringing to light the scientific action of the
divine Mind on human minds and bodies and giving   15
a better understanding of Soul and salvation. Jesus
healed sickness and sin by one and the same metaphysical
process.   18

The expression *mortal mind* is really a solecism, for
Mind is immortal, and Truth pierces the error of mortality

**Mind not
mortal**

as a sunbeam penetrates the cloud. Because,   21
in obedience to the immutable law of Spirit,
this so-called mind is self-destructive, I name it mortal.
Error soweth the wind and reapeth the whirlwind.   24

What is termed matter, being unintelligent, cannot say,
"I suffer, I die, I am sick, or I am well." It is the so-

**Matter
mindless**

called mortal mind which voices this and ap-   27
pears to itself to make good its claim. To
mortal sense, sin and suffering are real, but immortal
sense includes no evil nor pestilence. Because immortal   30
sense has no error of sense, it has no sense of error; therefore it is without a destructive element.

If brain, nerves, stomach, are intelligent, — if they talk 1
to us, tell us their condition, and report how they feel, —
then Spirit and matter, Truth and error, commingle 3
and produce sickness and health, good and evil, life and
death; and who shall say whether Truth or error is the
greater? 6

The sensations of the body must either be the sensations of a so-called mortal mind or of matter. Nerves

**Matter
sensationless**
are not mind. Is it not provable that Mind is 9
not *mortal* and that matter has no sensation?
Is it not equally true that matter does not appear in the
spiritual understanding of being? 12

The sensation of sickness and the impulse to sin seem
to obtain in mortal mind. When a tear starts, does not
this so-called mind produce the effect seen in the lachry- 15
mal gland? Without mortal mind, the tear could not
appear; and this action shows the nature of all so-called
material cause and effect. 18

It should no longer be said in Israel that "the fathers
have eaten sour grapes, and the children's teeth are set
on edge." Sympathy with error should disappear. The 21
transfer of the thoughts of one erring mind to another,
Science renders impossible.

If it is true that nerves have sensation, that matter has 24
intelligence, that the material organism causes the eyes to

**Nerves
painless**
see and the ears to hear, then, when the body
is dematerialized, these faculties must be lost, 27
for their immortality is not in Spirit; whereas the fact
is that only through dematerialization and spiritualization of thought can these faculties be conceived of as 30
immortal.

Nerves are not the source of pain or pleasure. We

suffer or enjoy in our dreams, but this pain or pleasure   1
is not communicated through a nerve. A tooth which has
been extracted sometimes aches again in belief, and the   3
pain seems to be in its old place. A limb which has been
amputated has continued in belief to pain the owner. If
the sensation of pain in the limb can return, can be pro-   6
longed, why cannot the limb reappear?

Why need pain, rather than pleasure, come to this mortal sense? Because the memory of pain is more vivid   9
than the memory of pleasure. I have seen an unwitting
attempt to scratch the end of a finger which had been cut
off for months. When the nerve is gone, which we say   12
was the occasion of pain, and the pain still remains, it
proves sensation to be in the mortal mind, not in matter.
Reverse the process; take away this so-called mind instead   15
of a piece of the flesh, and the nerves have no sensation.

Mortals have a modus of their own, undirected and unsustained by God. They produce a rose through seed and   18

**Human
falsities**

soil, and bring the rose into contact with the
olfactory nerves that they may smell it. In
legerdemain and credulous frenzy, mortals believe that   21
unseen spirits produce the flowers. God alone makes
and clothes the lilies of the field, and this He does by
means of Mind, not matter.   24

Because all the methods of Mind are not understood,
we say the lips or hands must move in order to convey

**No miracles
in Mind-
methods**

thought, that the undulations of the air convey   27
sound, and possibly that other methods involve
so-called miracles. The realities of being, its
normal action, and the origin of all things are unseen to   30
mortal sense; whereas the unreal and imitative movements of mortal belief, which would reverse the immortal

modus and action, are styled the real. Whoever con- 1
tradicts this mortal mind supposition of reality is called
a deceiver, or is said to be deceived. Of a man it has 3
been said, "As he thinketh in his heart, so is he;" hence
as a man spiritually *understandeth*, so is he in truth.

Mortal mind conceives of something as either liquid 6
or solid, and then classifies it materially. Immortal and

**Good
indefinable**

spiritual facts exist apart from this mortal and
material conception. God, good, is self-exist- 9
ent and self-expressed, though indefinable as a whole.
Every step towards goodness is a departure from materiality, and is a tendency towards God, Spirit. Material 12
theories partially paralyze this attraction towards infinite
and eternal good by an opposite attraction towards the
finite, temporary, and discordant. 15

Sound is a mental impression made on mortal belief.
The ear does not really hear. Divine Science reveals
sound as communicated through the senses of Soul — 18
through spiritual understanding.

Mozart experienced more than he expressed. The
rapture of his grandest symphonies was never heard. He 21

**Music,
rhythm of
head and
heart**

was a musician beyond what the world knew.
This was even more strikingly true of Bee-
thoven, who was so long hopelessly deaf. Men- 24
tal melodies and strains of sweetest music supersede conscious sound. Music is the rhythm of head and heart.
Mortal mind is the harp of many strings, discoursing 27
either discord or harmony according as the hand, which
sweeps over it, is human or divine.

Before human knowledge dipped to its depths into a 30
false sense of things, — into belief in material origins
which discard the one Mind and true source of being, —

it is possible that the impressions from Truth were as distinct as sound, and that they came as sound to the primitive prophets. If the medium of hearing is wholly spiritual, it is normal and indestructible.

If Enoch's perception had been confined to the evidence before his material senses, he could never have "walked with God," nor been guided into the demonstration of life eternal.

Adam, represented in the Scriptures as formed from dust, is an object-lesson for the human mind. The mate-

Adam and the senses

rial senses, like Adam, originate in matter and return to dust, — are proved non-intelligent. They go out as they came in, for they are still the error, not the truth of being. When it is learned that the spiritual sense, and not the material, conveys the impressions of Mind to man, then being will be understood and found to be harmonious.

We bow down to matter, and entertain finite thoughts of God like the pagan idolater. Mortals are inclined to

Idolatrous illusions

fear and to obey what they consider a material body more than they do a spiritual God. All material knowledge, like the original "tree of knowledge," multiplies their pains, for mortal illusions would rob God, slay man, and meanwhile would spread their table with cannibal tidbits and give thanks.

How transient a sense is mortal sight, when a wound on the retina may end the power of light and lens! But the

The senses of Soul

real sight or sense is not lost. Neither age nor accident can interfere with the senses of Soul, and there are no other real senses. It is evident that the body as matter has no sensation of its own, and there is no oblivion for Soul and its faculties. Spirit's senses are with-

out pain, and they are forever at peace. Nothing can hide 1
from them the harmony of all things and the might and
permanence of Truth. 3

If Spirit, Soul, could sin or be lost, then being and immortality would be lost, together with all the faculties of
Real being Mind; but being cannot be lost while God ex- 6
never lost ists. Soul and matter are at variance from the
very necessity of their opposite natures. Mortals are
unacquainted with the reality of existence, because matter 9
and mortality do not reflect the facts of Spirit.

Spiritual vision is not subordinate to geometric alti-
tudes. Whatever is governed by God, is never for an 12
instant deprived of the light and might of intelligence
and Life.

We are sometimes led to believe that darkness is as real 15
as light; but Science affirms darkness to be only a mortal
Light and sense of the absence of light, at the coming of
darkness which darkness loses the appearance of reality. 18
So sin and sorrow, disease and death, are the suppositional
absence of Life, God, and flee as phantoms of error before
truth and love. 21

With its divine proof, Science reverses the evidence of
material sense. Every quality and condition of mortality
is lost, swallowed up in immortality. Mortal man is the 24
antipode of immortal man in origin, in existence, and in his
relation to God.

Because he understood the superiority and immor- 27
tality of good, Socrates feared not the hemlock poison.
Faith of Even the faith of his philosophy spurned phys-
Socrates ical timidity. Having sought man's spiritual 30
state, he recognized the immortality of man. The ignorance and malice of the age would have killed the vener-

able philosopher because of his faith in Soul and his in-   1
difference to the body.

Who shall say that man is alive to-day, but may be dead   3
to-morrow? What has touched Life, God, to such

The serpent   strange issues? Here theories cease, and Sci-
of error   ence unveils the mystery and solves the prob-   6
lem of man. Error bites the heel of truth, but cannot kill
truth. Truth bruises the head of error — destroys error.
Spirituality lays open siege to materialism. On which   9
side are we fighting?

The understanding that the Ego is Mind, and that
there is but one Mind or intelligence, begins at once to   12

Servants   destroy the errors of mortal sense and to supply
and masters   the truth of immortal sense. This understanding makes the body harmonious; it makes the nerves,   15
bones, brain, etc., servants, instead of masters. If man
is governed by the law of divine Mind, his body is in submission to everlasting Life and Truth and Love. The   18
great mistake of mortals is to suppose that man, God's
image and likeness, is both matter and Spirit, both good
and evil.   21

If the decision were left to the corporeal senses, evil
would appear to be the master of good, and sickness to
be the rule of existence, while health would seem the   24
exception, death the inevitable, and life a paradox. Paul
asked: "What concord hath Christ with Belial?" (2 Cor-
inthians vi. 15.)   27

When you say, "Man's body is material," I say with
Paul: Be "willing rather to be absent from the body,

Personal   and to be present with the Lord." Give up   30
identity   your material belief of mind in matter, and
have but one Mind, even God; for this Mind forms its

own likeness. The loss of man's identity through the   1
understanding which Science confers is impossible; and
the notion of such a possibility is more absurd than to   3
conclude that individual musical tones are lost in the
origin of harmony.

Medical schools may inform us that the healing work   6
of Christian Science and Paul's peculiar Christian con-

Paul's experience   version and experience, — which prove Mind
to be scientifically distinct from matter, — are   9
indications of unnatural mental and bodily conditions,
even of catalepsy and hysteria; yet if we turn to the Scriptures, what do we read? Why, this: "If a man keep my   12
saying, he shall never see death!" and "Henceforth know
we no man after the flesh!"

That scientific methods are superior to others, is   15
seen by their effects. When you have once conquered

Fatigue is mental   a diseased condition of the body through
Mind, that condition never recurs, and you   18
have won a point in Science. When mentality gives
rest to the body, the next toil will fatigue you less, for
you are working out the problem of being in divine meta-   21
physics; and in proportion as you understand the control which Mind has over so-called matter, you will be
able to demonstrate this control. The scientific and   24
permanent remedy for fatigue is to learn the power of
Mind over the body or any illusion of physical weariness,
and so destroy this illusion, for matter cannot be weary   27
and heavy-laden.

You say, "Toil fatigues me." But what is this *me?*
Is it muscle or mind? Which is tired and so speaks?   30
Without mind, could the muscles be tired? Do the
muscles talk, or do you talk for them? Matter is non-

likeness. He reflects the infinite understanding, for I am 1
Infinity. The beauty of holiness, the perfection of being,

Testimony of Soul

imperishable glory, — all are Mine, for I am 3
God. I give immortality to man, for I am
Truth. I include and impart all bliss, for I am Love.
I give life, without beginning and without end, for I am 6
Life. I am supreme and give all, for I am Mind. I am
the substance of all, because I AM THAT I AM.

I hope, dear reader, I am leading you into the under- 9
standing of your divine rights, your heaven-bestowed har-

Heaven-bestowed prerogative

mony, — that, as you read, you see there is no
cause (outside of erring, mortal, material sense 12
which is not power) able to make you sick or
sinful; and I hope that you are conquering this false sense.
Knowing the falsity of so-called material sense, you can 15
assert your prerogative to overcome the belief in sin, disease, or death.

If you believe in and practise wrong knowingly, you 18
can at once change your course and do right. Matter can

Right endeavor possible

make no opposition to right endeavors against
sin or sickness, for matter is inert, mindless. 21
Also, if you believe yourself diseased, you can
alter this wrong belief and action without hindrance from
the body. 24

Do not believe in any supposed necessity for sin, disease, or death, knowing (as you ought to know) that God
never requires obedience to a so-called material law, for 27
no such law exists. The belief in sin and death is destroyed by the law of God, which is the law of Life instead of death, of harmony instead of discord, of Spirit 30
instead of the flesh.

The divine demand, "Be ye therefore perfect," is sci-

entific, and the human footsteps leading to perfection are 1
indispensable. Individuals are consistent who, watching

Patience and final perfection

and praying, can "run, and not be weary; . . . 3
walk, and not faint," who gain good rapidly
and hold their position, or attain slowly and
yield not to discouragement. God requires perfection, 6
but not until the battle between Spirit and flesh is fought
and the victory won. To stop eating, drinking, or being
clothed materially before the spiritual facts of existence 9
are gained step by step, is not legitimate. When we wait
patiently on God and seek Truth righteously, He directs
our path. Imperfect mortals grasp the ultimate of spir- 12
itual perfection slowly; but to *begin* aright and to continue the strife of demonstrating the great problem of
being, is doing much. 15

During the sensual ages, absolute Christian Science
may not be achieved prior to the change called death,
for we have not the power to demonstrate what we do 18
not understand. But the human self must be evangel-
ized. This task God demands us to accept lovingly
to-day, and to abandon so fast as practical the material, 21
and to work out the spiritual which determines the outward and actual.

If you venture upon the quiet surface of error and are 24
in sympathy with error, what is there to disturb the waters?
What is there to strip off error's disguise?

If you launch your bark upon the ever-agitated but 27
healthful waters of truth, you will encounter storms.

The cross and crown

Your good will be evil spoken of. This is the
cross. Take it up and bear it, for through it 30
you win and wear the crown. Pilgrim on earth, thy home
is heaven; stranger, thou art the guest of God.

Chapter 9

Creation

Thy throne is established of old:
Thou art from everlasting. — PSALMS.

For we know that the whole creation groaneth
and travaileth in pain together until now.
And not only they, but ourselves also,
which have the firstfruits of the Spirit,
even we ourselves groan within ourselves,
waiting for the adoption, to wit,
the redemption of our body. — PAUL.

Eternal Truth is changing the universe. As mortals drop off their mental swaddling-clothes, thought 1

Inadequate theories of creation   expands into expression. "Let there be light," 3
is the perpetual demand of Truth and Love,
changing chaos into order and discord into the
music of the spheres. The mythical human theories of 6
creation, anciently classified as the higher criticism, sprang
from cultured scholars in Rome and in Greece, but they
afforded no foundation for accurate views of creation by 9
the divine Mind.

Mortal man has made a covenant with his eyes to be-

Finite views of Deity   little Deity with human conceptions. In league 12
with material sense, mortals take limited views
of all things. That God is corporeal or material, no man
should affirm. 15

The human form, or physical finiteness, cannot be
made the basis of any true idea of the infinite Godhead.
Eye hath not seen Spirit, nor hath ear heard His voice. 18

Progress takes off human shackles. The finite must 1
yield to the infinite. Advancing to a higher plane of ac-

No material creation tion, thought rises from the material sense to 3
the spiritual, from the scholastic to the in-
spirational, and from the mortal to the immortal. All
things are created spiritually. Mind, not matter, is the 6
creator. Love, the divine Principle, is the Father and
Mother of the universe, including man.

The theory of three persons in one God (that is, a per- 9
Tritheism impossible sonal Trinity or Tri-unity) suggests polythe-
ism, rather than the one ever-present I AM.
"Hear, O Israel: the Lord our God is one Lord." 12

The everlasting I AM is not bounded nor compressed
within the narrow limits of physical humanity, nor can
No divine corporeality He be understood aright through mortal con- 15
cepts. The precise form of God must be of
small importance in comparison with the sublime question, What is infinite Mind or divine Love? 18

Who is it that demands our obedience? He who, in
the language of Scripture, "doeth according to His will
in the army of heaven, and among the inhabitants of the 21
earth; and none can stay His hand, or say unto Him,
What doest Thou?"

No form nor physical combination is adequate to rep- 24
resent infinite Love. A finite and material sense of God
leads to formalism and narrowness; it chills the spirit of
Christianity. 27

A limitless Mind cannot proceed from physical limita-
tions. Finiteness cannot present the idea or the vast-
Limitless Mind ness of infinity. A mind originating from a 30
finite or material source must be limited and
finite. Infinite Mind is the creator, and creation is the

infinite image or idea emanating from this Mind. If   1
Mind is within and without all things, then all is Mind;
and this definition is scientific.   3

If matter, so-called, is substance, then Spirit, matter's
unlikeness, must be shadow; and shadow cannot produce
Matter is not substance. The theory that Spirit is not the   6
substance
only substance and creator is pantheistic het-
erodoxy, which ultimates in sickness, sin, and death; it is
the belief in a bodily soul and a material mind, a soul   9
governed by the body and a mind in matter. This belief is shallow pantheism.

Mind creates His own likeness in ideas, and the sub-   12
stance of an idea is very far from being the supposed substance of non-intelligent matter. Hence the Father Mind
is not the father of matter. The material senses and   15
human conceptions would translate spiritual ideas into
material beliefs, and would say that an anthropomorphic
God, instead of infinite Principle, — in other words, divine 18
Love, — is the father of the rain, "who hath begotten the
drops of dew," who bringeth "forth Mazzaroth in his season," and guideth "Arcturus with his sons."   21

Finite mind manifests all sorts of errors, and thus
proves the material theory of mind in matter to be the
Inexhaustible antipode of Mind. Who hath found finite life   24
divine Love
or love sufficient to meet the demands of human
want and woe, — to still the desires, to satisfy the aspira-
tions? Infinite Mind cannot be limited to a finite form, 27
or Mind would lose its infinite character as inexhaustible
Love, eternal Life, omnipotent Truth.

It would require an infinite form to contain infinite   30
Mind. Indeed, the phrase *infinite form* involves a contradiction of terms. Finite man cannot be the image and

likeness of the infinite God. A mortal, corporeal, or   1
finite conception of God cannot embrace the glories of

limitless, incorporeal Life and Love. Hence   3
the unsatisfied human craving for something
better, higher, holier, than is afforded by a
material belief in a physical God and man. The insuffi-   6
ciency of this belief to supply the true idea proves the
falsity of material belief.

Man is more than a material form with a mind inside,   9

which must escape from its environments in
order to be immortal. Man reflects infinity,
and this reflection is the true idea of God.   12

God expresses in man the infinite idea forever develop-
ing itself, broadening and rising higher and higher from
a boundless basis. Mind manifests all that exists in   15
the infinitude of Truth. We know no more of man as
the true divine image and likeness, than we know of
God.   18

The infinite Principle is reflected by the infinite idea
and spiritual individuality, but the material so-called senses
have no cognizance of either Principle or its idea. The   21
human capacities are enlarged and perfected in proportion as humanity gains the true conception of man and
God.   24

Mortals have a very imperfect sense of the spiritual
man and of the infinite range of his thought. To him

belongs eternal Life. Never born and   27
never dying, it were impossible for man, under
the government of God in eternal Science, to fall from his
high estate.   30

Through spiritual sense you can discern the heart of
divinity, and thus begin to comprehend in Science the

generic term *man*. Man is not absorbed in Deity, and 1
man cannot lose his individuality, for he reflects eternal Life; nor is he an isolated, soli- 3
tary idea, for he represents infinite Mind, the sum of all
substance.

God's man discerned

In divine Science, man is the true image of God. The 6
divine nature was best expressed in Christ Jesus, who
threw upon mortals the truer reflection of God and lifted
their lives higher than their poor thought-models would 9
allow, — thoughts which presented man as fallen, sick,
sinning, and dying. The Christlike understanding of
scientific being and divine healing includes a perfect Prin- 12
ciple and idea, — perfect God and perfect man, — as the
basis of thought and demonstration.

If man was once perfect but has now lost his perfection, 15
then mortals have never beheld in man the reflex image
of God. The *lost* image is no image. The
true likeness cannot be lost in divine reflection. 18
Understanding this, Jesus said: "Be ye therefore perfect, even as your Father which is in heaven is
perfect." 21

The divine image not lost

Mortal thought transmits its own images, and forms
its offspring after human illusions. God, Spirit, works
spiritually, not materially. Brain or matter 24
never formed a human concept. Vibration is
not intelligence; hence it is not a creator. Immortal
ideas, pure, perfect, and enduring, are transmitted by 27
the divine Mind through divine Science, which corrects
error with truth and demands spiritual thoughts, divine
concepts, to the end that they may produce harmonious 30
results.

Immortal models

Deducing one's conclusions as to man from imperfec-

tion instead of perfection, one can no more arrive at the 1
true conception or understanding of man, and make himself like it, than the sculptor can perfect his outlines from 3
an imperfect model, or the painter can depict the form
and face of Jesus, while holding in thought the character
of Judas. 6

The conceptions of mortal, erring thought must give
way to the ideal of all that is perfect and eternal. Through

Spiritual discovery many generations human beliefs will be attain- 9
ing diviner conceptions, and the immortal and
perfect model of God's creation will finally be seen as
the only true conception of being. 12

Science reveals the possibility of achieving all good,
and sets mortals at work to discover what God has already
done; but distrust of one's ability to gain the goodness 15
desired and to bring out better and higher results, often
hampers the trial of one's wings and ensures failure at the
outset. 18

Mortals must change their ideals in order to improve

Requisite change of our ideals their models. A sick body is evolved from
sick thoughts. Sickness, disease, and death 21
proceed from fear. Sensualism evolves bad
physical and moral conditions.

Selfishness and sensualism are educated in mortal 24
mind by the thoughts ever recurring to one's self, by
conversation about the body, and by the expectation of
perpetual pleasure or pain from it; and this education 27
is at the expense of spiritual growth. If we array
thought in mortal vestures, it must lose its immortal
nature. 30

If we look to the body for pleasure, we find pain; for
Life, we find death; for Truth, we find error; for Spirit,

we find its opposite, matter. Now reverse this action.   1

Thoughts are things Look away from the body into Truth and Love,
the Principle of all happiness, harmony, and   3
immortality. Hold thought steadfastly to the enduring, the good, and the true, and you will bring these
into your experience proportionably to their occupancy   6
of your thoughts.

The effect of mortal mind on health and happiness is
seen in this: If one turns away from the body with such   9

Unreality of pain absorbed interest as to forget it, the body
experiences no pain. Under the strong im-
pulse of a desire to perform his part, a noted actor was   12
accustomed night after night to go upon the stage and
sustain his appointed task, walking about as actively
as the youngest member of the company. This old man   15
was so lame that he hobbled every day to the theatre, and
sat aching in his chair till his cue was spoken, — a signal
which made him as oblivious of physical infirmity as if   18
he had inhaled chloroform, though he was in the full possession of his so-called senses.

Detach sense from the body, or matter, which is only   21
a form of human belief, and you may learn the meaning

Immutable identity of man of God, or good, and the nature of the immutable and immortal. Breaking away from the   24
mutations of time and sense, you will neither
lose the solid objects and ends of life nor your own identity. Fixing your gaze on the realities supernal, you will   27
rise to the spiritual consciousness of being, even as the bird
which has burst from the egg and preens its wings for a
skyward flight.   30

We should forget our bodies in remembering good and
the human race. Good demands of man every hour, in

which to work out the problem of being. Consecration   1
to good does not lessen man's dependence on God, but

Forgetfulness
of self

heightens it. Neither does consecration di-   3
minish man's obligations to God, but shows
the paramount necessity of meeting them. Christian
Science takes naught from the perfection of God, but it   6
ascribes to Him the entire glory. By putting "off the old
man with his deeds," mortals "put on immortality."

We cannot fathom the nature and quality of God's   9
creation by diving into the shallows of mortal belief. We
must reverse our feeble flutterings — our efforts to find
life and truth in matter — and rise above the testimony   12
of the material senses, above the mortal to the immortal
idea of God. These clearer, higher views inspire the Godlike man to reach the absolute centre and circumference   15
of his being.

Job said: "I have heard of Thee by the hearing of the
ear: but now mine eye seeth Thee." Mortals will echo   18

The true
sense

Job's thought, when the supposed pain and
pleasure of matter cease to predominate. They
will then drop the false estimate of life and happiness, of   21
joy and sorrow, and attain the bliss of loving unselfishly,
working patiently, and conquering all that is unlike God.
Starting from a higher standpoint, one rises spontane-   24
ously, even as light emits light without effort; for "where
your treasure is, there will your heart be also."

The foundation of mortal discord is a false sense of   27
man's origin. To begin rightly is to end rightly. Every

Mind the
only cause

concept which seems to begin with the brain
begins falsely. Divine Mind is the only cause   30
or Principle of existence. Cause does not exist in matter,
in mortal mind, or in physical forms.

Mortals are egotists. They believe themselves to be 1
independent workers, personal authors, and even privi-

Human egotism

leged originators of something which Deity 3
would not or could not create. The creations
of mortal mind are material. Immortal spiritual man
alone represents the truth of creation. 6

When mortal man blends his thoughts of existence
with the spiritual and works only as God works,

Mortal man a mis-creator

he will no longer grope in the dark and cling 9
to earth because he has not tasted heaven.
Carnal beliefs defraud us. They make man an involuntary hypocrite, — producing evil when he would create 12
good, forming deformity when he would outline grace
and beauty, injuring those whom he would bless. He
becomes a general mis-creator, who believes he is a 15
semi-god. His "touch turns hope to dust, the dust we
all have trod." He might say in Bible language: "The
good that I would, I do not: but the evil which I would 18
not, *that I do.*"

There can be but one creator, who has created all.
Whatever seems to be a new creation, is but the discovery 21

No new creation

of some distant idea of Truth; else it is a
new multiplication or self-division of mortal thought, as when some finite sense peers from its 24
cloister with amazement and attempts to pattern the
infinite.

The multiplication of a human and mortal sense of per- 27
sons and things is not creation. A sensual thought, like
an atom of dust thrown into the face of spiritual im-
mensity, is dense blindness instead of a scientific eternal 30
consciousness of creation.

The fading forms of matter, the mortal body and ma-

terial earth, are the fleeting concepts of the human mind. 1
They have their day before the permanent facts and their

Mind's true camera perfection in Spirit appear. The crude crea- 3
tions of mortal thought must finally give place
to the glorious forms which we sometimes behold in the
camera of divine Mind, when the mental picture is spir- 6
itual and eternal. Mortals must look beyond fading,
finite forms, if they would gain the true sense of things.
Where shall the gaze rest but in the unsearchable realm 9
of Mind? We must look where we would walk, and we
must act as possessing all power from Him in whom we
have our being. 12

As mortals gain more correct views of God and man,
multitudinous objects of creation, which before were

Self-completeness invisible, will become visible. When we 15
realize that Life is Spirit, never in nor of
matter, this understanding will expand into self-completeness, finding all in God, good, and needing no other 18
consciousness.

Spirit and its formations are the only realities of being.
Matter disappears under the microscope of Spirit. Sin 21

Spiritual proofs of existence is unsustained by Truth, and sickness and
death were overcome by Jesus, who proved
them to be forms of error. Spiritual living 24
and blessedness are the only evidences, by which we can
recognize true existence and feel the unspeakable peace
which comes from an all-absorbing spiritual love. 27

When we learn the way in Christian Science and recognize man's spiritual being, we shall behold and understand God's creation, — all the glories of earth and heaven 30
and man.

The universe of Spirit is peopled with spiritual beings,

and its government is divine Science. Man is the off- 1
spring, not of the lowest, but of the highest qualities of

Godward gravitation Mind. Man understands spiritual existence 3
in proportion as his treasures of Truth and
Love are enlarged. Mortals must gravitate Godward,
their affections and aims grow spiritual, — they must near 6
the broader interpretations of being, and gain some proper
sense of the infinite, — in order that sin and mortality
may be put off. 9

This scientific sense of being, forsaking matter for
Spirit, by no means suggests man's absorption into Deity
and the loss of his identity, but confers upon man en- 12
larged individuality, a wider sphere of thought and action,
a more expansive love, a higher and more permanent
peace. 15

The senses represent birth as untimely and death as
irresistible, as if man were a weed growing apace or a

Mortal birth and death flower withered by the sun and nipped by 18
untimely frosts; but this is true only of a
mortal, not of a man in God's image and likeness. The
truth of being is perennial, and the error is unreal and 21
obsolete.

Who that has felt the loss of human peace has not gained
stronger desires for spiritual joy? The aspiration after 24

Blessings from pain heavenly good comes even before we discover
what belongs to wisdom and Love. The loss
of earthly hopes and pleasures brightens the ascending 27
path of many a heart. The pains of sense quickly inform
us that the pleasures of sense are mortal and that joy is
spiritual. 30

The pains of sense are salutary, if they wrench away
false pleasurable beliefs and transplant the affections

Decapitation of error

from sense to Soul, where the creations of God are good, 1
"rejoicing the heart." Such is the sword of
Science, with which Truth decapitates error, 3
materiality giving place to man's higher individuality and
destiny.

Uses of adversity

Would existence without personal friends be to you 6
a blank? Then the time will come when you will be
solitary, left without sympathy; but this
seeming vacuum is already filled with divine 9
Love. When this hour of development comes, even if
you cling to a sense of personal joys, spiritual Love will
force you to accept what best promotes your growth. 12
Friends will betray and enemies will slander, until the
lesson is sufficient to exalt you; for "man's extremity
is God's opportunity." The author has experienced the 15
foregoing prophecy and its blessings. Thus He teaches
mortals to lay down their fleshliness and gain spirituality.
This is done through self-abnegation. Universal Love 18
is the divine way in Christian Science.

The sinner makes his own hell by doing evil, and the
saint his own heaven by doing right. The opposite per- 21
secutions of material sense, aiding evil with evil, would
deceive the very elect.

Mortals must follow Jesus' sayings and his demonstra- 24
tions, which dominate the flesh. Perfect and infinite

Beatific presence

Mind enthroned is heaven. The evil beliefs
which originate in mortals are hell. Man is the 27
idea of Spirit; he reflects the beatific presence, illuming
the universe with light. Man is deathless, spiritual. He
is above sin or frailty. He does not cross the barriers 30
of time into the vast forever of Life, but he coexists with
God and the universe.

Every object in material thought will be destroyed, but 1
the spiritual idea, whose substance is in Mind, is eternal.

The infinitude of God The offspring of God start not from matter 3
or ephemeral dust. They are in and of Spirit,
divine Mind, and so forever continue. God is one. The
allness of Deity is His oneness. Generically man is one, 6
and specifically man means all men.

It is generally conceded that God is Father, eternal, self-
created, infinite. If this is so, the forever Father must 9
have had children prior to Adam. The great I AM made
all "that was made." Hence man and the spiritual universe coexist with God. 12

Christian Scientists understand that, in a religious
sense, they have the same authority for the appellative
mother, as for that of brother and sister. Jesus said: 15
"For whosoever shall do the will of my Father which
is in heaven, the same is my brother, and sister, and
mother." 18

When examined in the light of divine Science, mortals
present more than is detected upon the surface, since

Waymarks to eternal Truth inverted thoughts and erroneous beliefs must 21
be counterfeits of Truth. Thought is bor-
rowed from a higher source than matter, and
by reversal, errors serve as waymarks to the one Mind, 24
in which all error disappears in celestial Truth. The
robes of Spirit are "white and glistering," like the raiment
of Christ. Even in this world, therefore, "let thy gar- 27
ments be always white." "Blessed is the man that endureth [overcometh] temptation: for when he is tried,
[proved faithful], he shall receive the crown of life, 30
which the Lord hath promised to them that love him."
(James i. 12.)

Chapter 10

Science of Being

That which was from the beginning, which we have heard,
which we have seen with our eyes, which we have looked upon,
and our hands have handled, of the Word of life, . . .
That which we have seen and heard declare we unto you,
that ye also may have fellowship with us:
and truly our fellowship is with the Father,
and with His Son Jesus Christ. — JOHN, First Epistle.

Here I stand. I can do no otherwise;
so help me God! Amen! — MARTIN LUTHER.

I n the material world, thought has brought to light 1
with great rapidity many useful wonders. With
like activity have thought's swift pinions been rising 3
Materialistic towards the realm of the real, to the spiritual
challenge cause of those lower things which give impulse to inquiry. Belief in a material basis, from 6
which may be deduced all rationality, is slowly yielding
to the idea of a metaphysical basis, looking away from
matter to Mind as the cause of every effect. Material- 9
istic hypotheses challenge metaphysics to meet in final
combat. In this revolutionary period, like the shep-
herd-boy with his sling, woman goes forth to battle with 12
Goliath.

   In this final struggle for supremacy, semi-metaphysical systems afford no substantial aid to scientific meta- 15
Confusion physics, for their arguments are based on
confounded the false testimony of the material senses as
well as on the facts of Mind. These semi-metaphysical 18

268

systems are one and all pantheistic, and savor of Pan- 1
demonium, a house divided against itself.

From first to last the supposed coexistence of Mind 3
and matter and the mingling of good and evil have resulted from the philosophy of the serpent. Jesus' demonstrations sift the chaff from the wheat, and unfold the 6
unity and the reality of good, the unreality, the nothingness, of evil.

Human philosophy has made God manlike. Christian 9
Science makes man Godlike. The first is error; the latter

Divine metaphysics is truth. Metaphysics is above physics, and
matter does not enter into metaphysical prem- 12
ises or conclusions. The categories of metaphysics rest
on one basis, the divine Mind. Metaphysics resolves
things into thoughts, and exchanges the objects of sense 15
for the ideas of Soul.

These ideas are perfectly real and tangible to spiritual
consciousness, and they have this advantage over the ob- 18
jects and thoughts of material sense, — they are good and
eternal.

The testimony of the material senses is neither abso- 21
lute nor divine. I therefore plant myself unreservedly

Biblical foundations on the teachings of Jesus, of his apostles, of
the prophets, and on the testimony of the 24
Science of Mind. Other foundations there are none.
All other systems — systems based wholly or partly on
knowledge gained through the material senses — are reeds 27
shaken by the wind, not houses built on the rock.

The theories I combat are these: (1) that all is matter;

Rejected theories (2) that matter originates in Mind, and is as 30
real as Mind, possessing intelligence and life.
The first theory, that matter is everything, is quite as

reasonable as the second, that Mind and matter coexist   1
and cooperate. One only of the following statements can
be true: (1) that everything is matter; (2) that every-   3
thing is Mind. Which one is it?

Matter and Mind are opposites. One is contrary to
the other in its very nature and essence; hence both can-   6
not be real. If one is real, the other must be unreal. Only
by understanding that there is but one power, — not two
powers, matter and Mind, — are scientific and logical   9
conclusions reached. Few deny the hypothesis that intelligence, apart from man and matter, governs the universe; and it is generally admitted that this intelligence   12
is the eternal Mind or divine Principle, Love.

The prophets of old looked for something higher than

Prophetic
ignorance the systems of their times; hence their fore-   15
sight of the new dispensation of Truth. But
they knew not what would be the precise nature of the
teaching and demonstration of God, divine Mind, in His   18
more infinite meanings, — the demonstration which was
to destroy sin, sickness, and death, establish the definition
of omnipotence, and maintain the Science of Spirit.   21

The pride of priesthood is the prince of this world. It
has nothing in Christ. Meekness and charity have divine
authority. Mortals think wickedly; consequently they   24
are wicked. They think sickly thoughts, and so become
sick. If sin makes sinners, Truth and Love alone can
unmake them. If a sense of disease produces suffering   27
and a sense of ease antidotes suffering, disease is mental,
not material. Hence the fact that the human mind alone
suffers, is sick, and that the divine Mind alone heals.   30

The life of Christ Jesus was not miraculous, but it was
indigenous to his spirituality, — the good soil wherein the

seed of Truth springs up and bears much fruit. Christ's 1
Christianity is the chain of scientific being reappearing
in all ages, maintaining its obvious correspondence with 3
the Scriptures and uniting all periods in the design of
God. Neither emasculation, illusion, nor insubordination
exists in divine Science. 6

Jesus instructed his disciples whereby to heal the sick
through Mind instead of matter. He knew that the philosophy, Science, and proof of Christianity were in Truth, 9
casting out all inharmony.

In Latin the word rendered *disciple* signifies student;
and the word indicates that the power of healing was not 12

Studious disciples
a supernatural gift to those learners, but the
result of their cultivated spiritual understanding of the divine Science, which their Master demonstrated 15
by healing the sick and sinning. Hence the universal application of his saying: "Neither pray I for these alone,
but for them also which shall believe on me [understand 18
me] through their word."

Our Master said, "But the Comforter . . . shall
teach you all things." When the Science of Christianity 21

New Testament basis
appears, it will lead you into all truth. The
Sermon on the Mount is the essence of this
Science, and the eternal life, not the death of Jesus, is 24
its outcome.

Those, who are willing to leave their nets or to cast
them on the right side for Truth, have the opportunity 27

Modern evangel
now, as aforetime, to learn and to practise
Christian healing. The Scriptures contain it.
The spiritual import of the Word imparts this power. 30
But, as Paul says, "How shall they hear without a
preacher? and how shall they preach, except they be

sent?" If sent, how shall they preach, convert, and heal   1
multitudes, except the people hear?

The spiritual sense of truth must be gained before   3
Truth can be understood. This sense is assimilated only

Spirituality of Scripture

as we are honest, unselfish, loving, and meek.
In the soil of an "honest and good heart" the   6
seed must be sown; else it beareth not much fruit, for the
swinish element in human nature uproots it. Jesus said:
"Ye do err, not knowing the Scriptures." The spiritual   9
sense of the Scriptures brings out the scientific sense, and
is the new tongue referred to in the last chapter of Mark's
Gospel.   12

Jesus' parable of "the sower" shows the care our
Master took not to impart to dull ears and gross hearts
the spiritual teachings which dulness and grossness could   15
not accept. Reading the thoughts of the people, he said:
"Give not that which is holy unto the dogs, neither cast
ye your pearls before swine."   18

It is the spiritualization of thought and Christianization
of daily life, in contrast with the results of the ghastly farce

Unspiritual contrasts

of material existence; it is chastity and purity,   21
in contrast with the downward tendencies
and earthward gravitation of sensualism and impurity,
which really attest the divine origin and operation of Chris-   24
tian Science. The triumphs of Christian Science are recorded in the destruction of error and evil, from which are
propagated the dismal beliefs of sin, sickness, and death.   27

The divine Principle of the universe must interpret the
universe. God is the divine Principle of all that repre-

God the Principle of all

sents Him and of all that really exists. Chris-   30
tian Science, as demonstrated by Jesus, alone
reveals the natural, divine Principle of Science.

Matter and its claims of sin, sickness, and death are 1
contrary to God, and cannot emanate from Him. There
is no *material* truth. The physical senses can take no 3
cognizance of God and spiritual Truth. Human belief
has sought out many inventions, but not one of them
can solve the problem of being without the divine Prin- 6
ciple of divine Science. Deductions from material hypotheses are not scientific. They differ from real Science
because they are not based on the divine law. 9

Science versus sense Divine Science reverses the false testimony of the material senses, and thus tears away the foun-
dations of error. Hence the enmity between 12
Science and the senses, and the impossibility
of attaining perfect understanding till the errors of sense
are eliminated. 15

The so-called laws of matter and of medical science have
never made mortals whole, harmonious, and immortal.
Man is harmonious when governed by Soul. Hence the 18
importance of understanding the truth of being, which
reveals the laws of spiritual existence.

God never ordained a material law to annul the spiritual 21
law. If there were such a material law, it would oppose
Spiritual law the only law the supremacy of Spirit, God, and impugn the
wisdom of the creator. Jesus walked on the 24
waves, fed the multitude, healed the sick, and raised the
dead in direct opposition to material laws. His acts were
the demonstration of Science, overcoming the false claims 27
of material sense or law.

Science shows that material, conflicting mortal opinions and beliefs emit the effects of error at all times, but 30
this atmosphere of mortal mind cannot be destructive to
morals and health when it is opposed promptly and per-

sistently by Christian Science. Truth and Love antidote 1
this mental miasma, and thus invigorate and sustain ex-

Material knowledge illusive
istence. Unnecessary knowledge gained from 3
the five senses is only temporal, — the conception of mortal mind, the offspring of sense, not
of Soul, Spirit, — and symbolizes all that is evil and 6
perishable. *Natural science*, as it is commonly called, is
not really natural nor scientific, because it is deduced from
the evidence of the material senses. Ideas, on the con- 9
trary, are born of Spirit, and are not mere inferences
drawn from material premises.

The senses of Spirit abide in Love, and they demon- 12
strate Truth and Life. Hence Christianity and the Sci-

Five senses deceptive
ence which expounds it are based on spiritual
understanding, and they supersede the so- 15
called laws of matter. Jesus demonstrated this great
verity. When what we erroneously term the five physical
senses are misdirected, they are simply the manifested 18
beliefs of mortal mind, which affirm that life, substance,
and intelligence are material, instead of spiritual. These
false beliefs and their products constitute the flesh, and 21
the flesh wars against Spirit.

Divine Science is absolute, and permits no half-way
position in learning its Principle and rule — establishing 24

Impossible partnership
it by demonstration. The conventional firm,
called matter and mind, God never formed.
Science and understanding, governed by the unerring and 27
eternal Mind, destroy the imaginary copartnership, matter
and mind, formed only to be destroyed in a manner and
at a period as yet unknown. This suppositional partner- 30
ship is already obsolete, for matter, examined in the light
of divine metaphysics, disappears.

Matter has no life to lose, and Spirit never dies. A   1
partnership of mind with matter would ignore omnipres-

**Spirit the
starting-point**

ent and omnipotent Mind. This shows that   3
matter did not originate in God, Spirit, and is
not eternal. Therefore matter is neither substantial, living,
nor intelligent. The starting-point of divine Science is   6
that God, Spirit, is All-in-all, and that there is no other
might nor Mind, — that God is Love, and therefore He
is divine Principle.   9

To grasp the reality and order of being in its Science,
you must begin by reckoning God as the divine Principle

**Divine
synonyms**

of all that really is. Spirit, Life, Truth, Love,   12
combine as one, — and are the Scriptural names
for God. All substance, intelligence, wisdom, being, immortality, cause, and effect belong to God. These are   15
His attributes, the eternal manifestations of the infinite
divine Principle, Love. No wisdom is wise but His
wisdom; no truth is true, no love is lovely, no life is Life   18
but the divine; no good is, but the good God bestows.

Divine metaphysics, as revealed to spiritual understanding, shows clearly that all is Mind, and that Mind is   21

**The divine
completeness**

God, omnipotence, omnipresence, omniscience,
— that is, all power, all presence, all Science.
Hence all is in reality the manifestation of Mind.   24

Our material human theories are destitute of Science.
The true understanding of God is spiritual. It robs the
grave of victory. It destroys the false evidence that mis-   27
leads thought and points to other gods, or other so-called
powers, such as matter, disease, sin, and death, superior
or contrary to the one Spirit.   30

Truth, spiritually discerned, is scientifically understood.
It casts out error and heals the sick.

Having one God, one Mind, unfolds the power that 1
heals the sick, and fulfils these sayings of Scripture, "I
am the Lord that healeth thee," and "I have 3

Universal brotherhood

found a ransom." When the divine precepts
are understood, they unfold the foundation of fellowship,
in which one mind is not at war with another, but all have 6
one Spirit, God, one intelligent source, in accordance with
the Scriptural command: "Let this Mind be in you,
which was also in Christ Jesus." Man and his Maker 9
are correlated in divine Science, and real consciousness
is cognizant only of the things of God.

The realization that all inharmony is unreal brings 12
objects and thoughts into human view in their true light,
and presents them as beautiful and immortal. Harmony
in man is as real and immortal as in music. Discord is 15
unreal and mortal.

If God is admitted to be the only Mind and Life,
there ceases to be any opportunity for sin and death. 18

Perfection requisite

When we learn in Science how to be perfect
even as our Father in heaven is perfect,
thought is turned into new and healthy channels, — 21
towards the contemplation of things immortal and away
from materiality to the Principle of the universe, including harmonious man. 24

Material beliefs and spiritual understanding never
mingle. The latter destroys the former. Discord is the
nothingness named error. Harmony is the *somethingness* 27
named Truth.

Nature and revelation inform us that like produces

Like evolving like

like. Divine Science does not gather grapes 30
from thorns nor figs from thistles. Intelligence never produces non-intelligence; but matter is

ever non-intelligent and therefore cannot spring from   1
intelligence. To all that is unlike unerring and eternal
Mind, this Mind saith, "Thou shalt surely die;" and else-   3
where the Scripture says that dust returns to dust. The
non-intelligent relapses into its own unreality. Matter
never produces mind. The immortal never produces the   6
mortal. Good cannot result in evil. As God Himself is
good and is Spirit, goodness and spirituality must be immortal. Their opposites, evil and matter, are mortal   9
error, and error has no creator. If goodness and spirituality are real, evil and materiality are unreal and cannot be the outcome of an infinite God, good.   12

Natural history presents vegetables and animals as
preserving their original species, — like reproducing like.
A mineral is not produced by a vegetable nor the man   15
by the brute. In reproduction, the order of genus and
species is preserved throughout the entire round of nature.
This points to the spiritual truth and Science of being.   18
Error relies upon a reversal of this order, asserts that
Spirit produces matter and matter produces all the ills
of flesh, and therefore that good is the origin of evil.   21
These suppositions contradict even the order of material
so-called science.

The realm of the real is Spirit. The unlikeness of Spirit   24
is matter, and the opposite of the real is not divine, — it is

Material error   a human concept. Matter is an error of statement. This error in the premise leads to errors   27
in the conclusion in every statement into which it enters.
Nothing we can say or believe regarding matter is immortal, for matter is temporal and is therefore a mortal phe-   30
nomenon, a human concept, sometimes beautiful, always
erroneous.

Is Spirit the source or creator of matter? Science re- 1
veals nothing in Spirit out of which to create matter.

Substance Divine metaphysics explains away matter. 3
versus
supposition Spirit is the only substance and consciousness
recognized by divine Science. The material
senses oppose this, but there are no material senses, for 6
matter has no mind. In Spirit there is no matter, even
as in Truth there is no error, and in good no evil. It is
a false supposition, the notion that there is real substance- 9
matter, the opposite of Spirit. Spirit, God, is infinite,
all. Spirit can have no opposite.

That matter is substantial or has life and sensation, is 12
one of the false beliefs of mortals, and exists only in a
One cause supposititious mortal consciousness. Hence,
supreme as we approach Spirit and Truth, we lose the 15
consciousness of matter. The admission that there can
be material substance requires another admission, —
namely, that Spirit is not infinite and that matter is self- 18
creative, self-existent, and eternal. From this it would
follow that there are two eternal causes, warring forever
with each other; and yet we say that Spirit is supreme 21
and all-presence.

The belief of the eternity of matter contradicts the
demonstration of life as Spirit, and leads to the conclu- 24
sion that if man is material, he originated in matter and
must return to dust, — logic which would prove his an-
nihilation. 27

All that we term sin, sickness, and death is a mortal
belief. We define matter as error, because it is the oppo-
Substance site of life, substance, and intelligence. Mat- 30
is Spirit ter, with its mortality, cannot be substantial
if Spirit is substantial and eternal. Which ought to

his resurrection, and said: "Whosoever liveth and be- 1
lieveth in me shall never die."

That saying of our Master, "I and my Father are one," 3
separated him from the scholastic theology of the rabbis.

Hebrew theology His better understanding of God was a rebuke
to them. He knew of but one Mind and laid 6
no claim to any other. He knew that the Ego was Mind
instead of body and that matter, sin, and evil were not
Mind; and his understanding of this divine Science 9
brought upon him the anathemas of the age.

The opposite and false views of the people hid from
their sense Christ's sonship with God. They could not 12

The true sonship discern his spiritual existence. Their carnal
minds were at enmity with it. Their thoughts
were filled with mortal error, instead of with God's spirit- 15
ual idea as presented by Christ Jesus. The likeness of
God we lose sight of through sin, which beclouds the spiritual sense of Truth; and we realize this likeness only 18
when we subdue sin and prove man's heritage, the liberty
of the sons of God.

Jesus' spiritual origin and understanding enabled him 21
to demonstrate the facts of being, — to prove irrefutably

Immaculate conception how spiritual Truth destroys material error,
heals sickness, and overcomes death. The 24
divine conception of Jesus pointed to this truth and presented an illustration of creation. The history of Jesus
shows him to have been more spiritual than all other 27
earthly personalities.

Wearing in part a human form (that is, as it seemed
to mortal view), being conceived by a human mother, 30
Jesus was the mediator between Spirit and the flesh,
between Truth and error. Explaining and demonstrat-

ing the way of divine Science, he became the way of   1
salvation to all who accepted his word. From him mor-

Jesus as
mediator
tals may learn how to escape from evil. The   3
real man being linked by Science to his Maker,
mortals need only turn from sin and lose sight of mortal
selfhood to find Christ, the real man and his relation to   6
God, and to recognize the divine sonship. Christ, Truth,
was demonstrated through Jesus to prove the power of
Spirit over the flesh, — to show that Truth is made   9
manifest by its effects upon the human mind and body,
healing sickness and destroying sin.

Jesus represented Christ, the true idea of God. Hence   12
the warfare between this spiritual idea and perfunctory

Spiritual
government
religion, between spiritual clear-sightedness
and the blindness of popular belief, which led   15
to the conclusion that the spiritual idea could be killed
by crucifying the flesh. The Christ-idea, or the Christ-
man, rose higher to human view because of the crucifixion,   18
and thus proved that Truth was the master of death.
Christ presents the indestructible man, whom Spirit creates, constitutes, and governs. Christ illustrates that   21
blending with God, his divine Principle, which gives man
dominion over all the earth.

The spiritual idea of God, as presented by Jesus, was   24
scourged in person, and its Principle was rejected. That

Deadness
in sin
man was accounted a criminal who could
prove God's divine power by healing the   27
sick, casting out evils, spiritualizing materialistic beliefs,
and raising the dead, — those dead in trespasses and
sins, satisfied with the flesh, resting on the basis of mat-   30
ter, blind to the possibilities of Spirit and its correla-
tive truth.

Jesus uttered things which had been "secret from the   1
foundation of the world," — since material knowledge
usurped the throne of the creative divine Principle, insisted   3
on the might of matter, the force of falsity, the insignificance of spirit, and proclaimed an anthropomorphic God.

Whosoever lives most the life of Jesus in this age   6
and declares best the power of Christian Science, will
The cup drink of his Master's cup. Resistance to
of Jesus Truth will haunt his steps, and he will in-   9
cur the hatred of sinners, till "wisdom is justified of
her children." These blessed benedictions rest upon
Jesus' followers: "If the world hate you, ye know that   12
it hated me before it hated you;" "Lo, I am with you
alway," — that is, not only in all time, but in *all ways*
and conditions.   15

The individuality of man is no less tangible because
it is spiritual and because his life is not at the mercy of
matter. The understanding of his spiritual individuality   18
makes man more real, more formidable in truth, and enables him to conquer sin, disease, and death. Our Lord
and Master presented himself to his disciples after his   21
resurrection from the grave, as the self-same Jesus whom
they had loved before the tragedy on Calvary.

To the materialistic Thomas, looking for the ideal   24
Saviour in matter instead of in Spirit and to the testi-
Material mony of the material senses and the body,
skepticism more than to Soul, for an earnest of immor-   27
tality, — to him Jesus furnished the proof that he was
unchanged by the crucifixion. To this dull and doubt-
ing disciple Jesus remained a fleshly reality, so long as   30
the Master remained an inhabitant of the earth. Nothing but a display of matter could make existence real

to Thomas. For him to believe in matter was no task,   1
but for him to conceive of the substantiality of Spirit —
to know that nothing can efface Mind and immortality, in   3
which Spirit reigns — was more difficult.

Corporeal senses define diseases as realities; but the
Scriptures declare that God made all, even while the cor-   6

**What
the senses
originate**

poreal senses are saying that matter causes
disease and the divine Mind cannot or will
not heal it. The material senses originate and   9
support all that is material, untrue, selfish, or debased.
They would put soul into soil, life into limbo, and doom
all things to decay. We must silence this lie of material   12
sense with the truth of spiritual sense. We must cause
the error to cease that brought the belief of sin and death
and would efface the pure sense of omnipotence.   15

Is the sick man sinful above all others? No! but
so far as he is discordant, he is not the image of God.

**Sickness
as discord**

Weary of their material beliefs, from which   18
comes so much suffering, invalids grow more
spiritual, as the error — or belief that life is in matter —
yields to the reality of spiritual Life.   21

The Science of Mind denies the error of sensation in
matter, and heals with Truth. Medical science treats
disease as though disease were real, therefore right, and   24
attempts to heal it with matter. If disease is right it is
wrong to heal it. Material methods are temporary, and
are not adapted to elevate mankind.   27

The governor is not subjected to the governed. In
Science man is governed by God, divine Principle, as
numbers are controlled and proved by His laws. Intelli-   30
gence does not originate in numbers, but is manifested
through them. The body does not include soul, but man-

ifests mortality, a false sense of soul. The delusion that
there is life in matter has no kinship with the Life supernal.

Science depicts disease as error, as matter *versus*
Mind, and error reversed as subserving the facts of
Unscientific introspection health. To calculate one's life-prospects
from a material basis, would infringe upon
spiritual law and misguide human hope. Having faith
in the divine Principle of health and spiritually understanding God, sustains man under all circumstances;
whereas the lower appeal to the general faith in material
means (commonly called nature) must yield to the all-
might of infinite Spirit.

Throughout the infinite cycles of eternal existence,
Spirit and matter neither concur in man nor in the universe.

The varied doctrines and theories which presuppose
life and intelligence to exist in matter are so many ancient
God the only Mind and modern mythologies. Mystery, miracle,
sin, and death will disappear when it becomes
fairly understood that the divine Mind controls man and
man has no Mind but God.

The divine Science taught in the original language
of the Bible came through inspiration, and needs inspi-
Scriptures misinterpreted ration to be understood. Hence the misappre-
hension of the spiritual meaning of the Bible,
and the misinterpretation of the Word in
some instances by uninspired writers, who only wrote
down what an inspired teacher had said. A misplaced
word changes the sense and misstates the Science of
the Scriptures, as, for instance, to name Love as merely
an attribute of God; but we can by special and proper
capitalization speak of the love of Love, meaning by that
what the beloved disciple meant in one of his epistles,

when he said, "God is love." Likewise we can speak of   1
the truth of Truth and of the life of Life, for Christ plainly
declared, "I am the way, the truth, and the life."   3
Metaphors abound in the Bible, and names are often
expressive of spiritual ideas. The most distinguished

Interior
meaning

theologians in Europe and America agree that   6
the Scriptures have both a spiritual and literal meaning. In Smith's Bible Dictionary it is said:
"The spiritual interpretation of Scripture must rest   9
upon both the literal and moral;" and in the learned
article on Noah in the same work, the familiar text,
Genesis vi. 3, "And the Lord said, My spirit shall not   12
always strive with man, for that he also is flesh," is quoted
as follows, from the original Hebrew: "And Jehovah
said, My spirit shall not forever rule [or be humbled] in   15
men, seeing that they are [or, in their error they are]
but flesh." Here the original text declares plainly the
spiritual fact of being, even man's eternal and harmo-   18
nious existence as image, idea, instead of matter (however transcendental such a thought appears), and avers
that this fact is not forever to be humbled by the belief   21
that man is flesh and matter, for according to that error
man is mortal.
The one important interpretation of Scripture is the   24
spiritual. For example, the text, "In my flesh shall I

Job, on the
resurrection

see God," gives a profound idea of the divine power to heal the ills of the flesh, and   27
encourages mortals to hope in Him who healeth all our
diseases; whereas this passage is continually quoted
as if Job intended to declare that even if disease and   30
worms destroyed his body, yet in the latter days he should
stand in celestial perfection before Elohim, still clad

in material flesh, — an interpretation which is just the op- 1
posite of the true, as may be seen by studying the book
of Job. As Paul says, in his first epistle to the Corin- 3
thians, "Flesh and blood cannot inherit the kingdom of
God."

The Hebrew Lawgiver, slow of speech, despaired of 6
making the people understand what should be revealed

Fear of the serpent overcome

to him. When, led by wisdom to cast down his
rod, he saw it become a serpent, Moses fled be- 9
fore it; but wisdom bade him come back and
handle the serpent, and then Moses' fear departed. In
this incident was seen the actuality of Science. Matter 12
was shown to be a belief only. The serpent, evil, under
wisdom's bidding, was destroyed through understanding
divine Science, and this proof was a staff upon which to 15
lean. The illusion of Moses lost its power to alarm him,
when he discovered that what he apparently saw was really
but a phase of mortal belief. 18

It was scientifically demonstrated that leprosy was a
creation of mortal mind and not a condition of matter,

Leprosy healed

when Moses first put his hand into his bosom 21
and drew it forth white as snow with the dread
disease, and presently restored his hand to its natural condition by the same simple process. God had lessened 24
Moses' fear by this proof in divine Science, and the in-
ward voice became to him the voice of God, which said:
"It shall come to pass, if they will not believe thee, neither 27
hearken to the voice of the first sign, that they will believe
the voice of the latter sign." And so it was in the coming
centuries, when the Science of being was demonstrated 30
by Jesus, who showed his students the power of Mind by
changing water into wine, and taught them how to handle

serpents unharmed, to heal the sick and cast out evils in   1
proof of the supremacy of Mind.

When understanding changes the standpoints of life and   3
intelligence from a material to a spiritual basis, we shall

Standpoints changed   gain the reality of Life, the control of Soul over
sense, and we shall perceive Christianity, or   6
Truth, in its divine Principle. This must be the climax
before harmonious and immortal man is obtained and his
capabilities revealed. It is highly important — in view   9
of the immense work to be accomplished before this recog-
nition of divine Science can come — to turn our thoughts
towards divine Principle, that finite belief may be pre-   12
pared to relinquish its error.

Man's wisdom finds no satisfaction in sin, since God
has sentenced sin to suffer. The necromancy of yester-   15

Saving the inebriate   day foreshadowed the mesmerism and hypnotism of to-day. The drunkard thinks he enjoys
drunkenness, and you cannot make the inebriate leave   18
his besottedness, until his physical sense of pleasure yields
to a higher sense. Then he turns from his cups, as
the startled dreamer who wakens from an incubus in-   21
curred through the pains of distorted sense. A man who
likes to do wrong — finding pleasure in it and refraining
from it only through fear of consequences — is neither   24
a temperate man nor a reliable religionist.

The sharp experiences of belief in the supposititious life
of matter, as well as our disappointments and ceaseless   27

Uses of suffering   woes, turn us like tired children to the arms
of divine Love. Then we begin to learn Life
in divine Science. Without this process of weaning,   30
"Canst thou by searching find out God?" It is easier
to desire Truth than to rid one's self of error. Mortals

may seek the understanding of Christian Science, but they will not be able to glean from Christian Science the facts of being without striving for them. This strife consists in the endeavor to forsake error of every kind and to possess no other consciousness but good.

A bright outlook

Through the wholesome chastisements of Love, we are helped onward in the march towards righteousness, peace, and purity, which are the landmarks of Science. Beholding the infinite tasks of truth, we pause, — wait on God. Then we push onward, until boundless thought walks enraptured, and conception unconfined is winged to reach the divine glory.

Need and supply

In order to apprehend more, we must put into practice what we already know. We must recollect that Truth is demonstrable when understood, and that good is not understood until demonstrated. If "faithful over a few things," we shall be made rulers over many; but the one unused talent decays and is lost. When the sick or the sinning awake to realize their need of what they have not, they will be receptive of divine Science, which gravitates towards Soul and away from material sense, removes thought from the body, and elevates even mortal mind to the contemplation of something better than disease or sin. The true idea of God gives the true understanding of Life and Love, robs the grave of victory, takes away all sin and the delusion that there are other minds, and destroys mortality.

Childlike receptivity

The effects of Christian Science are not so much seen as felt. It is the "still, small voice" of Truth uttering itself. We are either turning away from this utterance, or we are listening to it and going up higher. Willingness to become as a little child and

to leave the old for the new, renders thought receptive of   1
the advanced idea. Gladness to leave the false landmarks
and joy to see them disappear, — this disposition helps   3
to precipitate the ultimate harmony. The purification
of sense and self is a proof of progress. "Blessed are the
pure in heart: for they shall see God."   6

Unless the harmony and immortality of man are becoming more apparent, we are not gaining the true idea
Narrow   of God; and the body will reflect what gov-   9
pathway   erns it, whether it be Truth or error,
understanding or belief, Spirit or matter. Therefore
"acquaint now thyself with Him, and be at peace."   12
Be watchful, sober, and vigilant. The way is straight
and narrow, which leads to the understanding that God
is the only Life. It is a warfare with the flesh, in which   15
we must conquer sin, sickness, and death, either here
or hereafter, — certainly before we can reach the goal
of Spirit, or life in God.   18

Paul was not at first a disciple of Jesus but a persecutor of Jesus' followers. When the truth first appeared
Paul's   to him in Science, Paul was made blind,   21
enlightenment   and his blindness was felt; but spiritual
light soon enabled him to follow the example and teachings of Jesus, healing the sick and preaching Christian-   24
ity throughout Asia Minor, Greece, and even in imperial
Rome.

Paul writes, "If Christ [Truth] be not risen, then is   27
our preaching vain." That is, if the idea of the supremacy of Spirit, which is the true conception of being,
come not to your thought, you cannot be benefited by   30
what I say.

Jesus said substantially, "He that believeth in me

shall not see death." That is, he who perceives the

true idea of Life loses his belief in death. He who has

Abiding in Life the true idea of good loses all sense of evil,

and by reason of this is being ushered into the

undying realities of Spirit. Such a one abideth in Life, —

life obtained not of the body incapable of supporting life,

but of Truth, unfolding its own immortal idea. Jesus

gave the true idea of being, which results in infinite bless-

ings to mortals.

In Colossians (iii. 4) Paul writes: "When Christ, who

is our life, shall appear [be manifested], then shall ye also

Indestructible being appear [be manifested] with him in glory."

When spiritual being is understood in all its

perfection, continuity, and might, then shall man be found

in God's image. The absolute meaning of the apostolic

words is this: Then shall man be found, in His likeness,

perfect as the Father, indestructible in Life, "hid with

Christ in God," — with Truth in divine Love, where

human sense hath not seen man.

Paul had a clear sense of the demands of Truth upon

mortals physically and spiritually, when he said: "Pre-

Consecration required sent your bodies a living sacrifice, holy, ac-

ceptable unto God, which is your reasonable

service." But he, who is begotten of the beliefs of the

flesh and serves them, can never reach in this world the

divine heights of our Lord. The time cometh when

the spiritual origin of man, the divine Science which

ushered Jesus into human presence, will be understood

and demonstrated.

When first spoken in any age, Truth, like the light,

"shineth in darkness, and the darkness comprehended

it not." A false sense of life, substance, and mind

hides the divine possibilities, and conceals scientific   1
demonstration.

If we wish to follow Christ, Truth, it must be in the   3
way of God's appointing. Jesus said, "He that believeth

Loving God
supremely
on me, the works that I do shall he do also."
He, who would reach the source and find the   6
divine remedy for every ill, must not try to climb the hill
of Science by some other road. All nature teaches God's
love to man, but man cannot love God supremely and set   9
his whole affections on spiritual things, while loving the
material or trusting in it more than in the spiritual.

We must forsake the foundation of material systems,   12
however time-honored, if we would gain the Christ as
our only Saviour. Not partially, but fully, the great
healer of mortal mind is the healer of the body.   15

The purpose and motive to live aright can be gained
now. This point won, you have started as you should.
You have begun at the numeration-table of Christian   18
Science, and nothing but wrong intention can hinder your
advancement. Working and praying with true motives,
your Father will open the way. "Who did hinder you,   21
that ye should not obey the truth?"

Saul of Tarsus beheld the way — the Christ, or Truth
— only when his uncertain sense of right yielded to a   24

Conversion
of Saul
spiritual sense, which is always right. Then
the man was changed. Thought assumed a
nobler outlook, and his life became more spiritual. He   27
learned the wrong that he had done in persecuting Christians, whose religion he had not understood, and in humility he took the new name of Paul. He beheld for the   30
first time the true idea of Love, and learned a lesson in
divine Science.

Reform comes by understanding that there is no abid- 1
ing pleasure in evil, and also by gaining an affection for
good according to Science, which reveals the immortal 3
fact that neither pleasure nor pain, appetite nor passion,
can exist in or of matter, while divine Mind can and does
destroy the false beliefs of pleasure, pain, or fear and all 6
the sinful appetites of the human mind.

What a pitiful sight is malice, finding pleasure in revenge! Evil is sometimes a man's highest conception 9

**Image of
the beast**
of right, until his grasp on good grows stronger.
Then he loses pleasure in wickedness, and it
becomes his torment. The way to escape the misery of 12
sin is to cease sinning. There is no other way. Sin is
the image of the beast to be effaced by the sweat of agony.
It is a moral madness which rushes forth to clamor with 15
midnight and tempest.

To the physical senses, the strict demands of Christian

**Peremptory
demands**
Science seem peremptory; but mortals are has- 18
tening to learn that Life is God, good, and that
evil has in reality neither place nor power in the human or
the divine economy. 21

Fear of punishment never made man truly honest.
Moral courage is requisite to meet the wrong and to

**Moral
courage**
proclaim the right. But how shall we re- 24
form the man who has more animal than
moral courage, and who has not the true idea of good?
Through human consciousness, convince the mortal of 27
his mistake in seeking material means for gaining happiness. Reason is the most active human faculty. Let
that inform the sentiments and awaken the man's dor- 30
mant sense of moral obligation, and by degrees he will
learn the nothingness of the pleasures of human sense

and the grandeur and bliss of a spiritual sense, which 1
silences the material or corporeal. Then he not only will
be saved, but *is* saved. 3

Mortals suppose that they can live without goodness,
when God is good and the only real Life. What is the

**Final
destruction
of error**

result? Understanding little about the divine 6
Principle which saves and heals, mortals get
rid of sin, sickness, and death only in belief. These errors
are not thus really destroyed, and must therefore cling 9
to mortals until, here or hereafter, they gain the true understanding of God in the Science which destroys human
delusions about Him and reveals the grand realities of 12
His allness.

This understanding of man's power, when he is
equipped by God, has sadly disappeared from Christian 15

**Promise
perpetual**

history. For centuries it has been dormant, a
lost element of Christianity. Our missionaries
carry the Bible to India, but can it be said that they 18
explain it practically, as Jesus did, when hundreds of
persons die there annually from serpent-bites? Understanding spiritual law and knowing that there is no mate- 21
rial law, Jesus said: "These signs shall follow them that
believe, . . . they shall take up serpents, and if they
drink any deadly thing, it shall not hurt them. They 24
shall lay hands on the sick, and they shall recover." It
were well had Christendom believed and obeyed this
sacred saying. 27

Jesus' promise is perpetual. Had it been given only
to his immediate disciples, the Scriptural passage would
read *you*, not *they*. The purpose of his great life-work 30
extends through time and includes universal humanity.
Its Principle is infinite, reaching beyond the pale of a

single period or of a limited following. As time moves   1
on, the healing elements of pure Christianity will be fairly
dealt with; they will be sought and taught, and will glow   3
in all the grandeur of universal goodness.

A little leaven leavens the whole lump. A little understanding of Christian Science proves the truth of all that   6

Imitation of Jesus

I say of it. Because you cannot walk on the
water and raise the dead, you have no right to
question the great might of divine Science in these direc-   9
tions. Be thankful that Jesus, who was the true demon-
strator of Science, did these things, and left his example for
us. In Science we can use only what we understand. We   12
must prove our faith by demonstration.

One should not tarry in the storm if the body is freez-
ing, nor should he remain in the devouring flames. Un-   15
til one is able to prevent bad results, he should avoid their
occasion. To be discouraged, is to resemble a pupil in
addition, who attempts to solve a problem of Euclid, and   18
denies the rule of the problem because he fails in his first
effort.

There is no hypocrisy in Science. Principle is impera-   21
tive. You cannot mock it by human will. Science is a

Error destroyed, not pardoned

divine demand, not a human. Always right,
its divine Principle never repents, but main-   24
tains the claim of Truth by quenching error.
The pardon of divine mercy is the destruction of error. If
men understood their real spiritual source to be all bless-   27
edness, they would struggle for recourse to the spiritual
and be at peace; but the deeper the error into which mortal mind is plunged, the more intense the opposition to   30
spirituality, till error yields to Truth.

Human resistance to divine Science weakens in pro-

portion as mortals give up error for Truth and the un- 1
derstanding of being supersedes mere belief. Until the

The hopeful outlook author of this book learned the vastness of 3
Christian Science, the fixedness of mortal illu-
sions, and the human hatred of Truth, she cherished
sanguine hopes that Christian Science would meet with 6
immediate and universal acceptance.

When the following platform is understood and the
letter and the spirit bear witness, the infallibility of divine 9
metaphysics will be demonstrated.

I. God is infinite, the only Life, substance, Spirit, or
Soul, the only intelligence of the universe, including man. 12

The deific supremacy Eye hath neither seen God nor His image and
likeness. Neither God nor the perfect man
can be discerned by the material senses. The individ- 15
uality of Spirit, or the infinite, is unknown, and thus a
knowledge of it is left either to human conjecture or to the
revelation of divine Science. 18

II. God is what the Scriptures declare Him to be, —
Life, Truth, Love. Spirit is divine Principle, and divine

The deific definitions Principle is Love, and Love is Mind, and 21
Mind is not both good and bad, for God is
Mind; therefore there is in reality one Mind only, be-
cause there is one God. 24

III. The notion that both evil and good are real is a
delusion of material sense, which Science annihilates.

Evil obsolete Evil is nothing, no thing, mind, nor power. 27
As manifested by mankind it stands for a lie,
nothing claiming to be something, — for lust, dishonesty,
selfishness, envy, hypocrisy, slander, hate, theft, adultery, 30
murder, dementia, insanity, inanity, devil, hell, with all
the etceteras that word includes.

IV. God is divine Life, and Life is no more confined 1
to the forms which reflect it than substance is in its

Life the creator shadow. If life were in mortal man or mate- 3
rial things, it would be subject to their limi-
tations and would end in death. Life is Mind, the creator
reflected in His creations. If He dwelt within what He 6
creates, God would not be reflected but absorbed, and the
Science of being would be forever lost through a mortal
sense, which falsely testifies to a beginning and an 9
end.

V. The Scriptures imply that God is All-in-all. From
this it follows that nothing possesses reality nor existence 12

Allness of Spirit except the divine Mind and His ideas. The
Scriptures also declare that God is Spirit.
Therefore in Spirit all is harmony, and there can be no 15
discord; all is Life, and there is no death. Everything
in God's universe expresses Him.

VI. God is individual, incorporeal. He is divine Prin- 18
ciple, Love, the universal cause, the only creator, and

The universal cause there is no other self-existence. He is all-
inclusive, and is reflected by all that is real 21
and eternal and by nothing else. He fills all space, and
it is impossible to conceive of such omnipresence and individuality except as infinite Spirit or Mind. Hence all 24
is Spirit and spiritual.

VII. Life, Truth, and Love constitute the triune Person
called God, — that is, the triply divine Principle, Love. 27

Divine trinity They represent a trinity in unity, three in
one, — the same in essence, though multi-
form in office: God the Father-Mother; Christ the spirit- 30
ual idea of sonship; divine Science or the Holy Comforter.
These three express in divine Science the threefold, essen-

tial nature of the infinite. They also indicate the divine   1
Principle of scientific being, the intelligent relation of God
to man and the universe.   3

VIII. Father-Mother is the name for Deity, which indicates His tender relationship to His spiritual creation.

Father-
Mother

As the apostle expressed it in words which he   6
quoted with approbation from a classic poet:
"For we are also His offspring."

IX. Jesus was born of Mary. Christ is the true idea   9
voicing good, the divine message from God to men speak-

The Son
of God

ing to the human consciousness. The Christ
is incorporeal, spiritual, — yea, the divine   12
image and likeness, dispelling the illusions of the senses;
the Way, the Truth, and the Life, healing the sick and
casting out evils, destroying sin, disease, and death. As   15
Paul says: "There is one God, and one mediator between
God and men, the man Christ Jesus." The corporeal
man Jesus was human.   18

X. Jesus demonstrated Christ; he proved that Christ

Holy Ghost
or Comforter

is the divine idea of God — the Holy Ghost,
or Comforter, revealing the divine Principle,   21
Love, and leading into all truth.

XI. Jesus was the son of a virgin. He was appointed
to speak God's word and to appear to mortals in such   24

Christ Jesus

a form of humanity as they could understand
as well as perceive. Mary's conception of
him was spiritual, for only purity could reflect Truth   27
and Love, which were plainly incarnate in the good and
pure Christ Jesus. He expressed the highest type of
divinity, which a fleshly form could express in that age.   30
Into the real and ideal man the fleshly element cannot
enter. Thus it is that Christ illustrates the coincidence,

or spiritual agreement, between God and man in His   1
image.

XII. The word *Christ* is not properly a synonym for   3
Jesus, though it is commonly so used. Jesus was a human

Messiah
or Christ

name, which belonged to him in common with
other Hebrew boys and men, for it is identical   6
with the name Joshua, the renowned Hebrew leader. On
the other hand, Christ is not a name so much as the divine
title of Jesus. Christ expresses God's spiritual, eternal   9
nature. The name is synonymous with Messiah, and alludes to the spirituality which is taught, illustrated, and
demonstrated in the life of which Christ Jesus was the   12
embodiment. The proper name of our Master in the
Greek was Jesus the Christ; but Christ Jesus better signifies the Godlike.   15

XIII. The advent of Jesus of Nazareth marked the
first century of the Christian era, but the Christ is

The divine
Principle
and idea

without beginning of years or end of days.   18
Throughout all generations both before and
after the Christian era, the Christ, as the spiritual idea, — the reflection of God, — has come with some   21
measure of power and grace to all prepared to receive
Christ, Truth. Abraham, Jacob, Moses, and the prophets
caught glorious glimpses of the Messiah, or Christ, which   24
baptized these seers in the divine nature, the essence of
Love. The divine image, idea, or Christ was, is, and
ever will be inseparable from the divine Principle, God.   27
Jesus referred to this unity of his spiritual identity thus:
"Before Abraham was, I am;" "I and my Father are
one;" "My Father is greater than I." The one Spirit   30
includes all identities.

XIV. By these sayings Jesus meant, not that the hu-

man Jesus was or is eternal, but that the divine idea or   1
Christ was and is so and therefore antedated Abraham;

not that the corporeal Jesus was one with the   3
Father, but that the spiritual idea, Christ,
dwells forever in the bosom of the Father, God, from
which it illumines heaven and earth; not that the Father   6
is greater than Spirit, which is God, but greater, infinitely
greater, than the fleshly Jesus, whose earthly career was
brief.   9

XV. The invisible Christ was imperceptible to the
so-called personal senses, whereas Jesus appeared as a

bodily existence. This dual personality of the   12
unseen and the seen, the spiritual and material, the eternal Christ and the corporeal Jesus manifest
in flesh, continued until the Master's ascension, when   15
the human, material concept, or Jesus, disappeared,
while the spiritual self, or Christ, continues to exist in
the eternal order of divine Science, taking away the sins   18
of the world, as the Christ has always done, even before
the human Jesus was incarnate to mortal eyes.

XVI. This was "the Lamb slain from the foundation   21
of the world," — slain, that is, according to the testi-

mony of the corporeal senses, but undying in
the deific Mind. The Revelator represents the   24
Son of man as saying (Revelation i. 17, 18): "I am the
first and the last: I am he that liveth, and was dead
[not understood]; and, behold, I am alive for evermore,   27
[Science has explained me]." This is a mystical statement of the eternity of the Christ, and is also a reference
to the human sense of Jesus crucified.   30

XVII. Spirit being God, there is but one Spirit, for
there can be but one infinite and therefore one God.

There are neither spirits many nor gods many. There   1
is no evil in Spirit, because God is Spirit. The theory,

Infinite Spirit

that Spirit is distinct from matter but must   3
pass through it, or into it, to be individualized,
would reduce God to dependency on matter, and establish
a basis for pantheism.   6

XVIII. Spirit, God, has created all in and of Himself. Spirit never created matter. There is nothing in

The only substance

Spirit out of which matter could be made,   9
for, as the Bible declares, without the Logos,
the Æon or Word of God, "was not anything made
that was made." Spirit is the only substance, the in-   12
visible and indivisible infinite God. Things spiritual and
eternal are substantial. Things material and temporal
are insubstantial.   15

XIX. Soul and Spirit being one, God and Soul are
one, and this one never included in a limited mind or a

Soul and Spirit one

limited body. Spirit is eternal, divine. Noth-   18
ing but Spirit, Soul, can evolve Life, for Spirit
is more than all else. Because Soul is immortal, it does
not exist in mortality. Soul must be incorporeal to be   21
Spirit, for Spirit is not finite. Only by losing the false
sense of Soul can we gain the eternal unfolding of Life as
immortality brought to light.   24

XX. Mind is the divine Principle, Love, and can produce nothing unlike the eternal Father-Mother, God.

The one divine Mind

Reality is spiritual, harmonious, immutable,   27
immortal, divine, eternal. Nothing unspiritual can be real, harmonious, or eternal. Sin, sickness,
and mortality are the suppositional antipodes of Spirit,   30
and must be contradictions of reality.

XXI. The Ego is deathless and limitless, for limits

would imply and impose ignorance. Mind is the I AM, 1
or infinity. Mind never enters the finite. Intelligence

The divine Ego never passes into non-intelligence, or matter. 3
Good never enters into evil, the unlimited into
the limited, the eternal into the temporal, nor the immortal into mortality. The divine Ego, or individuality, 6
is reflected in all spiritual individuality from the infinitesimal to the infinite.

XXII. Immortal man was and is God's image or idea, 9
even the infinite expression of infinite Mind, and immor-

The real manhood tal man is coexistent and coeternal with that
Mind. He has been forever in the eternal 12
Mind, God; but infinite Mind can never be in man, but
is reflected by man. The spiritual man's consciousness
and individuality are reflections of God. They are the 15
emanations of Him who is Life, Truth, and Love. Immortal man is not and never was material, but always
spiritual and eternal. 18

XXIII. God is indivisible. A portion of God could
not enter man; neither could God's fulness be reflected

Indivisibility of the infinite by a single man, else God would be manifestly 21
finite, lose the deific character, and become
less than God. Allness is the measure of the infinite, and
nothing less can express God. 24

XXIV. God, the divine Principle of man, and man in
God's likeness are inseparable, harmonious, and eternal.

God the parent Mind The Science of being furnishes the rule of per- 27
fection, and brings immortality to light. God
and man are not the same, but in the order of divine Science, God and man coexist and are eternal. God is the 30
parent Mind, and man is God's spiritual offspring.

XXV. God is individual and personal in a scientific

sense, but not in any anthropomorphic sense. Therefore 1
man, reflecting God, cannot lose his individuality; but as

Man reflects the perfect God

material sensation, or a soul in the body, blind 3
mortals do lose sight of spiritual individuality.
Material personality is not realism; it is not
the reflection or likeness of Spirit, the perfect God. Sen- 6
sualism is not bliss, but bondage. For true happiness,
man must harmonize with his Principle, divine Love; the
Son must be in accord with the Father, in conformity with 9
Christ. According to divine Science, man is in a degree
as perfect as the Mind that forms him. The truth of being makes man harmonious and immortal, while error is 12
mortal and discordant.

XXVI. Christian Science demonstrates that none but

Purity the path to perfection

the pure in heart can see God, as the gospel 15
teaches. In proportion to his purity is man
perfect; and perfection is the order of celestial
being which demonstrates Life in Christ, Life's spiritual 18
ideal.

XXVII. The true idea of man, as the reflection of the
invisible God, is as incomprehensible to the limited senses 21
as is man's infinite Principle. The visible uni-

True idea of man

verse and material man are the poor counter-
feits of the invisible universe and spiritual man. Eternal 24
things (verities) are God's thoughts as they exist in the
spiritual realm of the real. Temporal things are the
thoughts of mortals and are the unreal, being the oppo- 27
site of the real or the spiritual and eternal.

XXVIII. Subject sickness, sin, and death to the rule

Truth demonstrated

of health and holiness in Christian Science, 30
and you ascertain that this Science is demon-
strably true, for it heals the sick and sinning as no

other system can. Christian Science, rightly under-   1
stood, leads to eternal harmony. It brings to light the
only living and true God and man as made in His like-   3
ness; whereas the opposite belief — that man originates
in matter and has beginning and end, that he is both
soul and body, both good and evil, both spiritual and   6
material — terminates in discord and mortality, in the
error which must be destroyed by Truth. The mortality
of material man proves that error has been ingrafted   9
into the premises and conclusions of material and mortal
humanity.

XXIX. The word *Adam* is from the Hebrew *adamah*,   12
signifying the *red color of the ground, dust, nothingness.*

**Adam not
ideal man**
Divide the name Adam into two syllables,
and it reads, *a dam*, or obstruction. This   15
suggests the thought of something fluid, of mortal mind
in solution. It further suggests the thought of that
"darkness . . . upon the face of the deep," when mat-   18
ter or dust was deemed the agent of Deity in creating
man, — when matter, as that which is accursed, stood
opposed to Spirit. Here *a dam* is not a mere play upon   21
words; it stands for obstruction, error, even the supposed separation of man from God, and the obstacle
which the serpent, sin, would impose between man and   24
his creator. The dissection and definition of words,
aside from their metaphysical derivation, is not scientific. Jehovah declared the ground was accursed; and   27
from this ground, or matter, sprang Adam, notwithstanding God had blessed the earth "for man's sake."
From this it follows that Adam was not the ideal man   30
for whom the earth was blessed. The ideal man was
revealed in due time, and was known as Christ Jesus.

XXX. The destruction of sin is the divine method of 1
pardon. Divine Life destroys death, Truth destroys

Divine pardon

error, and Love destroys hate. Being de- 3
stroyed, sin needs no other form of forgiveness.
Does not God's pardon, destroying any one sin, prophesy
and involve the final destruction of all sin? 6

XXXI. Since God is All, there is no room for His
unlikeness. God, Spirit, alone created all, and called it

Evil not produced by God

good. Therefore evil, being contrary to good, 9
is unreal, and cannot be the product of God.
A sinner can receive no encouragement from the fact that
Science demonstrates the unreality of evil, for the sinner 12
would make a reality of sin, — would make that real
which is unreal, and thus heap up "wrath against the
day of wrath." He is joining in a conspiracy against 15
himself, — against his own awakening to the awful unreality by which he has been deceived. Only those, who
repent of sin and forsake the unreal, can fully understand 18
the unreality of evil.

XXXII. As the mythology of pagan Rome has yielded
to a more spiritual idea of Deity, so will our material 21

Basis of health and immortality

theories yield to spiritual ideas, until the finite
gives place to the infinite, sickness to health,
sin to holiness, and God's kingdom comes "in 24
earth, as it is in heaven." The basis of all health, sin-
lessness, and immortality is the great fact that God is
the only Mind; and this Mind must be not merely be- 27
lieved, but it must be understood. To get rid of sin
through Science, is to divest sin of any supposed mind
or reality, and never to admit that sin can have intelli- 30
gence or power, pain or pleasure. You conquer error by
denying its verity. Our various theories will never lose

their imaginary power for good or evil, until we lose our 1
faith in them and make life its own proof of harmony
and God. 3

This text in the book of Ecclesiastes conveys the
Christian Science thought, especially when the word
duty, which is not in the original, is omitted: "Let 6
us hear the conclusion of the whole matter: Fear God,
and keep His commandments: for this is the whole
duty of man." In other words: Let us hear the con- 9
clusion of the whole matter: love God and keep His
commandments: for this is the whole of man in His
image and likeness. Divine Love is infinite. Therefore 12
all that really exists is in and of God, and manifests His
love.

"Thou shalt have no other gods before me." (Exodus 15
xx. 3.) The First Commandment is my favorite text.
It demonstrates Christian Science. It inculcates the tri-
unity of God, Spirit, Mind; it signifies that man shall 18
have no other spirit or mind but God, eternal good, and
that all men shall have one Mind. The divine Principle
of the First Commandment bases the Science of being, by 21
which man demonstrates health, holiness, and life eternal.
One infinite God, good, unifies men and nations; constitutes the brotherhood of man; ends wars; fulfils the 24
Scripture, "Love thy neighbor as thyself;" annihilates
pagan and Christian idolatry, — whatever is wrong in
social, civil, criminal, political, and religious codes; 27
equalizes the sexes; annuls the curse on man, and leaves
nothing that can sin, suffer, be punished or destroyed.

Chapter 11

Some Objections
Answered

And because I tell you the truth, ye believe me not.
Which of you convinceth me of sin?
And if I say the truth, why do ye not believe me? — JESUS.

But if the spirit of Him that raised up Jesus from the dead dwell in you,
He that raised up Christ from the dead shall also quicken
your mortal bodies by His spirit that dwelleth in you. — PAUL.

he strictures on this volume would condemn to oblivion the truth, which is raising up thousands from helplessness to strength and elevating them from a theoretical to a practical Christianity. These criticisms are generally based on detached sentences or clauses separated from their context. Even the Scriptures, which grow in beauty and consistency from one grand root, appear contradictory when subjected to such usage. Jesus said, "Blessed are the pure in heart: for they shall see God" [Truth].

In Christian Science mere opinion is valueless. Proof is essential to a due estimate of this subject. Sneers at

Supported by facts

the application of the word *Science* to Christianity cannot prevent that from being scientific which is based on divine Principle, demonstrated according to a divine given rule, and subjected to proof. The facts are so absolute and numerous in support of Christian Science, that misrepresentation and denuncia-

341

tion cannot overthrow it. Paul alludes to "doubtful dis- 1
putations." The hour has struck when proof and demonstration, instead of opinion and dogma, are summoned to 3
the support of Christianity, "making wise the simple."

In the result of some unqualified condemnations of
scientific Mind-healing, one may see with sorrow the sad 6

Commands of Jesus

effects on the sick of denying Truth. He that
decries this Science does it presumptuously,
in the face of Bible history and in defiance of the direct 9
command of Jesus, "Go ye into all the world, and preach
the gospel," to which command was added the promise
that his students should cast out evils and heal the sick. 12
He bade the seventy disciples, as well as the twelve,
heal the sick in any town where they should be hospitably
received. 15

If Christianity is not scientific, and Science is not of
God, then there is no invariable law, and truth becomes
an accident. Shall it be denied that a system 18

Christianity scientific

which works according to the Scriptures has
Scriptural authority?

Christian Science awakens the sinner, reclaims the 21
infidel, and raises from the couch of pain the helpless
invalid. It speaks to the dumb the words of

Argument of good works

Truth, and they answer with rejoicing. It 24
causes the deaf to hear, the lame to walk, and the blind
to see. Who would be the first to disown the Christli-
ness of good works, when our Master says, "By their 27
fruits ye shall know them"?

If Christian Scientists were teaching or practising
pharmacy or obstetrics according to the common theo- 30
ries, no denunciations would follow them, even if their
treatment resulted in the death of a patient. The people

If we are Christians on all moral questions, but are in
darkness as to the physical exemption which Christian-

**Disease far
more docile
than iniquity**

ity includes, then we must have more faith
in God on this subject and be more alive to
His promises. It is easier to cure the most
malignant disease than it is to cure sin. The author has
raised up the dying, partly because they were willing to
be restored, while she has struggled long, and perhaps in
vain, to lift a student out of a chronic sin. Under all
modes of pathological treatment, the sick recover more
rapidly from disease than does the sinner from his sin.
Healing is easier than teaching, if the teaching is faithfully
done.

The fear of disease and the love of sin are the sources
of man's enslavement. "The fear of the Lord

**Love frees
from fear**

is the beginning of wisdom," but the Scriptures
also declare, through the exalted thought of John, that
"perfect Love casteth out fear."

The fear occasioned by ignorance can be cured; but
to remove the effects of fear produced by sin, you must
rise above both fear and sin. Disease is expressed not
so much by the lips as in the functions of the body. Establish the scientific sense of health, and you relieve the
oppressed organ. The inflammation, decomposition, or
deposit will abate, and the disabled organ will resume its
healthy functions.

When the blood rushes madly through the veins or
languidly creeps along its frozen channels, we call these

**Mind
circulates
blood**

conditions disease. This is a misconception.
Mortal mind is producing the propulsion or the
languor, and we prove this to be so when by mental means
the circulation is changed, and returns to that standard

which mortal mind has decided upon as essential for   1
health. Anodynes, counter-irritants, and depletion never
reduce inflammation scientifically, but the truth of being,   3
whispered into the ear of mortal mind, will bring relief.

Hatred and its effects on the body are removed by
Love. Because mortal mind seems to be conscious, the   6

Mind can
destroy all ills

sick say: "How can my mind cause a disease
I never thought of and knew nothing about,
until it appeared on my body?" The author has an-   9
swered this question in her explanation of disease as originating in human belief before it is consciously apparent
on the body, which is in fact the objective state of mortal   12
mind, though it is called matter. This mortal blindness
and its sharp consequences show our need of divine metaphysics. Through immortal Mind, or Truth, we can   15
destroy all ills which proceed from mortal mind.

Ignorance of the cause or approach of disease is no
argument against the mental origin of disease. You con-   18
fess to ignorance of the future and incapacity to preserve
your own existence, and this belief helps rather than
hinders disease. Such a state of mind induces sickness.   21
It is like walking in darkness on the edge of a precipice.
You cannot forget the belief of danger, and your steps
are less firm because of your fear, and ignorance of mental   24
cause and effect.

Heat and cold are products of mortal mind. The body,
when bereft of mortal mind, at first cools, and after-   27

Temperature
is mental

wards it is resolved into its primitive mortal
elements. Nothing that lives ever dies, and
vice versa. Mortal mind produces animal heat, and then   30
expels it through the abandonment of a belief, or increases it to the point of self-destruction. Hence it is

mortal mind, not matter, which says, "I die." Heat 1
would pass from the body as painlessly as gas dissipates
into the air when it evaporates but for the belief that in- 3
flammation and pain must accompany the separation of
heat from the body.

Chills and heat are often the form in which fever mani- 6
fests itself. Change the mental state, and the chills and
fever disappear. The old-school physician

Science versus hypnotism

proves this when his patient says, "I am better," 9
but the patient believes that matter, not mind,
has helped him. The Christian Scientist demonstrates
that divine Mind heals, while the hypnotist dispossesses 12
the patient of his individuality in order to control him.
No person is benefited by yielding his mentality to any
mental despotism or malpractice. All unscientific mental 15
practice is erroneous and powerless, and should be understood and so rendered fruitless. The genuine Christian
Scientist is adding to his patient's mental and moral power, 18
and is increasing his patient's spirituality while restoring
him physically through divine Love.

Palsy is a belief that matter governs mortals, and can 21
paralyze the body, making certain portions of

Cure for palsy

it motionless. Destroy the belief, show mortal
mind that muscles have no power to be lost, for Mind is 24
supreme, and you cure the palsy.

Consumptive patients always show great hopeful-
ness and courage, even when they are supposed to be in 27
hopeless danger. This state of mind seems

Latent fear diagnosed

anomalous except to the expert in Christian
Science. This mental state is not understood, simply 30
because it is a stage of fear so excessive that it amounts
to fortitude. The belief in consumption presents to mor-

tal thought a hopeless state, an image more terrifying than
that of most other diseases. The patient turns involun-
tarily from the contemplation of it, but though unacknowledged, the latent fear and the despair of recovery remain
in thought.

Just so is it with the greatest sin. It is the most subtle,
and does its work almost self-deceived. The diseases

Insidious
concepts

deemed dangerous sometimes come from the
most hidden, undefined, and insidious beliefs.
The pallid invalid, whom you declare to be wasting away
with consumption of the blood, should be told that blood
never gave life and can never take it away, — that Life is
Spirit, and that there is more life and immortality in one
good motive and act, than in all the blood which ever
flowed through mortal veins and simulated a corporeal
sense of life.

If the body is material, it cannot, for that very reason,
suffer with a fever. Because the so-called material body

Remedy
for fever

is a mental concept and governed by mortal
mind, it manifests only what that so-called
mind expresses. Therefore the efficient remedy is to
destroy the patient's false belief by both silently and audibly arguing the true facts in regard to harmonious
being, — representing man as healthy instead of diseased,
and showing that it is impossible for matter to suffer, to
feel pain or heat, to be thirsty or sick. Destroy fear,
and you end fever. Some people, mistaught as to Mind-
science, inquire when it will be safe to check a fever.
Know that in Science you cannot check a fever after ad-
mitting that it must have its course. To fear and admit
the power of disease, is to paralyze mental and scientific
demonstration.

If your patient believes in taking cold, mentally con- 1
vince him that matter cannot take cold, and that thought
governs this liability. If grief causes suffering, convince 3
the sufferer that affliction is often the source of joy, and
that he should rejoice always in ever-present Love.

Invalids flee to tropical climates in order to save their 6
lives, but they come back no better than when they went

Climate harmless away. Then is the time to cure them through
Christian Science, and prove that they can 9
be healthy in all climates, when their fear of climate is
exterminated.

Through different states of mind, the body becomes 12
suddenly weak or abnormally strong, showing mortal

Mind governs body mind to be the producer of strength or weakness. A sudden joy or grief has caused what 15
is termed instantaneous death. Because a belief originates unseen, the mental state should be continually
watched that it may not produce blindly its bad effects. 18
The author never knew a patient who did not recover
when the belief of the disease had gone. Remove the
leading error or governing fear of this lower so-called mind, 21
and you remove the cause of all disease as well as the morbid or excited action of any organ. You also remove in
this way what are termed organic diseases as readily as 24
functional difficulties.

The cause of all so-called disease is mental, a mortal
fear, a mistaken belief or conviction of the necessity and 27
power of ill-health; also a fear that Mind is helpless to
defend the life of man and incompetent to control it. Without this ignorant human belief, any circumstance is of it- 30
self powerless to produce suffering. It is latent belief in
disease, as well as the fear of disease, which associates sick-

ness with certain circumstances and causes the two to   1
appear conjoined, even as poetry and music are reproduced in union by human memory. Disease has no in-   3
telligence. Unwittingly you sentence yourself to suffer.
The understanding of this will enable you to commute this
self-sentence, and meet every circumstance with truth.   6
Disease is less than mind, and Mind can control it.

Without the so-called human mind, there can be no
inflammatory nor torpid action of the system. Remove   9

Latent power the error, and you destroy its effects. By
looking a tiger fearlessly in the eye, Sir Charles
Napier sent it cowering back into the jungle. An ani-   12
mal may infuriate another by looking it in the eye, and
both will fight for nothing. A man's gaze, fastened
fearlessly on a ferocious beast, often causes the beast to   15
retreat in terror. This latter occurrence represents the
power of Truth over error, — the might of intelligence
exercised over mortal beliefs to destroy them; whereas   18
hypnotism and hygienic drilling and drugging, adopted
to cure matter, is represented by two material erroneous
bases.   21

Disease is not an intelligence to dispute the empire of
Mind or to dethrone Mind and take the government into

Disease powerless its own hands. Sickness is not a God-given,   24
nor a self-constituted material power, which
copes astutely with Mind and finally conquers it. God
never endowed matter with power to disable Life or to   27
chill harmony with a long and cold night of discord.
Such a power, without the divine permission, is incon-
ceivable; and if such a power could be divinely directed,   30
it would manifest less wisdom than we usually find displayed in human governments.

Jurisdiction
of Mind

If disease can attack and control the body without   1
the consent of mortals, sin can do the same, for both
are errors, announced as partners in the be-   3
ginning. The Christian Scientist finds only
effects, where the ordinary physician looks for causes.
The real jurisdiction of the world is in Mind, controlling   6
every effect and recognizing all causation as vested in
divine Mind.

A felon, on whom certain English students experi-   9
mented, fancied himself bleeding to death, and died because of that belief, when only a stream of
warm water was trickling over his arm. Had   12
he known his sense of bleeding was an illusion, he would
have risen above the false belief. Let the despairing invalid, inspecting the hue of her blood on a cambric hand-   15
kerchief, think of the experiment of those Oxford boys,
who caused the death of a man, when not a drop of his
blood was shed. Then let her learn the opposite state-   18
ment of Life as taught in Christian Science, and she will
understand that she is not dying on account of the state of
her blood, but is suffering from her belief that blood is   21
destroying her life. The so-called vital current does not
affect the invalid's health, but her belief produces the
very results she dreads.   24

Fevers are errors of various types. The quickened
pulse, coated tongue, febrile heat, dry skin, pain in the
head and limbs, are pictures drawn on the   27
body by a mortal mind. The images, held in
this disturbed mind, frighten conscious thought. Unless
the fever-picture, drawn by millions of mortals and im-   30
aged on the body through the belief that mind is in matter
and discord is as real as harmony, is destroyed through

**Jurisdiction
of Mind**

**Power of
imagination**

**Fevers the
effect of fear**

Science, it may rest at length on some receptive thought,   1
and become a fever case, which ends in a belief called
death, which belief must be finally conquered by eternal   3
Life. Truth is always the victor. Sickness and sin fall
by their own weight. Truth is the rock of ages, the head-
stone of the corner, "but on whomsoever it shall fall, it   6
will grind him to powder."

Contending for the evidence or indulging the demands
of sin, disease, or death, we virtually contend against   9

**Misdirected
contention**

the control of Mind over body, and deny the
power of Mind to heal. This false method
is as though the defendant should argue for the plaintiff   12
in favor of a decision which the defendant knows will
be turned against himself.

The physical effects of fear illustrate its illusion. Gaz-   15
ing at a chained lion, crouched for a spring, should not

**Benefits of
metaphysics**

terrify a man. The body is affected only with
the belief of disease produced by a so-called   18
mind ignorant of the truth which chains disease. Nothing but the power of Truth can prevent the fear of
error, and prove man's dominion over error.   21

Many years ago the author made a spiritual discovery, the scientific evidence of which has accumulated to

**A higher
discovery**

prove that the divine Mind produces in man   24
health, harmony, and immortality. Gradu-
ally this evidence will gather momentum and clearness,
until it reaches its culmination of scientific statement and   27
proof. Nothing is more disheartening than to believe
that there is a power opposite to God, or good, and that
God endows this opposing power with strength to be used   30
against Himself, against Life, health, harmony.

Every law of matter or the body, supposed to govern

man, is rendered null and void by the law of Life, God. 1
Ignorant of our God-given rights, we submit to unjust

Ignorance of our rights

decrees, and the bias of education enforces 3
this slavery. Be no more willing to suffer the
illusion that you are sick or that some disease is develop-
ing in the system, than you are to yield to a sinful temp- 6
tation on the ground that sin has its necessities.

When infringing some supposed law, you say that
there is danger. This fear is the danger and induces the 9

No laws of matter

physical effects. We cannot in reality suffer
from breaking anything except a moral or
spiritual law. The so-called laws of mortal belief are 12
destroyed by the understanding that Soul is immortal,
and that mortal mind cannot legislate the times, periods,
and types of disease, with which mortals die. God is the 15
lawmaker, but He is not the author of barbarous codes.
In infinite Life and Love there is no sickness, sin, nor
death, and the Scriptures declare that we live, move, and 18
have our being in the infinite God.

Think less of the enactments of mortal mind, and you
will sooner grasp man's God-given dominion. You must 21

God-given dominion

understand your way out of human theories
relating to health, or you will never believe
that you are quite free from some ailment. The har- 24
mony and immortality of man will never be reached
without the understanding that Mind is not in matter.
Let us banish sickness as an outlaw, and abide by the 27
rule of perpetual harmony, — God's law. It is man's
moral right to annul an unjust sentence, a sentence never
inflicted by divine authority. 30

Christ Jesus overruled the error which would impose
penalties for transgressions of the physical laws of

health; he annulled supposed laws of matter, opposed   1
to the harmonies of Spirit, lacking divine authority and having only human approval for   3
their sanction.

If half the attention given to hygiene were given to the
study of Christian Science and to the spiritualization of   6
thought, this alone would usher in the millen-
nium. Constant bathing and rubbing to alter
the secretions or to remove unhealthy exhalations from   9
the cuticle receive a useful rebuke from Jesus' precept,
"Take no thought . . . for the body." We must beware
of making clean merely the outside of the platter.   12

He, who is ignorant of what is termed hygienic law, is
more receptive of spiritual power and of faith in one
God, than is the devotee of supposed hygienic   15
law, who comes to teach the so-called ignorant one. Must we not then consider the so-called law
of matter a canon "more honored in the breach than   18
the observance"? A patient thoroughly booked in medical theories is more difficult to heal through Mind than
one who is not. This verifies the saying of our Master: 21
"Whosoever shall not receive the kingdom of God as a
little child, shall in no wise enter therein."

One whom I rescued from seeming spiritual oblivion,   24
in which the senses had engulfed him, wrote to me: "I
should have died, but for the glorious Principle you teach,
— supporting the power of Mind over the body and show-   27
ing me the nothingness of the so-called pleasures and pains
of sense. The treatises I had read and the medicines I
had taken only abandoned me to more hopeless suffering   30
and despair. Adherence to hygiene was useless. Mortal
mind needed to be set right. The ailment was not bodily,

but mental, and I was cured when I learned my way in 1
Christian Science."

We need a clean body and a clean mind, — a body 3
rendered pure by Mind as well as washed by water.

A clean mind and body One says: "I take good care of my body."
To do this, the pure and exalting influence of 6
the divine Mind on the body is requisite, and the Christian
Scientist takes the best care of his body when he leaves
it most out of his thought, and, like the Apostle Paul, is 9
"willing rather to be absent from the body, and to be present with the Lord."

A hint may be taken from the emigrant, whose filth 12
does not affect his happiness, because mind and body
rest on the same basis. To the mind equally gross, dirt
gives no uneasiness. It is the native element of such a 15
mind, which is symbolized, and not chafed, by its sur-
roundings; but impurity and uncleanliness, which do
not trouble the gross, could not be borne by the refined. 18
This shows that the mind must be clean to keep the body
in proper condition.

The tobacco-user, eating or smoking poison for half a 21
century, sometimes tells you that the weed preserves
Beliefs illusive his health, but does this make it so? Does his
assertion prove the use of tobacco to be a salu- 24
brious habit, and man to be the better for it? Such instances only prove the illusive physical effect of a false
belief, confirming the Scriptural conclusion concerning a 27
man, "As he thinketh in his heart, so is he."

The movement-cure — pinching and pounding the poor
body, to make it sensibly well when it ought to be in- 30
sensibly so — is another medical mistake, resulting from
the common notion that health depends on inert matter

instead of on Mind. Can matter, or what is termed   1
matter, either feel or act without mind?

We should relieve our minds from the depressing thought   3
that we have transgressed a material law and must of

Corporeal
penalties
necessity pay the penalty. Let us reassure
ourselves with the law of Love. God never   6
punishes man for doing right, for honest labor, or for
deeds of kindness, though they expose him to fatigue,
cold, heat, contagion. If man seems to incur the penalty   9
through matter, this is but a belief of mortal mind, not
an enactment of wisdom, and man has only to enter his
protest against this belief in order to annul it. Through   12
this action of thought and its results upon the body, the
student will prove to himself, by small beginnings, the
grand verities of Christian Science.   15

If exposure to a draught of air while in a state of
perspiration is followed by chills, dry cough, influenza,

Not matter,
but Mind
congestive symptoms in the lungs, or hints of   18
inflammatory rheumatism, your Mind-remedy
is safe and sure. If you are a Christian Scientist, such
symptoms are not apt to follow exposure; but if you   21
believe in laws of matter and their fatal effects when
transgressed, you are not fit to conduct your own case or
to destroy the bad effects of your belief. When the fear   24
subsides and the conviction abides that you have broken
no law, neither rheumatism, consumption, nor any other
disease will ever result from exposure to the weather. In   27
Science this is an established fact which all the evidence
before the senses can never overrule.

Sickness, sin, and death must at length quail before   30
the divine rights of intelligence, and then the power
of Mind over the entire functions and organs of the

human system will be acknowledged. It is proverbial
that Florence Nightingale and other philanthropists en-

Benefit of philanthropy gaged in humane labors have been able to
undergo without sinking fatigues and expo-
sures which ordinary people could not endure. The explanation lies in the support which they derived from
the divine law, rising above the human. The spiritual
demand, quelling the material, supplies energy and endurance surpassing all other aids, and forestalls the
penalty which our beliefs would attach to our best
deeds. Let us remember that the eternal law of right,
though it can never annul the law which makes sin its
own executioner, exempts man from all penalties but
those due for wrong-doing.

Constant toil, deprivations, exposures, and all untow-
ard conditions, *if without sin*, can be experienced with-

Honest toil has no penalty out suffering. Whatever it is your duty to do,
you can do without harm to yourself. If you
sprain the muscles or wound the flesh, your
remedy is at hand. Mind decides whether or not the
flesh shall be discolored, painful, swollen, and inflamed.

You say that you have not slept well or have overeaten.
You are a law unto yourself. Saying this and believing

Our sleep and food it, you will suffer in proportion to your belief
and fear. Your sufferings are not the penalty
for having broken a law of matter, for it is a law of mortal
mind which you have disobeyed. You say or think, because you have partaken of salt fish, that you must be
thirsty, and you are thirsty accordingly, while the opposite belief would produce the opposite result.

Any supposed information, coming from the body or
from inert matter as if either were intelligent, is an illu-

sion of mortal mind, — one of its dreams. Realize that   1

**Doubtful
evidence**

the evidence of the senses is not to be accepted
in the case of sickness, any more than it is in   3
the case of sin.

Expose the body to certain temperatures, and belief
says that you may catch cold and have catarrh; but no   6

**Climate
and belief**

such result occurs without mind to demand
it and produce it. So long as mortals declare
that certain states of the atmosphere produce catarrh,   9
fever, rheumatism, or consumption, those effects will
follow, — not because of the climate, but on account of
the belief. The author has in too many instances healed   12
disease through the action of Truth on the minds of mortals, and the corresponding effects of Truth on the body,
not to know that this is so.   15

A blundering despatch, mistakenly announcing the
death of a friend, occasions the same grief that the friend's

**Erroneous
despatch**

real death would bring. You think that your   18
anguish is occasioned by your loss. Another
despatch, correcting the mistake, heals your grief, and
you learn that your suffering was merely the result of   21
your belief. Thus it is with all sorrow, sickness, and
death. You will learn at length that there is no cause
for grief, and divine wisdom will then be understood.   24
Error, not Truth, produces all the suffering on earth.

If a Christian Scientist had said, while you were labor-
ing under the influence of the belief of grief, "Your sor-   27

**Mourning
causeless**

row is without cause," you would not have
understood him, although the correctness of
the assertion might afterwards be proved to you. So,   30
when our friends pass from our sight and we lament,
that lamentation is needless and causeless. We shall

perceive this to be true when we grow into the under-   1
standing of Life, and know that there is no death.

Because mortal mind is kept active, must it pay the   3
penalty in a softened brain? Who dares to say that actual

Mind heals brain-disease Mind can be overworked? When we reach
our limits of mental endurance, we conclude   6
that intellectual labor has been carried sufficiently far;
but when we realize that immortal Mind is ever active,
and that spiritual energies can neither wear out nor can   9
so-called material law trespass upon God-given powers
and resources, we are able to rest in Truth, refreshed by
the assurances of immortality, opposed to mortality.   12

Our thinkers do not die early because they faithfully
perform the natural functions of being. If printers and

Right never punishable authors have the shortest span of earthly ex-   15
istence, it is not because they occupy the most
important posts and perform the most vital functions in
society. That man does not pay the severest penalty   18
who does the most good. By adhering to the realities of
eternal existence, — instead of reading disquisitions on
the inconsistent supposition that death comes in obedience   21
to the law of life, and that God punishes man for doing
good, — one cannot suffer as the result of any labor of
love, but grows stronger because of it. It is a law of so-   24
called mortal mind, misnamed matter, which causes all
things discordant.

The history of Christianity furnishes sublime proofs   27
of the supporting influence and protecting power bestowed

Christian history on man by his heavenly Father, omnipotent
Mind, who gives man faith and understanding   30
whereby to defend himself, not only from temptation, but
from bodily suffering.

The Christian martyrs were prophets of Christian   1
Science. Through the uplifting and consecrating power
of divine Truth, they obtained a victory over the corpo-   3
real senses, a victory which Science alone can explain.
Stolidity, which is a resisting state of mortal mind, suffers
less, only because it knows less of material law.   6

The Apostle John testified to the divine basis of Christian Science, when dire inflictions failed to destroy his
body. Idolaters, believing in more than one mind, had   9
"gods many," and thought that they could kill the body
with matter, independently of mind.

Admit the common hypothesis that food is the nutri-   12
ment of life, and there follows the necessity for another

Sustenance spiritual

admission in the opposite direction, — that
food has power to destroy Life, God, through   15
a deficiency or an excess, a quality or a quantity. This
is a specimen of the ambiguous nature of all material
health-theories. They are self-contradictory and self-de-   18
structive, constituting a "kingdom divided against itself,"
which is "brought to desolation." If food was prepared
by Jesus for his disciples, it cannot destroy life.   21

The fact is, food does not affect the absolute Life of
man, and this becomes self-evident, when we learn that

God sustains man

God is our Life. Because sin and sickness are   24
not qualities of Soul, or Life, we have hope in
immortality; but it would be foolish to venture beyond
our present understanding, foolish to stop eating until   27
we gain perfection and a clear comprehension of the living
Spirit. In that perfect day of understanding, we shall
neither eat to live nor live to eat.   30

If mortals think that food disturbs the harmonious
functions of mind and body, either the food or this thought

and cannot transmit good or evil intelligence to man, and   1
God, the only Mind, does not produce pain in matter.
The act of yielding one's thoughts to the undue contem-   3
plation of physical wants or conditions induces those very
conditions. A single requirement, beyond what is necessary to meet the simplest needs of the babe is harmful.   6
Mind regulates the condition of the stomach, bowels, and
food, the temperature of children and of men, and matter
does not. The wise or unwise views of parents and other   9
persons on these subjects produce good or bad effects on
the health of children.

The daily ablutions of an infant are no more natural   12
nor necessary than would be the process of taking a fish

Ablutions for cleanliness

out of water every day and covering it with dirt
in order to make it thrive more vigorously in its   15
own element. "Cleanliness is next to godliness," but
washing should be only for the purpose of keeping the
body clean, and this can be effected without scrubbing the   18
whole surface daily. Water is not the natural habitat of
humanity. I insist on bodily cleanliness within and without. I am not patient with a speck of dirt; but in caring   21
for an infant one need not wash his little body all over each
day in order to keep it sweet as the new-blown flower.

Giving drugs to infants, noticing every symptom of   24
flatulency, and constantly directing the mind to such

Juvenile ailments

signs, — that mind being laden with illusions
about disease, health-laws, and death, — these   27
actions convey mental images to children's budding
thoughts, and often stamp them there, making it probable
at any time that such ills may be reproduced in the very   30
ailments feared. A child may have worms, if you say so,
or any other malady, timorously held in the beliefs con-

cerning his body. Thus are laid the foundations of the   1
belief in disease and death, and thus are children educated
into discord.   3

The treatment of insanity is especially interesting.
However obstinate the case, it yields more readily than

Cure of insanity   do most diseases to the salutary action of   6
truth, which counteracts error. The argu-
ments to be used in curing insanity are the same as in
other diseases: namely, the impossibility that matter,   9
brain, can control or derange mind, can suffer or cause
suffering; also the fact that truth and love will establish
a healthy state, guide and govern mortal mind or the   12
thought of the patient, and destroy all error, whether it is
called dementia, hatred, or any other discord.

To fix truth steadfastly in your patients' thoughts, ex-   15
plain Christian Science to them, but not too soon, — not
until your patients are prepared for the explanation, —
lest you array the sick against their own interests by troub-   18
ling and perplexing their thought. The Christian Scientist's argument rests on the Christianly scientific basis of
being. The Scripture declares, "The Lord He is God   21
[good]; there is none else beside Him." Even so, harmony
is universal, and discord is unreal. Christian Science declares that Mind is substance, also that matter neither   24
feels, suffers, nor enjoys. Hold these points strongly in
view. Keep in mind the verity of being, — that man is
the image and likeness of God, in whom all being is   27
painless and permanent. Remember that man's perfection is real and unimpeachable, whereas imperfection is
blameworthy, unreal, and is not brought about by divine   30
Love.

Matter cannot be inflamed. Inflammation is fear, an

excited state of mortals which is not normal. Immor- 1
tal Mind is the only cause; therefore disease is neither a

Matter is not inflamed

cause nor an effect. Mind in every case is the 3
eternal God, good. Sin, disease, and death
have no foundations in Truth. Inflammation as a mortal belief quickens or impedes the action of the system, 6
because thought moves quickly or slowly, leaps or halts
when it contemplates unpleasant things, or when the individual looks upon some object which he dreads. In- 9
flammation never appears in a part which mortal thought
does not reach. That is why opiates relieve inflammation.
They quiet the thought by inducing stupefaction and by 12
resorting to matter instead of to Mind. Opiates do not
remove the pain in any scientific sense. They only render mortal mind temporarily less fearful, till it can master 15
an erroneous belief.

Note how thought makes the face pallid. It either re-
tards the circulation or quickens it, causing a pale or 18

Truth calms the thought

flushed cheek. In the same way thought increases or diminishes the secretions, the action
of the lungs, of the bowels, and of the heart. The mus- 21
cles, moving quickly or slowly and impelled or palsied by
thought, represent the action of all the organs of the human system, including brain and viscera. To remove 24
the error producing disorder, you must calm and instruct
mortal mind with immortal Truth.

Etherization will apparently cause the body to dis- 27
appear. Before the thoughts are fully at rest, the limbs

Effects of etherization

will vanish from consciousness. Indeed, the
whole frame will sink from sight along with 30
surrounding objects, leaving the pain standing forth as
distinctly as a mountain-peak, as if it were a separate

bodily member. At last the agony also vanishes. This 1
process shows the pain to be in the mind, for the inflammation is not suppressed; and the belief of pain will 3
presently return, unless the mental image occasioning
the pain be removed by recognizing the truth of being.

A hypodermic injection of morphine is administered 6
to a patient, and in twenty minutes the sufferer is qui-

Sedatives
valueless

etly asleep. To him there is no longer any
pain. Yet any physician — allopathic, homœ- 9
opathic, botanic, eclectic — will tell you that the troublesome material cause is unremoved, and that when the
soporific influence of the opium is exhausted, the pa- 12
tient will find himself in the same pain, unless the belief
which occasions the pain has meanwhile been changed.
Where is the pain while the patient sleeps? 15

The material body, which you call me, is mortal mind,
and this mind is material in sensation, even as the body,

The so-called
physical ego

which has originated from this material sense 18
and been developed according to it, is material. This materialism of parent and child is only in
mortal mind, as the dead body proves; for when the 21
mortal has resigned his body to dust, the body is no
longer the parent, even in appearance.

The sick know nothing of the mental process by 24
which they are depleted, and next to nothing of the

Evil thought
depletes

metaphysical method by which they can be
healed. If they ask about their disease, tell 27
them only what is best for them to know. Assure them
that they think too much about their ailments, and
have already heard too much on that subject. Turn 30
their thoughts away from their bodies to higher objects. Teach them that their being is sustained by

Spirit, not by matter, and that they find health, peace,   1
and harmony in God, divine Love.

Give sick people credit for sometimes knowing more   3
than their doctors. Always support their trust in the

Helpful encouragement power of Mind to sustain the body. Never
tell the sick that they have more courage   6
than strength. Tell them rather, that their strength
is in proportion to their courage. If you make the sick
realize this great truism, there will be no reaction from   9
over-exertion or from excited conditions. Maintain
the facts of Christian Science, — that Spirit is God, and
therefore cannot be sick; that what is termed matter   12
cannot be sick; that all causation is Mind, acting
through spiritual law. Then hold your ground with
the unshaken understanding of Truth and Love, and   15
you will win. When you silence the witness against your
plea, you destroy the evidence, for the disease disappears. The evidence before the corporeal senses is not   18
the Science of immortal man.

To the Christian Science healer, sickness is a dream
from which the patient needs to be awakened. Dis-   21
Disease to be made unreal ease should not appear real to the physician,
since it is demonstrable that the way to
cure the patient is to make disease unreal to him. To   24
do this, the physician must understand the unreality
of disease in Science.

Explain audibly to your patients, as soon as they can   27
bear it, the complete control which Mind holds over the
body. Show them how mortal mind seems to induce
disease by certain fears and false conclusions, and how   30
divine Mind can cure by opposite thoughts. Give your
patients an underlying understanding to support them

and to shield them from the baneful effects of their own   1
conclusions. Show them that the conquest over sickness,
as well as over sin, depends on mentally destroying all   3
belief in material pleasure or pain.

Stick to the truth of being in contradistinction to the
error that life, substance, or intelligence can be in matter.   6

Christian pleading Plead with an honest conviction of truth and
a clear perception of the unchanging, unerr-
ing, and certain effect of divine Science. Then, if your   9
fidelity is half equal to the truth of your plea, you will
heal the sick.

It must be clear to you that sickness is no more   12
the reality of being than is sin. This mortal dream

Truthful arguments of sickness, sin, and death should cease
through Christian Science. Then one dis-   15
ease would be as readily destroyed as another. Whatever the belief is, if arguments are used to destroy it,
the belief must be repudiated, and the negation must ex-   18
tend to the supposed disease and to whatever decides its
type and symptoms. Truth is affirmative, and confers
harmony. All metaphysical logic is inspired by this sim-   21
ple rule of Truth, which governs all reality. By the
truthful arguments you employ, and especially by the
spirit of Truth and Love which you entertain, you will   24
heal the sick.

Include moral as well as physical belief in your efforts
to destroy error. Cast out all manner of evil. "Preach   27

Morality required the gospel to every creature." Speak the
truth to every form of error. Tumors, ulcers,
tubercles, inflammation, pain, deformed joints, are wak-   30
ing dream-shadows, dark images of mortal thought, which
flee before the light of Truth.

A moral question may hinder the recovery of the sick. [1] Lurking error, lust, envy, revenge, malice, or hate will perpetuate or even create the belief in disease. Errors [3] of all sorts tend in this direction. Your true course is to destroy the foe, and leave the field to God, Life, Truth, and Love, remembering that God and His ideas alone [6] are real and harmonious.

Relapse unnecessary

If your patient from any cause suffers a relapse, meet the cause mentally and courageously, knowing that [9] there can be no reaction in Truth. Neither disease itself, sin, nor fear has the power to cause disease or a relapse. Disease has no intelligence [12] with which to move itself about or to change itself from one form to another. If disease moves, mind, not matter, moves it; therefore be sure that you move it off. [15] Meet every adverse circumstance as its master. Observe mind instead of body, lest aught unfit for development enter thought. Think less of material conditions [18] and more of spiritual.

Mind produces all action. If the action proceeds from Truth, from immortal Mind, there is harmony; but mor- [21] tal mind is liable to any phase of belief. A

Conquer beliefs and fears

relapse cannot in reality occur in mortals or so-called mortal minds, for there is but one [24] Mind, one God. Never fear the mental malpractitioner, the mental assassin, who, in attempting to rule mankind, tramples upon the divine Principle of metaphysics, for God [27] is the only power. To succeed in healing, you must conquer your own fears as well as those of your patients, and rise into higher and holier consciousness. [30]

If it is found necessary to treat against relapse, know that disease or its symptoms cannot change forms, nor

go from one part to another, for Truth destroys disease. 1
There is no metastasis, no stoppage of harmonious

True government of man

action, no paralysis. Truth not error, Love 3
not hate, Spirit not matter, governs man. If
students do not readily heal themselves, they should
early call an experienced Christian Scientist to aid 6
them. If they are unwilling to do this for themselves,
they need only to know that error cannot produce this
unnatural reluctance. 9

Instruct the sick that they are not helpless victims,
for if they will only accept Truth, they can resist disease

Positive reassurance

and ward it off, as positively as they can the 12
temptation to sin. This fact of Christian Science should be explained to invalids when they are in a
fit mood to receive it, — when they will not array them- 15
selves against it, but are ready to become receptive to the
new idea. The fact that Truth overcomes both disease
and sin reassures depressed hope. It imparts a healthy 18
stimulus to the body, and regulates the system. It increases or diminishes the action, as the case may require,
better than any drug, alterative, or tonic. 21

Mind is the natural stimulus of the body, but erroneous belief, taken at its best, is not promotive of health

Proper stimulus

or happiness. Tell the sick that they can 24
meet disease fearlessly, if they only realize
that divine Love gives them all power over every physical
action and condition. 27

If it becomes necessary to startle mortal mind to break
its dream of suffering, vehemently tell your patient that

Awaken the patient

he must awake. Turn his gaze from the false 30
evidence of the senses to the harmonious facts
of Soul and immortal being. Tell him that he suffers

only as the insane suffer, from false beliefs. The only
difference is, that insanity implies belief in a diseased
brain, while physical ailments (so-called) arise from the
belief that other portions of the body are deranged. De-
rangement, or *disarrangement*, is a word which conveys
the true definition of all human belief in ill-health, or disturbed harmony. Should you thus startle mortal mind
in order to remove its beliefs, afterwards make known
to the patient your motive for this shock, showing him
that it was to facilitate recovery.

How to treat a crisis

If a crisis occurs in your treatment, you must treat
the patient less for the disease and more for the mental
disturbance or fermentation, and subdue the
symptoms by removing the belief that this
chemicalization produces pain or disease. Insist vehemently on the great fact which covers the whole ground,
that God, Spirit, is all, and that there is none beside
Him. There is *no disease.* When the supposed suffering is gone from mortal mind, there can be no pain; and
when the fear is destroyed, the inflammation will sub-
side. Calm the excitement sometimes induced by chemicalization, which is the alterative effect produced by
Truth upon error, and sometimes explain the symptoms
and their cause to the patient.

No perversion of Mind-science

It is no more Christianly scientific to see disease than
it is to experience it. If you would destroy the sense
of disease, you should not build it up by
wishing to see the forms it assumes or by
employing a single material application for
its relief. The perversion of Mind-science is like asserting that the products of eight multiplied by five, and
of seven by ten, are both forty, and that their combined

sum is fifty, and then calling the process mathematics.   1
Wiser than his persecutors, Jesus said: "If I by Beelzebub cast out devils, by whom do your children cast them   3
out?"

If the reader of this book observes a great stir throughout his whole system, and certain moral and physical   6
Effect of
this book   symptoms seem aggravated, these indications
are favorable. Continue to read, and the book
will become the physician, allaying the tremor which   9
Truth often brings to error when destroying it.

Patients, unfamiliar with the cause of this commotion
and ignorant that it is a favorable omen, may be alarmed.   12
Disease   If such be the case, explain to them the law
neutralized   of this action. As when an acid and alkali
meet and bring out a third quality, so mental and moral   15
chemistry changes the material base of thought, giving
more spirituality to consciousness and causing it to depend
less on material evidence. These changes which go on   18
in mortal mind serve to reconstruct the body. Thus
Christian Science, by the alchemy of Spirit, destroys sin
and death.   21

Let us suppose two parallel cases of bone-disease, both
similarly produced and attended by the same symptoms.
Bone-healing   A surgeon is employed in one case, and a   24
by surgery   Christian Scientist in the other. The surgeon, holding that matter forms its own conditions and
renders them fatal at certain points, entertains fears and   27
doubts as to the ultimate outcome of the injury. Not
holding the reins of government in his own hands, he
believes that something stronger than Mind — namely,   30
matter — governs the case. His treatment is therefore
tentative. This mental state invites defeat. The belief

that he has met his master in matter and may not be 1
able to mend the bone, increases his fear; yet this belief
should not be communicated to the patient, either ver- 3
bally or otherwise, for this fear greatly diminishes the
tendency towards a favorable result. Remember that the
unexpressed belief oftentimes affects a sensitive patient 6
more strongly than the expressed thought.

Scientific corrective

The Christian Scientist, understanding scientifically
that all is Mind, commences with mental causation, the 9
truth of being, to destroy the error. This corrective is an alterative, reaching to every part
of the human system. According to Scripture, it searches 12
"the joints and marrow," and it restores the harmony of
man.

Coping with difficulties

The matter-physician deals with matter as both his foe 15
and his remedy. He regards the ailment as weakened or
strengthened according to the evidence which
matter presents. The metaphysician, making 18
Mind his basis of operation irrespective of matter and
regarding the truth and harmony of being as superior to
error and discord, has rendered himself strong, instead 21
of weak, to cope with the case; and he proportionately
strengthens his patient with the stimulus of courage and
conscious power. Both Science and consciousness are 24
now at work in the economy of being according to the law
of Mind, which ultimately asserts its absolute supremacy.

Formation from thought

Ossification or any abnormal condition or derange- 27
ment of the body is as directly the action of mortal
mind as is dementia or insanity. Bones have
only the substance of thought which forms 30
them. They are only phenomena of the mind of mortals. The so-called substance of bone is formed first

by the parent's mind, through self-division. Soon the   1
child becomes a separate, individualized mortal mind,
which takes possession of itself and its own thoughts of   3
bones.

Accidents are unknown to God, or immortal Mind,

and we must leave the mortal basis of belief   6
and unite with the one Mind, in order to
change the notion of chance to the proper sense
of God's unerring direction and thus bring out harmony.   9

Under divine Providence there can be no accidents,
since there is no room for imperfection in perfection.

In medical practice objections would be raised if one   12
doctor should administer a drug to counteract the work-

ing of a remedy prescribed by another doctor.
It is equally important in metaphysical prac-   15
tice that the *minds* which surround your patient should
not act against your influence by continually expressing
such opinions as may alarm or discourage, — either by   18
giving antagonistic advice or through unspoken thoughts
resting on your patient. While it is certain that the
divine Mind can remove any obstacle, still you need the   21
ear of your auditor. It is not more difficult to make yourself heard mentally while others are thinking about your
patients or conversing with them, if you understand   24
Christian Science — the oneness and the allness of divine
Love; but it is well to be alone with God and the sick
when treating disease.   27

To prevent or to cure scrofula and other so-called hereditary diseases, you must destroy the belief in these ills

and the faith in the possibility of their trans-   30
mission. The patient may tell you that he
has a humor in the blood, a scrofulous diathesis. His

parents or some of his progenitors farther back have so 1
believed. Mortal mind, not matter, induces this conclusion and its results. You will have humors, just so 3
long as you believe them to be safety-valves or to be
ineradicable.

If the case to be mentally treated is consumption, take 6
up the leading points included (according to belief) in

Nothing to consume this disease. Show that it is not inherited;
that inflammation, tubercles, hemorrhage, and 9
decomposition are beliefs, images of mortal thought su-
perimposed upon the body; that they are not the truth
of man; that they should be treated as error and put out 12
of thought. Then these ills will disappear.

If the body is diseased, this is but one of the beliefs of
mortal mind. Mortal man will be less mortal, when he 15

The lungs re-formed learns that matter never sustained existence
and can never destroy God, who is man's Life.
When this is understood, mankind will be more spiritual 18
and know that there is nothing to consume, since Spirit,
God, is All-in-all. What if the belief is consumption?
God is more to a man than his belief, and the less we ac- 21
knowledge matter or its laws, the more immortality we
possess. Consciousness constructs a better body when
faith in matter has been conquered. Correct material 24
belief by spiritual understanding, and Spirit will form
you anew. You will never fear again except to offend
God, and you will never believe that heart or any por- 27
tion of the body can destroy you.

If you have sound and capacious lungs and want

Soundness maintained them to remain so, be always ready with the 30
mental protest against the opposite belief in
heredity. Discard all notions about lungs, tubercles, in-

herited consumption, or disease arising from any cir- 1
cumstance, and you will find that mortal mind, when
instructed by Truth, yields to divine power, which steers 3
the body into health.

The discoverer of Christian Science finds the path less
difficult when she has the high goal always before her 6

Our footsteps heavenward

thoughts, than when she counts her footsteps
in endeavoring to reach it. When the destination is desirable, expectation speeds our progress. The 9
struggle for Truth makes one strong instead of weak,
resting instead of wearying one. If the belief in death
were obliterated, and the understanding obtained that 12
there is no death, this would be a "tree of life," known
by its fruits. Man should renew his energies and endeavors, and see the folly of hypocrisy, while also learn- 15
ing the necessity of working out his own salvation. When
it is learned that disease cannot destroy life, and that
mortals are not saved from sin or sickness by death, this 18
understanding will quicken into newness of life. It will
master either a desire to die or a dread of the grave,
and thus destroy the great fear that besets mortal 21
existence.

The relinquishment of all faith in death and also of
the fear of its sting would raise the standard of health 24

Christian standard

and morals far beyond its present elevation,
and would enable us to hold the banner of
Christianity aloft with unflinching faith in God, in Life 27
eternal. Sin brought death, and death will disappear
with the disappearance of sin. Man is immortal, and
the body cannot die, because matter has no life to sur- 30
render. The human concepts named matter, death, disease, sickness, and sin are all that can be destroyed.

If it is true that man lives, this fact can never change 1
in Science to the opposite belief that man dies. Life is
Life not
contingent
on matter
the law of Soul, even the law of the spirit of 3
Truth, and Soul is never without its represent-
ative. Man's individual being can no more
die nor disappear in unconsciousness than can Soul, for 6
both are immortal. If man believes in death now, he
must disbelieve in it when learning that there is no reality
in death, since the truth of being is deathless. The be- 9
lief that existence is contingent on matter must be met
and mastered by Science, before Life can be understood
and harmony obtained. 12

Death is but another phase of the dream that existence can be material. Nothing can interfere with the
Mortality
vanquished
harmony of being nor end the existence of 15
man in Science. Man is the same after as
before a bone is broken or the body guillotined. If man
is never to overcome death, why do the Scriptures say, 18
"The last enemy that shall be destroyed is death"? The
tenor of the Word shows that we shall obtain the victory
over death in proportion as we overcome sin. The great 21
difficulty lies in ignorance of what God is. God, Life,
Truth, and Love make man undying. Immortal Mind,
governing all, must be acknowledged as supreme in the 24
physical realm, so-called, as well as in the spiritual.

Called to the bed of death, what material remedy has
man when all such remedies have failed? Spirit is his 27
No death
nor inaction
last resort, but it should have been his first
and only resort. The dream of death must
be mastered by Mind here or hereafter. Thought 30
will waken from its own material declaration, "I am
dead," to catch this trumpet-word of Truth, "There

is no death, no inaction, diseased action, overaction, nor 1
reaction."

Life is real, and death is the illusion. A demonstra- 3
tion of the facts of Soul in Jesus' way resolves the dark

Vision
opening
visions of material sense into harmony and
immortality. Man's privilege at this supreme 6
moment is to prove the words of our Master: "If a man
keep my saying, he shall never see death." To divest
thought of false trusts and material evidences in order 9
that the spiritual facts of being may appear, — this is
the great attainment by means of which we shall sweep
away the false and give place to the true. Thus we may 12
establish in truth the temple, or body, "whose builder
and maker is God."

We should consecrate existence, not "to the unknown 15
God" whom we "ignorantly worship," but to the eternal

Intelligent
consecration
builder, the everlasting Father, to the Life
which mortal sense cannot impair nor mortal 18
belief destroy. We must realize the ability of mental
might to offset human misconceptions and to replace them
with the life which is spiritual, not material. 21

The great spiritual fact must be brought out that man
is, not *shall be*, perfect and immortal. We must hold

The present
immortality
forever the consciousness of existence, and 24
sooner or later, through Christ and Christian
Science, we must master sin and death. The evidence
of man's immortality will become more apparent, as ma- 27
terial beliefs are given up and the immortal facts of being
are admitted.

The author has healed hopeless organic disease, and 30
raised the dying to life and health through the understanding of God as the only Life. It is a sin to believe

that aught can overpower omnipotent and eternal Life, 1
and this Life must be brought to light by the understand-

Careful guidance ing that there is no death, as well as by other 3
graces of Spirit. We must begin, however,
with the more simple demonstrations of control, and
the sooner we begin the better. The final demonstration 6
takes time for its accomplishment. When walking, we
are guided by the eye. We look before our feet, and if
we are wise, we look beyond a single step in the line of 9
spiritual advancement.

The corpse, deserted by thought, is cold and decays,
but it never suffers. Science declares that man is sub- 12

Clay replying to the potter ject to Mind. Mortal mind affirms that mind
is subordinate to the body, that the body is
dying, that it must be buried and decomposed 15
into dust; but mortal mind's affirmation is not true.
Mortals waken from the dream of death with bodies unseen by those who think that they bury the body. 18

If man did not exist before the material organization
began, he could not exist after the body is disintegrated.

Continuity of existence If we live after death and are immortal, we 21
must have lived before birth, for if Life ever
had any beginning, it must also have an ending, even according to the calculations of natural science. Do you 24
believe this? No! Do you understand it? No! This
is why you doubt the statement and do not demonstrate
the facts it involves. We must have faith in all the say- 27
ings of our Master, though they are not included in the
teachings of the schools, and are not understood generally by our ethical instructors. 30

Jesus said (John viii. 51), "If a man keep my saying,
he shall never see death." That statement is not con-

fined to spiritual life, but includes all the phenomena of   1
existence. Jesus demonstrated this, healing the dying

Life all-inclusive and raising the dead. Mortal mind must part   3
with error, must put off itself with its deeds,
and immortal manhood, the Christ ideal, will appear.
Faith should enlarge its borders and strengthen its base   6
by resting upon Spirit instead of matter. When man
gives up his belief in death, he will advance more rapidly
towards God, Life, and Love. Belief in sickness and   9
death, as certainly as belief in sin, tends to shut out the
true sense of Life and health. When will mankind wake
to this great fact in Science?   12

I here present to my readers an allegory illustrative
of the law of divine Mind and of the supposed laws of matter and hygiene, an allegory in which the plea of Christian   15
Science heals the sick.

Suppose a mental case to be on trial, as cases are tried
in court. A man is charged with having committed liver-   18

A mental court case complaint. The patient feels ill, ruminates,
and the trial commences. Personal Sense is
the plaintiff. Mortal Man is the defendant. False Belief   21
is the attorney for Personal Sense. Mortal Minds, Materia Medica, Anatomy, Physiology, Hypnotism, Envy,
Greed and Ingratitude, constitute the jury. The court-   24
room is filled with interested spectators, and Judge
Medicine is on the bench.

The evidence for the prosecution being called for, a   27
witness testifies thus: —

I represent Health-laws. I was present on certain nights
when the prisoner, or patient, watched with a sick friend.   30
Although I have the superintendence of human affairs, I
was personally abused on those occasions. I was told that

I must remain silent until called for at this trial, when I 1
would be allowed to testify in the case. Notwithstanding
my rules to the contrary, the prisoner watched with the sick 3
every night in the week. When the sick mortal was thirsty,
the prisoner gave him drink. During all this time the prisoner attended to his daily labors, partaking of food at ir- 6
regular intervals, sometimes going to sleep immediately
after a heavy meal. At last he committed liver-complaint,
which I considered criminal, inasmuch as this offence is 9
deemed punishable with death. Therefore I arrested Mortal Man in behalf of the state (namely, the body) and cast
him into prison. 12

At the time of the arrest the prisoner summoned Physiology, Materia Medica, and Hypnotism to prevent his punishment. The struggle on their part was long. Materia 15
Medica held out the longest, but at length all these assist-
ants resigned to me, Health-laws, and I succeeded in getting Mortal Man into close confinement until I should 18
release him.

The next witness is called: —

I am Coated Tongue. I am covered with a foul fur, 21
placed on me the night of the liver-attack. Morbid Secretion hypnotized the prisoner and took control of his mind,
making him despondent. 24

Another witness takes the stand and testifies: —

I am Sallow Skin. I have been dry, hot, and chilled by
turns since the night of the liver-attack. I have lost my 27
healthy hue and become unsightly, although nothing on my
part has occasioned this change. I practise daily ablutions
and perform my functions as usual, but I am robbed of my 30
good looks.

The next witness testifies: — 1

I am Nerve, the State Commissioner for Mortal Man.
I am intimately acquainted with the plaintiff, Personal 3
Sense, and know him to be truthful and upright, whereas
Mortal Man, the prisoner at the bar, is capable of falsehood. I was witness to the crime of liver-complaint. I 6
knew the prisoner would commit it, for I convey messages
from my residence in matter, *alias* brain, to body.

Another witness is called for by the Court of Error 9
and says: —

I am Mortality, Governor of the Province of Body, in
which Mortal Man resides. In this province there is a stat- 12
ute regarding disease, — namely, that he upon whose person disease is found shall be treated as a criminal and
punished with death. 15

The Judge asks if by doing good to his neighbor, it is
possible for man to become diseased, transgress the laws,
and merit punishment, and Governor Mortality replies in 18
the affirmative.
Another witness takes the stand and testifies: —

I am Death. I was called for, shortly after the report of 21
the crime, by the officer of the Board of Health, who protested that the prisoner had abused him, and that my presence was required to confirm his testimony. One of the 24
prisoner's friends, Materia Medica, was present when I
arrived, endeavoring to assist the prisoner to escape from
the hands of justice, *alias* nature's so-called law; but my 27
appearance with a message from the Board of Health
changed the purpose of Materia Medica, and he decided at
once that the prisoner should die. 30

The testimony for the plaintiff, Personal Sense, being 1
closed, Judge Medicine arises, and with great solemnity

Judge Medicine charges the jury
addresses the jury of Mortal Minds. He an- 3
alyzes the offence, reviews the testimony, and
explains the law relating to liver-complaint.

His conclusion is, that laws of nature render disease 6
homicidal. In compliance with a stern duty, his Honor,
Judge Medicine, urges the jury not to allow their judgment to be warped by the irrational, unchristian sugges- 9
tions of Christian Science. The jury must regard in such
cases only the evidence of Personal Sense against Mortal
Man. 12

As the Judge proceeds, the prisoner grows restless. His
sallow face blanches with fear, and a look of despair and
death settles upon it. The case is given to the jury. A 15
brief consultation ensues, and the jury returns a verdict
of "Guilty of liver-complaint in the first degree."

Judge Medicine then proceeds to pronounce the solemn 18
sentence of death upon the prisoner. Because he has

Mortal Man sentenced
loved his neighbor as himself, Mortal Man has
been guilty of benevolence in the first degree, 21
and this has led him into the commission of the second
crime, liver-complaint, which material laws condemn as
homicide. For this crime Mortal Man is sentenced to 24
be tortured until he is dead. "May God have mercy on
your soul," is the Judge's solemn peroration.

The prisoner is then remanded to his cell (sick-bed), 27
and Scholastic Theology is sent for to prepare the frightened sense of Life, God, — which sense must be immortal,
— for *death*. 30

Ah! but Christ, Truth, the spirit of Life and the
friend of Mortal Man, can open wide those prison doors

and set the captive free. Swift on the wings of divine 1
Love, there comes a despatch: "Delay the execution;

Appeal to
a higher
tribunal
the prisoner is not guilty." Consternation fills 3
the prison-yard. Some exclaim, "It is contrary to law and justice." Others say,
"The law of Christ supersedes *our* laws; let us follow 6
Christ."

After much debate and opposition, permission is obtained for a trial in the Court of Spirit, where Christian 9

Counsel for
defence
Science is allowed to appear as counsel for
the unfortunate prisoner. Witnesses, judges,
and jurors, who were at the previous Court of Error, 12
are now summoned to appear before the bar of Justice
and eternal Truth.

When the case for Mortal Man *versus* Personal Sense 15
is opened, Mortal Man's counsel regards the prisoner
with the utmost tenderness. The counsel's earnest,
solemn eyes, kindling with hope and triumph, look up- 18
ward. Then Christian Science turns suddenly to the
supreme tribunal, and opens the argument for the
defence: — 21

The prisoner at the bar has been unjustly sentenced.
His trial was a tragedy, and is morally illegal. Mortal
Man has had no proper counsel in the case. All the testi- 24
mony has been on the side of Personal Sense, and we shall
unearth this foul conspiracy against the liberty and life of
Man. The only valid testimony in the case shows the 27
alleged crime never to have been committed. The prisoner is not proved "worthy of death, or of bonds."

Your Honor, the lower court has sentenced Mortal Man 30
to die, but God made Man immortal and amenable to
Spirit only. Denying justice to the body, that court com-

mended man's immortal Spirit to heavenly mercy, — Spirit 1
which is God Himself and Man's only lawgiver! Who or
what has sinned? Has the body or has Mortal Mind 3
committed a criminal deed? Counsellor False Belief has
argued that the body should die, while Reverend Theology
would console conscious Mortal Mind, which alone is capa- 6
ble of sin and suffering. The body committed no offence.
Mortal Man, in obedience to higher law, helped his fellow-
man, an act which should result in good to himself as well 9
as to others.

The law of our Supreme Court decrees that whosoever
sinneth shall die; but good deeds are immortal, bringing 12
joy instead of grief, pleasure instead of pain, and life
instead of death. If liver-complaint was committed by
trampling on Laws of Health, this was a good deed, for the 15
agent of those laws is an outlaw, a destroyer of Mortal
Man's liberty and rights. Laws of Health should be sentenced to die. 18

Watching beside the couch of pain in the exercise of a
love that "is the fulfilling of the law," — doing "unto
others as ye would that they should do unto you," — this 21
is no infringement of law, for no demand, human or divine,
renders it just to punish a man for acting justly. If mortals sin, our Supreme Judge in equity decides what penalty 24
is due for the sin, and Mortal Man can suffer only for his
sin. For naught else can he be punished, according to the
law of Spirit, God. 27

Then what jurisdiction had his Honor, Judge Medicine,
in this case? To him I might say, in Bible language, "Sit-
test thou to judge . . . after the law, and commandest . . . 30
to be smitten contrary to the law?" The only jurisdiction
to which the prisoner can submit is that of Truth, Life, and
Love. If they condemn him not, neither shall Judge Medi- 33
cine condemn him; and I ask that the prisoner be restored
to the liberty of which he has been unjustly deprived.

The principal witness (the officer of the Health-laws)   1
deposed that he was an eye-witness to the good deeds for
which Mortal Man is under sentence of death. After be-   3
traying him into the hands of your law, the Health-agent
disappeared, to reappear however at the trial as a witness
against Mortal Man and in the interest of Personal Sense,   6
a murderer. Your Supreme Court must find the prisoner on the night of the alleged offence to have been acting
within the limits of the divine law, and in obedience   9
thereto. Upon this statute hangs all the law and testimony.
Giving a cup of cold water in Christ's name, is a Christian
service. Laying down his life for a good deed, Mortal Man   12
should find it again. Such acts bear their own justification, and are under the protection of the Most High.

Prior to the night of his arrest, the prisoner summoned   15
two professed friends, Materia Medica and Physiology, to
prevent his committing liver-complaint, and thus save him
from arrest. But they brought with them Fear, the sheriff,   18
to precipitate the result which they were called to prevent.
It was Fear who handcuffed Mortal Man and would now
punish him. You have left Mortal Man no alternative.   21
He must obey your law, fear its consequences, and be punished for his fear. His friends struggled hard to rescue the
prisoner from the penalty they considered justly due, but   24
they were compelled to let him be taken into custody, tried,
and condemned. Thereupon Judge Medicine sat in judgment on the case, and substantially charged the jury, twelve   27
Mortal Minds, to find the prisoner guilty. His Honor sentenced Mortal Man to die for the very deeds which the divine law compels man to commit. Thus the Court of Error   30
construed obedience to the law of divine Love as disobedience to the law of Life. Claiming to protect Mortal Man
in right-doing, that court pronounced a sentence of death   33
for doing right.

One of the principal witnesses, Nerve, testified that he

Science that all inharmony of mortal mind or body is illu- 1
sion, possessing neither reality nor identity though seeming
to be real and identical. 3

The Science of Mind disposes of all evil. Truth, God,
is not the father of error. Sin, sickness, and death are
Christ the ideal Truth to be classified as effects of error. Christ 6
came to destroy the belief of sin. The God-
principle is omnipresent and omnipotent. God is everywhere, and nothing apart from Him is present or has 9
power. Christ is the ideal Truth, that comes to heal
sickness and sin through Christian Science, and attributes
all power to God. Jesus is the name of the man who, 12
more than all other men, has presented Christ, the true
idea of God, healing the sick and the sinning and destroying the power of death. Jesus is the human man, and 15
Christ is the divine idea; hence the duality of Jesus the
Christ.

In an age of ecclesiastical despotism, Jesus introduced 18
the teaching and practice of Christianity, affording the
Jesus not God proof of Christianity's truth and love; but to
reach his example and to test its unerring Sci- 21
ence according to his rule, healing sickness, sin, and
death, a better understanding of God as divine Principle, Love, rather than personality or the man Jesus, is 24
required.

Jesus established what he said by demonstration,
thus making his acts of higher importance than his 27
Jesus not understood words. He proved what he taught. This
is the Science of Christianity. Jesus *proved*
the Principle, which heals the sick and casts out error, 30
to be divine. Few, however, except his students understood in the least his teachings and their glorious

proofs, — namely, that Life, Truth, and Love (the Prin- 1
ciple of this unacknowledged Science) destroy all error,
evil, disease, and death. 3

The reception accorded to Truth in the early Christian era is repeated to-day. Whoever introduces the
Miracles Science of Christianity will be scoffed at and 6
rejected scourged with worse cords than those which
cut the flesh. To the ignorant age in which it first
appears, Science seems to be a mistake, — hence the 9
misinterpretation and consequent maltreatment which
it receives. Christian marvels (and *marvel* is the simple meaning of the Greek word rendered *miracle* in the 12
New Testament) will be misunderstood and misused
by many, until the glorious Principle of these marvels is
gained. 15

If sin, sickness, and death are as real as Life, Truth,
and Love, then they must all be from the same source;
Divine God must be their author. Now Jesus came 18
fulfilment to destroy sin, sickness, and death; yet the
Scriptures aver, "I am not come to destroy, but to fulfil."
Is it possible, then, to believe that the evils which Jesus 21
lived to destroy are real or the offspring of the divine
will?

Despite the hallowing influence of Truth in the de- 24
struction of error, must error still be immortal? Truth
Truth spares all that is true. If evil is real, Truth
destroys falsity must make it so; but error, not Truth, is 27
the author of the unreal, and the unreal vanishes,
while all that is real is eternal. The apostle says that
the mission of Christ is to "destroy the works of the 30
devil." Truth destroys falsity and error, for light and
darkness cannot dwell together. Light extinguishes the

darkness, and the Scripture declares that there is "no 1
night there." To Truth there is no error, — all is Truth.
To infinite Spirit there is no matter, — all is Spirit, divine 3
Principle and its idea.

Question. — What is man?
Answer. — Man is not matter; he is not made up of 6
brain, blood, bones, and other material elements. The

**Fleshly
factors unreal**

Scriptures inform us that man is made in
the image and likeness of God. Matter is 9
not that likeness. The likeness of Spirit cannot be so
unlike Spirit. Man is spiritual and perfect; and because he is spiritual and perfect, he must be so under- 12
stood in Christian Science. Man is idea, the image, of
Love; he is not physique. He is the compound idea of
God, including all right ideas; the generic term for 15
all that reflects God's image and likeness; the conscious
identity of being as found in Science, in which man is
the reflection of God, or Mind, and therefore is eternal; 18
that which has no separate mind from God; that which
has not a single quality underived from Deity; that which
possesses no life, intelligence, nor creative power of his 21
own, but reflects spiritually all that belongs to his Maker.

And God said: "Let us make man in our image, after
our likeness; and let them have dominion over the fish 24
of the sea, and over the fowl of the air, and over the cattle,
and over all the earth, and over every creeping thing that
creepeth upon the earth." 27

Man is incapable of sin, sickness, and death. The

**Man
unfallen**

real man cannot depart from holiness, nor
can God, by whom man is evolved, engender 30
the capacity or freedom to sin. A mortal sinner is not

God's man. Mortals are the counterfeits of immortals.   1
They are the children of the wicked one, or the one evil,
which declares that man begins in dust or as a material   3
embryo. In divine Science, God and the real man are
inseparable as divine Principle and idea.

Error, urged to its final limits, is self-destroyed.   6
Error will cease to claim that soul is in body, that life

**Mortals are
not immortals**

and intelligence are in matter, and that
this matter is man. God is the Principle of   9
man, and man is the idea of God. Hence man is not
mortal nor material. Mortals will disappear, and immortals, or the children of God, will appear as the only   12
and eternal verities of man. Mortals are not fallen children of God. They never had a perfect state of being,
which may subsequently be regained. They were, from   15
the beginning of mortal history, "conceived in sin and
brought forth in iniquity." Mortality is finally swallowed
up in immortality. Sin, sickness, and death must dis-   18
appear to give place to the facts which belong to immortal
man.

Learn this, O mortal, and earnestly seek the spiritual   21
status of man, which is outside of all material selfhood.

**Imperishable
identity**

Remember that the Scriptures say of mortal
man: "As for man, his days are as grass: as   24
a flower of the field, so he flourisheth. For the wind
passeth over it, and it is gone; and the place thereof shall
know it no more."   27

When speaking of God's children, not the children of
men, Jesus said, "The kingdom of God is within you;"

**The kingdom
within**

that is, Truth and Love reign in the real   30
man, showing that man in God's image is
unfallen and eternal. Jesus beheld in Science the per-

fect man, who appeared to him where sinning mortal   1
man appears to mortals. In this perfect man the Saviour
saw God's own likeness, and this correct view of man   3
healed the sick. Thus Jesus taught that the kingdom
of God is intact, universal, and that man is pure and holy.
Man is not a material habitation for Soul; he is himself   6
spiritual. Soul, being Spirit, is seen in nothing imperfect
nor material.

Whatever is material is mortal. To the five corporeal   9
senses, man appears to be matter and mind united; but

Material
body never
God's idea

Christian Science reveals man as the idea of
God, and declares the corporeal senses to be   12
mortal and erring illusions. Divine Science
shows it to be impossible that a material body, though
interwoven with matter's highest stratum, misnamed   15
mind, should be man, — the genuine and perfect man,
the immortal idea of being, indestructible and eternal.
Were it otherwise, man would be annihilated.   18

Question. — What are body and Soul?
Answer. — Identity is the reflection of Spirit, the reflection in multifarious forms of the living Principle,   21

Reflection
of Spirit

Love. Soul is the substance, Life, and intelligence of man, which is individualized, but not
in matter. Soul can never reflect anything inferior to   24
Spirit.

Man is the expression of Soul. The Indians caught

Man
inseparable
from Spirit

some glimpses of the underlying reality, when   27
they called a certain beautiful lake "the smile
of the Great Spirit." Separated from man,
who expresses Soul, Spirit would be a nonentity; man,   30
divorced from Spirit, would lose his entity. But there is,

there can be, no such division, for man is coexistent with   1
God.

What evidence of Soul or of immortality have you   3
within mortality? Even according to the teachings of

A vacant
domicile

natural science, man has never beheld Spirit
or Soul leaving a body or entering it. What   6
basis is there for the theory of indwelling spirit, except
the claim of mortal belief? What would be thought of
the declaration that a house was inhabited, and by a cer-   9
tain class of persons, when no such persons were ever seen
to go into the house or to come out of it, nor were they
even visible through the windows? Who can see a soul   12
in the body?

Question. — Does brain think, and do nerves feel, and
is there intelligence in matter?   15
Answer. — No, not if God is true and mortal man a
liar. The assertion that there can be pain or pleasure

Harmonious
functions

in matter is erroneous. That body is most   18
harmonious in which the discharge of the natural functions is least noticeable. How can intelligence
dwell in matter when matter is non-intelligent and   21
brain-lobes cannot think? Matter cannot perform the
functions of Mind. Error says, "I am man;" but this
belief is mortal and far from actual. From beginning   24
to end, whatever is mortal is composed of material human beliefs and of nothing else. That only is real which
reflects God. St. Paul said, "But when it pleased God,   27
who separated me from my mother's womb, and called me
by His grace, . . . I conferred not with flesh and blood."

Mortal man is really a self-contradictory phrase, for   30
man is not mortal, "neither indeed can be;" man is im-

mortal. If a child is the offspring of physical sense and   1
not of Soul, the child must have a material, not a spirit-

ual origin. With what truth, then, could the   3
Scriptural rejoicing be uttered by any mother,
"I have gotten a man from the Lord"? On the contrary, if aught comes from God, it cannot be mortal and   6
material; it must be immortal and spiritual.

Matter is neither self-existent nor a product of Spirit.
An image of mortal thought, reflected on the retina, is   9

all that the eye beholds. Matter cannot see,
feel, hear, taste, nor smell. It is not self-
cognizant, — cannot feel itself, see itself, nor   12
understand itself. Take away so-called mortal mind,
which constitutes matter's supposed selfhood, and matter
can take no cognizance of matter. Does that which we   15
call dead ever see, hear, feel, or use any of the physical
senses?

"In the beginning God created the heaven and the   18
earth. And the earth was without form, and void; and

darkness was upon the face of the deep."
(Genesis i. 1, 2.) In the vast forever, in the   21
Science and truth of being, the only facts are Spirit
and its innumerable creations. Darkness and chaos
are the imaginary opposites of light, understanding,   24
and eternal harmony, and they are the elements of
nothingness.

We admit that black is not a color, because it reflects   27
no light. So evil should be denied identity or power,

because it has none of the divine hues. Paul
says: "For the invisible things of Him, from   30
the creation of the world, are clearly seen, being understood by the things that are made." (Romans i. 20.)

When the substance of Spirit appears in Christian Sci- 1
ence, the nothingness of matter is recognized. Where
the spirit of God is, and there is no place where God is 3
not, evil becomes nothing, — the opposite of the something of Spirit. If there is no spiritual reflection, then
there remains only the darkness of vacuity and not a trace 6
of heavenly tints.

Nerves are an element of the belief that there is sensation in matter, whereas matter is devoid of sensation. 9

**Harmony
from Spirit**

Consciousness, as well as action, is governed
by Mind, — is in God, the origin and governor of all that Science reveals. Material sense has 12
its realm apart from Science in the unreal. Harmonious
action proceeds from Spirit, God. Inharmony has no
Principle; its action is erroneous and presupposes man 15
to be in matter. Inharmony would make matter the
cause as well as the effect of intelligence, or Soul, thus
attempting to separate Mind from God. 18

Man is not God, and God is not man. Again, God,
or good, never made man capable of sin. It is the oppo-

**Evil
non-existent**

site of good — that is, evil — which seems to 21
make men capable of wrong-doing. Hence,
evil is but an illusion, and it has no real basis. Evil is a
false belief. God is not its author. The supposititious 24
parent of evil is a lie.

The Bible declares: "All things were made by Him
[the divine Word]; and without Him was not anything 27

**Vapor and
nothingness**

made that was made." This is the eternal
verity of divine Science. If sin, sickness, and
death were understood as nothingness, they would dis- 30
appear. As vapor melts before the sun, so evil would
vanish before the reality of good. One must hide the

other. How important, then, to choose good as the   1
reality! Man is tributary to God, Spirit, and to nothing
else. God's being is infinity, freedom, harmony, and   3
boundless bliss. "Where the Spirit of the Lord is,
there is liberty." Like the archpriests of yore, man is
free "to enter into the holiest," — the realm of God.   6

Material sense never helps mortals to understand
Spirit, God. Through spiritual sense only, man com-

The fruit forbidden prehends and loves Deity. The various con-   9
tradictions of the Science of Mind by the ma-
terial senses do not change the unseen Truth, which remains forever intact. The forbidden fruit of knowledge,   12
against which wisdom warns man, is the testimony of
error, declaring existence to be at the mercy of death,
and good and evil to be capable of commingling. This   15
is the significance of the Scripture concerning this "tree
of the knowledge of good and evil," — this growth of
material belief, of which it is said: "In the day that thou   18
eatest thereof thou shalt surely die." Human hypotheses
first assume the reality of sickness, sin, and death, and
then assume the necessity of these evils because of their   21
admitted actuality. These human verdicts are the pro-
curers of all discord.

If Soul sins, it must be mortal. Sin has the elements   24
of self-destruction. It cannot sustain itself. If sin is

Sense and pure Soul supported, God must uphold it, and this is
impossible, since Truth cannot support error.   27
Soul is the divine Principle of man and never sins, —
hence the immortality of Soul. In Science we learn that
it is material sense, not Soul, which sins; and it will be   30
found that it is the sense of sin which is lost, and not a
sinful soul. When reading the Scriptures, the substitu-

tion of the word *sense* for *soul* gives the exact meaning in   1
a majority of cases.

Human thought has adulterated the meaning of the   3
word *soul* through the hypothesis that soul is both an evil

Soul defined   and a good intelligence, resident in matter.

The proper use of the word *soul* can always   6
be gained by substituting the word *God,* where the deific
meaning is required. In other cases, use the word *sense,*
and you will have the scientific signification. As used   9
in Christian Science, Soul is properly the synonym of
Spirit, or God; but out of Science, soul is identical with
sense, with material sensation.   12

Question. — Is it important to understand these ex-
planations in order to heal the sick?

Answer. — It is, since Christ is "the way" and the   15
truth casting out all error. Jesus called himself "the

Sonship of Jesus   Son of man," but not the son of Joseph. As
woman is but a species of the genera, he was   18
literally the Son of Man. Jesus was the highest human
concept of the perfect man. He was inseparable from
Christ, the Messiah, — the divine idea of God outside   21
the flesh. This enabled Jesus to demonstrate his control over matter. Angels announced to the Wisemen of
old this dual appearing, and angels whisper it, through   24
faith, to the hungering heart in every age.

Sickness is part of the error which Truth casts out.
Error will not expel error. Christian Science is the law   27

Sickness erroneous   of Truth, which heals the sick on the basis
of the one Mind or God. It can heal in no
other way, since the human, mortal mind so-called is not   30
a healer, but causes the belief in disease.

Then comes the question, how do drugs, hygiene, and 1
animal magnetism heal? It may be affirmed that they

True healing transcendent do not heal, but only relieve suffering tempo- 3
rarily, exchanging one disease for another.
We classify disease as error, which nothing but Truth or
Mind can heal, and this Mind must be divine, not human. 6
Mind transcends all other power, and will ultimately supersede all other means in healing. In order to heal by
Science, you must not be ignorant of the moral and spir- 9
itual demands of Science nor disobey them. Moral ignorance or sin affects your demonstration, and hinders its
approach to the standard in Christian Science. 12

After the author's sacred discovery, she affixed the
name "Science" to Christianity, the name "error" to

Terms adopted by the author corporeal sense, and the name "substance" to 15
Mind. Science has called the world to battle
over this issue and its demonstration, which
heals the sick, destroys error, and reveals the universal 18
harmony. To those natural Christian Scientists, the ancient worthies, and to Christ Jesus, God certainly revealed
the spirit of Christian Science, if not the absolute letter. 21

Because the Science of Mind seems to bring into dis-
honor the ordinary scientific schools, which wrestle with

Science the way material observations alone, this Science has 24
met with opposition; but if any system honors
God, it ought to receive aid, not opposition, from all thinking persons. And Christian Science does honor God as 27
no other theory honors Him, and it does this in the way
of His appointing, by doing many wonderful works
through the divine name and nature. One must fulfil 30
one's mission without timidity or dissimulation, for to be
well done, the work must be done unselfishly. Christianity

will never be based on a divine Principle and so found to   1
be unerring, until its absolute Science is reached. When
this is accomplished, neither pride, prejudice, bigotry,   3
nor envy can wash away its foundation, for it is built upon
the rock, Christ.

Question. — Does Christian Science, or metaphysical   6
healing, include medication, material hygiene, mesmerism, hypnotism, theosophy, or spiritualism?
Answer. — Not one of them is included in it. In di-   9
vine Science, the supposed laws of matter yield to the
law of Mind. What are termed natural

Mindless
methods
  science and material laws are the objective   12
states of mortal mind. The physical universe expresses
the conscious and unconscious thoughts of mortals.
Physical force and mortal mind are one. Drugs and   15
hygiene oppose the supremacy of the divine Mind.
Drugs and inert matter are unconscious, mindless. Certain results, supposed to proceed from drugs, are really   18
caused by the faith in them which the false human consciousness is educated to feel.

    Mesmerism is mortal, material illusion. Animal mag-   21
netism is the voluntary or involuntary action of error

Animal
magnetism
error
  in all its forms; it is the human antipode
of divine Science. Science must triumph   24
over material sense, and Truth over error, thus putting
an end to the hypotheses involved in all false theories
and practices.   27

Question. — Is materiality the concomitant of spirituality, and is material sense a necessary preliminary to
the understanding and expression of Spirit?   30

Answer. — If error is necessary to define or to reveal 1
Truth, the answer is yes; but not otherwise. *Material*

Error only ephemeral *sense* is an absurd phrase, for matter has no 3
sensation. Science declares that Mind, not
matter, sees, hears, feels, speaks. Whatever contradicts
this statement is the false sense, which ever betrays 6
mortals into sickness, sin, and death. If the unimpor-
tant and evil appear, only soon to disappear because
of their uselessness or their iniquity, then these ephem- 9
eral views of error ought to be obliterated by Truth.
Why malign Christian Science for instructing mortals how
to make sin, disease, and death appear more and more 12
unreal?

Emerge gently from matter into Spirit. Think not
to thwart the spiritual ultimate of all things, but come 15

Scientific translations naturally into Spirit through better health and
morals and as the result of spiritual growth.
Not death, but the understanding of Life, makes man im- 18
mortal. The belief that life can be in matter or soul in
body, and that man springs from dust or from an egg,
is the result of the mortal error which Christ, or Truth, 21
destroys by fulfilling the spiritual law of being, in which
man is perfect, even as the "Father which is in heaven
is perfect." If thought yields its dominion to other 24
powers, it cannot outline on the body its own beautiful
images, but it effaces them and delineates foreign agents,
called disease and sin. 27

The heathen gods of mythology controlled war and
agriculture as much as nerves control sensation or

Material beliefs muscles measure strength. To say that 30
strength is in matter, is like saying that the
power is in the lever. The notion of any life or intelli-

gence in matter is without foundation in fact, and you   1
can have no faith in falsehood when you have learned
falsehood's true nature.   3

Suppose one accident happens to the eye, another to
the ear, and so on, until every corporeal sense is quenched.

Sense *versus* Soul

What is man's remedy? To die, that he may   6
regain these senses? Even then he must gain
spiritual understanding and spiritual sense in order to
possess immortal consciousness. Earth's preparatory   9
school must be improved to the utmost. In reality man
never dies. The belief that he dies will not establish his
scientific harmony. Death is not the result of Truth but   12
of error, and one error will not correct another.

Jesus proved by the prints of the nails, that his body
was the same immediately after death as before. If death   15

Death an error

restores sight, sound, and strength to man,
then death is not an enemy but a better friend
than Life. Alas for the blindness of belief, which makes   18
harmony conditional upon death and matter, and yet
supposes Mind unable to produce harmony! So long
as this error of belief remains, mortals will continue mor-   21
tal in belief and subject to chance and change.

Sight, hearing, all the spiritual senses of man, are
eternal. They cannot be lost. Their reality and immor-   24

Permanent sensibility

tality are in Spirit and understanding, not in
matter, — hence their permanence. If this
were not so, man would be speedily annihilated. If the   27
five corporeal senses were the medium through which
to understand God, then palsy, blindness, and deafness
would place man in a terrible situation, where he would   30
be like those "having no hope, and without God in the
world;" but as a matter of fact, these calamities often

drive mortals to seek and to find a higher sense of happi- 1
ness and existence.

Life is deathless. Life is the origin and ultimate of 3
man, never attainable through death, but gained by walk-

Exercise of Mind-faculties ing in the pathway of Truth both before and
after that which is called death. There is more 6
Christianity in seeing and hearing spiritually
than materially. There is more Science in the perpetual
exercise of the Mind-faculties than in their loss. Lost 9
they cannot be, while Mind remains. The apprehension
of this gave sight to the blind and hearing to the deaf centuries ago, and it will repeat the wonder. 12

Question. — You speak of belief. Who or what is it
that believes?

Answer. — Spirit is all-knowing; this precludes the 15
need of believing. Matter cannot believe, and Mind

Understanding versus belief understands. The body cannot believe. The
believer and belief are one and are mortal. 18
Christian evidence is founded on Science or
demonstrable Truth, flowing from immortal Mind, and
there is in reality no such thing as *mortal* mind. Mere 21
belief is blindness without Principle from which to explain the reason of its hope. The belief that life is sentient and intelligent matter is erroneous. 24

The Apostle James said, "Show me thy faith without
thy works, and I will show thee my faith by my works."
The understanding that Life is God, Spirit, lengthens 27
our days by strengthening our trust in the deathless
reality of Life, its almightiness and immortality.

This faith relies upon an understood Principle. This 30
Principle makes whole the diseased, and brings out the

enduring and harmonious phases of things. The result   1
of our teachings is their sufficient confirmation. When,

Confirmation by healing   on the strength of these instructions, you are   3
able to banish a severe malady, the cure shows
that you understand this teaching, and therefore you receive the blessing of Truth.   6

The Hebrew and Greek words often translated *belief*
differ somewhat in meaning from that conveyed by the

Belief and firm trust   English verb *believe;* they have more the sig-   9
nificance of faith, understanding, trust, con-
stancy, firmness. Hence the Scriptures often appear in
our common version to approve and endorse belief, when   12
they mean to enforce the necessity of understanding.

Question. — Do the five corporeal senses constitute
man?   15
Answer. — Christian Science sustains with immortal
proof the impossibility of any material sense, and defines

All faculties from Mind   these so-called senses as *mortal beliefs,* the   18
testimony of which cannot be true either of
man or of his Maker. The corporeal senses can take no
cognizance of spiritual reality and immortality. Nerves   21
have no more sensation, apart from what belief bestows upon them, than the fibres of a plant. Mind alone
possesses all faculties, perception, and comprehension.   24
Therefore mental endowments are not at the mercy of
organization and decomposition, — otherwise the very
worms could unfashion man. If it were possible for the   27
real senses of man to be injured, Soul could reproduce
them in all their perfection; but they cannot be disturbed nor destroyed, since they exist in immortal Mind,   30
not in matter.

Nothing can be novel to eternal Mind, the author of all 1
things, who from all eternity knoweth His own ideas.

Perfection of creation Deity was satisfied with His work. How could 3
He be otherwise, since the spiritual creation
was the outgrowth, the emanation, of His infinite self-
containment and immortal wisdom? 6

Genesis ii. 1. Thus the heavens and the earth were
finished, and all the host of them.

Thus the ideas of God in universal being are complete 9
and forever expressed, for Science reveals infinity and

Infinity measureless the fatherhood and motherhood of Love. Hu-
man capacity is slow to discern and to grasp 12
God's creation and the divine power and presence which
go with it, demonstrating its spiritual origin. Mortals
can never know the infinite, until they throw off the old 15
man and reach the spiritual image and likeness. What
can fathom infinity! How shall we declare Him, till,
in the language of the apostle, "we all come in the unity 18
of the faith, and of the knowledge of the Son of God, unto
a perfect man, unto the measure of the stature of the fulness of Christ"? 21

Genesis ii. 2. And on the seventh day God ended His
work which He had made; and He rested on the seventh
day from all His work which He had made. 24

God rests in action. Imparting has not impoverished,

Resting in holy work can never impoverish, the divine Mind. No
exhaustion follows the action of this Mind, 27
according to the apprehension of divine Science. The

highest and sweetest rest, even from a human standpoint, 1
is in holy work.

Unfathomable Mind is expressed. The depth, breadth, 3
height, might, majesty, and glory of infinite Love fill all
Love and man
coexistent space. That is enough! Human language
can repeat only an infinitesimal part of what 6
exists. The absolute ideal, man, is no more seen nor
comprehended by mortals, than is his infinite Principle,
Love. Principle and its idea, man, are coexistent and 9
eternal. The numerals of infinity, called *seven days*, can
never be reckoned according to the calendar of time.
These days will appear as mortality disappears, and they 12
will reveal eternity, newness of Life, in which all sense of
error forever disappears and thought accepts the divine
infinite calculus. 15

Genesis ii. 4, 5. These are the generations of the heavens
and of the earth when they were created, in the day that the
Lord God [Jehovah] made the earth and the heavens, and 18
every plant of the field before it was in the earth, and every
herb of the field before it grew: for the Lord God [Jehovah]
had not caused it to rain upon the earth, and there was not 21
a man to till the ground.

Here is the emphatic declaration that God creates all
through Mind, not through matter, — that the plant 24
Growth is
from Mind grows, not because of seed or soil, but because
growth is the eternal mandate of Mind. Mor-
tal thought drops into the ground, but the immortal creat- 27
ing thought is from above, not from beneath. Because
Mind makes all, there is nothing left to be made by a
lower power. Spirit acts through the Science of Mind, 30
never causing man to till the ground, but making him

superior to the soil. Knowledge of this lifts man above   1
the sod, above earth and its environments, to conscious
spiritual harmony and eternal being.   3

Here the inspired record closes its narrative of being
that is without beginning or end. All that is made is

Spiritual the work of God, and all is good. We leave   6
narrative this brief, glorious history of spiritual creation
(as stated in the first chapter of Genesis) in the hands of
God, not of man, in the keeping of Spirit, not matter, —   9
joyfully acknowledging now and forever God's supremacy,
omnipotence, and omnipresence.

The harmony and immortality of man are intact. We   12
should look away from the opposite supposition that man
is created materially, and turn our gaze to the spiritual
record of creation, to that which should be engraved on   15
the understanding and heart "with the point of a diamond"
and the pen of an angel.

The reader will naturally ask if there is nothing more   18
about creation in the book of Genesis. Indeed there is,
but the continued account is mortal and material.

Genesis ii. 6. But there went up a mist from the earth,   21
and watered the whole face of the ground.

The Science and truth of the divine creation have been
presented in the verses already considered, and now the   24

The story opposite error, a material view of creation, is
of error to be set forth. The second chapter of Genesis contains a statement of this material view of God and   27
the universe, a statement which is the exact opposite of
scientific truth as before recorded. The history of error
or matter, if veritable, would set aside the omnipotence   30

of Spirit; but it is the false history in contradistinction   1
to the true.

The Science of the first record proves the falsity of   3
the second. If one is true, the other is false, for they are
antagonistic. The first record assigns all

The two records

might and government to God, and endows   6
man out of God's perfection and power. The second
record chronicles man as mutable and mortal, — as having broken away from Deity and as revolving in an orbit   9
of his own. Existence, separate from divinity, Science
explains as impossible.

This second record unmistakably gives the history of   12
error in its externalized forms, called life and intelligence in matter. It records pantheism, opposed to the
supremacy of divine Spirit; but this state of things is   15
declared to be temporary and this man to be mortal, —
dust returning to dust.

In this erroneous theory, matter takes the place of Spirit.   18
Matter is represented as the life-giving principle of the
earth. Spirit is represented as entering mat-

Erroneous representation

ter in order to create man. God's glowing   21
denunciations of man when not found in His
image, the likeness of Spirit, convince reason and coincide
with revelation in declaring this material creation false.   24

This latter part of the second chapter of Genesis, which
portrays Spirit as supposedly cooperating with matter in

Hypothetical reversal

constructing the universe, is based on some   27
hypothesis of error, for the Scripture just pre-
ceding declares God's work to be finished. Does Life,
Truth, and Love produce death, error, and hatred? Does   30
the creator condemn His own creation? Does the unerring Principle of divine law change or repent? It can-

not be so. Yet one might so judge from an unintelligent 1
perusal of the Scriptural account now under comment.

Because of its false basis, the mist of obscurity evolved 3
by error deepens the false claim, and finally declares that

Mist, or false claim

God knows error and that error can improve
His creation. Although presenting the exact 6
opposite of Truth, the lie claims to be truth. The creations of matter arise from a mist or false claim, or from
mystification, and not from the firmament, or under- 9
standing, which God erects between the true and false.
In error everything comes from beneath, not from above.
All is material myth, instead of the reflection of 12
Spirit.

It may be worth while here to remark that, according
to the best scholars, there are clear evidences of two dis- 15

Distinct documents

tinct documents in the early part of the book of
Genesis. One is called the Elohistic, because
the Supreme Being is therein called Elohim. The other 18
document is called the Jehovistic, because Deity therein is
always called Jehovah, — or Lord God, as our common
version translates it. 21

Throughout the first chapter of Genesis and in three
verses of the second, — in what we understand to be the

Jehovah or Elohim

spiritually scientific account of creation, — it is 24
Elohim (God) who creates. From the fourth
verse of chapter two to chapter five, the creator is called
Jehovah, or the Lord. The different accounts become 27
more and more closely intertwined to the end of chapter
twelve, after which the distinction is not definitely trace-
able. In the historic parts of the Old Testament, it is 30
usually Jehovah, peculiarly the divine sovereign of the
Hebrew people, who is referred to.

Gods of the heathen

The idolatry which followed this material mythology is   1
seen in the Phœnician worship of Baal, in the Moabitish
god Chemosh, in the Moloch of the Amorites,   3
in the Hindoo Vishnu, in the Greek Aphro-
dite, and in a thousand other so-called deities.

It was also found among the Israelites, who constantly   6
went after "strange gods." They called the Supreme

Jehovah a tribal deity

Being by the national name of Jehovah. In
that name of Jehovah, the true idea of God   9
seems almost lost. God becomes "a man of war," a
tribal god to be worshipped, rather than Love, the divine
Principle to be lived and loved.   12

Genesis ii. 7. And the Lord God [Jehovah] formed man
of the dust of the ground, and breathed into his nostrils
the breath of life; and man became a living soul.   15

Creation reversed

Did the divine and infinite Principle become a finite
deity, that He should now be called Jehovah? With
a single command, Mind had made man,   18
both male and female. How then could a
material organization become the basis of man? How
could the non-intelligent become the medium of Mind,   21
and error be the enunciator of Truth? Matter is not
the reflection of Spirit, yet God is reflected in all His
creation. Is this addition to His creation real or un-   24
real? Is it the truth, or is it a lie concerning man and
God?

It must be a lie, for God presently curses the ground.   27
Could Spirit evolve its opposite, matter, and give matter
ability to sin and suffer? Is Spirit, God, injected into
dust, and eventually ejected at the demand of matter?   30
Does Spirit enter dust, and lose therein the divine nature

and omnipotence? Does Mind, God, enter matter to be- 1
come there a mortal sinner, animated by the breath of
God? In this narrative, the validity of matter is opposed, 3
not the validity of Spirit or Spirit's creations. Man reflects God; *mankind* represents the Adamic race, and is
a human, not a divine, creation. 6

The following are some of the equivalents of the term
man in different languages. In the Saxon, *mankind, a*

Definitions
of man

woman, any one; in the Welsh, *that which rises* 9
up, — the primary sense being *image, form;* in
the Hebrew, *image, similitude;* in the Icelandic, *mind.*
The following translation is from the Icelandic: — 12

And God said, Let us make man after our mind and
our likeness; and God shaped man after His mind; after
God's mind shaped He him; and He shaped them male and 15
female.

In the Gospel of John, it is declared that all things were
made through the Word of God, "and without Him [the 18

No baneful
creation

logos, or *word*] was not anything made that
was made." Everything good or worthy, God
made. Whatever is valueless or baneful, He did not 21
make, — hence its unreality. In the Science of Genesis
we read that He saw everything which He had made,
"and, behold, it was very good." The corporeal senses 24
declare otherwise; and if we give the same heed to the
history of error as to the records of truth, the Scriptural
record of sin and death favors the false conclusion of the 27
material senses. Sin, sickness, and death must be deemed
as devoid of reality as they are of good, God.

Genesis ii. 9. And out of the ground made the Lord God 30
[Jehovah] to grow every tree that is pleasant to the sight,

and good for food; the tree of life also, in the midst of the   1
garden, and the tree of knowledge of good and evil.

The previous and more scientific record of creation   3
declares that God made "every plant of the field before it was in the earth." This opposite

declaration, this statement that life issues   6
from matter, contradicts the teaching of the first chapter, — namely, that all Life is God. Belief is less than
understanding. Belief involves theories of material hear-   9
ing, sight, touch, taste, and smell, termed the five senses.
The appetites and passions, sin, sickness, and death,
follow in the train of this error of a belief in intelligent   12
matter.

The first mention of evil is in the legendary Scriptural
text in the second chapter of Genesis. God pronounced   15

good all that He created, and the Scriptures
declare that He created all. The "tree of
life" stands for the idea of Truth, and the sword which   18
guards it is the type of divine Science. The "tree of
knowledge" stands for the erroneous doctrine that the
knowledge of evil is as real, hence as God-bestowed, as   21
the knowledge of good. Was evil instituted through God,
Love? Did He create this fruit-bearer of sin in contradiction of the first creation? This second biblical account   24
is a picture of error throughout.

Genesis ii. 15. And the Lord God [Jehovah] took the
man, and put him into the garden of Eden, to dress it and   27
to keep it.

The name Eden, according to Cruden, means *pleasure,
delight.* In this text Eden stands for the mortal, mate-   30

rial body. God could not put Mind into matter nor in-   1
finite Spirit into finite form to dress it and
keep it, — to make it beautiful or to cause it   3
to live and grow. Man is God's reflection, needing no
cultivation, but ever beautiful and complete.

Genesis ii. 16, 17. And the Lord God [Jehovah] com-   6
manded the man, saying, Of every tree of the garden thou
mayest freely eat: but of the tree of the knowledge of good
and evil, thou shalt not eat of it: for in the day that thou   9
eatest thereof thou shalt surely die.

Here the metaphor represents God, Love, as tempting
man, but the Apostle James says: "God cannot be   12
tempted with evil, neither tempteth He any
man." It is true that a knowledge of evil would
make man mortal. It is plain also that mate-   15
rial perception, gathered from the corporeal senses, constitutes evil and mortal knowledge. But is it true that God,
good, made "the tree of life" to be the tree of death to His   18
own creation? Has evil the reality of good? Evil is unreal because it is a lie, — false in every statement.

Genesis ii. 19. And out of the ground the Lord God   21
[Jehovah] formed every beast of the field, and every fowl
of the air; and brought them unto Adam to see what he
would call them: and whatsoever Adam called every living   24
creature, that was the name thereof.

Here the lie represents God as repeating creation, but
doing so materially, not spiritually, and ask-   27
ing a prospective sinner to help Him. Is the
Supreme Being retrograding, and is man giving up his
dignity? Was it requisite for the formation of man   30

Marginal notes:

Garden of
Eden

No temptation
from God

Creation's
counterfeit

that dust should become sentient, when all being is the   1
reflection of the eternal Mind, and the record declares
that God has already created man, both male and   3
female? That Adam gave the name and nature of
animals, is solely mythological and material. It cannot be true that man was ordered to create man anew   6
in partnership with God; this supposition was a dream,
a myth.

Genesis ii. 21, 22. And the Lord God [Jehovah, Yawah]   9
caused a deep sleep to fall upon Adam, and he slept: and
He took one of his ribs, and closed up the flesh instead
thereof; and the rib, which the Lord God [Jehovah] had   12
taken from man, made He a woman, and brought her unto
the man.

Here falsity, error, credits Truth, God, with inducing   15
a sleep or hypnotic state in Adam in order to perform a
surgical operation on him and thereby create

Hypnotic
surgery   woman. This is the first record of magnet-   18
ism. Beginning creation with darkness instead of light,
— materially rather than spiritually, — error now simu-
lates the work of Truth, mocking Love and declar-   21
ing what great things error has done. Beholding the
creations of his own dream and calling them real and
God-given, Adam — *alias* error — gives them names.   24
Afterwards he is supposed to become the basis of the
creation of woman and of his own kind, calling them
mankind, — that is, a kind of man.   27

But according to this narrative, surgery was first per-

Mental
midwifery   formed mentally and without instruments;
and this may be a useful hint to the medical   30
faculty. Later in human history, when the forbidden

fruit was bringing forth fruit of its own kind, there 1
came a suggestion of change in the *modus operandi*, —
that man should be born of woman, not woman again 3
taken from man. It came about, also, that instruments
were needed to assist the birth of mortals. The first
system of suggestive obstetrics has changed. Another 6
change will come as to the nature and origin of man,
and this revelation will destroy the *dream* of existence,
reinstate reality, usher in Science and the glorious fact 9
of creation, that both man and woman proceed from
God and are His eternal children, belonging to no lesser
parent. 12

Genesis iii. 1–3. Now the serpent was more subtle than
any beast of the field which the Lord God [Jehovah] had
made. And he said unto the woman, Yea, hath God said, 15
Ye shall not eat of every tree of the garden? And the
woman said unto the serpent, We may eat of the fruit of
the trees of the garden: but of the fruit of the tree which is 18
in the midst of the garden, God hath said, Ye shall not eat
of it, neither shall ye touch it, lest ye die.

Whence comes a talking, lying serpent to tempt the 21
children of divine Love? The serpent enters into the

Mythical serpent metaphor only as evil. We have nothing in the
animal kingdom which represents the species 24
described, — a talking serpent, — and should rejoice that
evil, by whatever figure presented, contradicts itself and
has neither origin nor support in Truth and good. Seeing 27
this, we should have faith to fight all claims of evil, because we know that they are worthless and unreal.

Adam, the synonym for error, stands for a belief of 30
material mind. He begins his reign over man some-

what mildly, but he increases in falsehood and his days   1
Error or Adam   become shorter. In this development, the immortal, spiritual law of Truth is made manifest   3
as forever opposed to mortal, material sense.

In divine Science, man is sustained by God, the divine
Principle of being. The earth, at God's command, brings   6
Divine providence   forth food for man's use. Knowing this, Jesus
once said, "Take no thought for your life,
what ye shall eat, or what ye shall drink," — presuming   9
not on the prerogative of his creator, but recognizing God,
the Father and Mother of all, as able to feed and clothe
man as He doth the lilies.   12

Genesis iii. 4, 5. And the serpent said unto the woman,
Ye shall not surely die: for God doth know that in the day
ye eat thereof, then your eyes shall be opened; and ye shall   15
be as gods, knowing good and evil.

This myth represents error as always asserting its superiority over truth, giving the lie to divine Science and   18
Error's assumption   saying, through the material senses: "I can
open your eyes. I can do what God has not
done for you. Bow down to me and have another god.   21
Only admit that I am real, that sin and sense are more
pleasant to the eyes than spiritual Life, more to be desired than Truth, and I shall know you, and you will be   24
mine." Thus Spirit and flesh war.

The history of error is a dream-narrative. The dream
has no reality, no intelligence, no mind; therefore the   27
Scriptural allegory   dreamer and dream are one, for neither is
true nor real. *First*, this narrative supposes
that something springs from nothing, that matter pre-   30
cedes mind. *Second*, it supposes that mind enters matter,

and matter becomes living, substantial, and intelligent.   1
The order of this allegory — the belief that everything
springs from dust instead of from Deity — has been main-   3
tained in all the subsequent forms of belief. This is the
error, — that mortal man starts materially, that non-
intelligence becomes intelligence, that mind and soul are   6
both right and wrong.

It is well that the upper portions of the brain represent
the higher moral sentiments, as if hope were ever prophe-   9

Higher hope

sying thus: The human mind will sometime
rise above all material and physical sense, exchanging it for spiritual perception, and exchanging hu-   12
man concepts for the divine consciousness. Then man
will recognize his God-given dominion and being.

If, in the beginning, man's body originated in non-   15
intelligent dust, and mind was afterwards put into body

Biological inventions

by the creator, why is not this divine order
still maintained by God in perpetuating the   18
species? Who will say that minerals, vegetables, and
animals have a propagating property of their own?
Who dares to say either that God is in matter or that   21
matter exists without God? Has man sought out other
creative inventions, and so changed the method of his
Maker?   24

Which institutes Life, — matter or Mind? Does Life
begin with Mind or with matter? Is Life sustained by
matter or by Spirit? Certainly not by both, since flesh   27
wars against Spirit and the corporeal senses can take no
cognizance of Spirit. The mythologic theory of material life at no point resembles the scientifically Christian   30
record of man as created by Mind in the image and likeness of God and having dominion over all the earth. Did

God at first create one man unaided, — that is, Adam, —   1
but afterwards require the union of the two sexes in order
to create the rest of the human family? No! God makes   3
and governs all.

All human knowledge and material sense must be
gained from the five corporeal senses. Is this knowledge   6

Progeny
cursed

safe, when eating its first fruits brought death?
"In the day that thou eatest thereof thou shalt
surely die," was the prediction in the story under consid-   9
eration. Adam and his progeny were cursed, not blessed;
and this indicates that the divine Spirit, or Father, con-
demns material man and remands him to dust.   12

Genesis iii. 9, 10. And the Lord God [Jehovah] called
unto Adam, and said unto him, Where art thou? And he
said, I heard Thy voice in the garden, and I was afraid,   15
because I was naked; and I hid myself.

Knowledge and pleasure, evolved through material
sense, produced the immediate fruits of fear and shame.   18

Shame the
effect of sin

Ashamed before Truth, error shrank abashed
from the divine voice calling out to the cor-
poreal senses. Its summons may be thus paraphrased: 21
"Where art thou, man? Is Mind in matter? Is Mind
capable of error as well as of truth, of evil as well as of
good, when God is All and He is Mind and there is but   24
one God, hence one Mind?"

Fear was the first manifestation of the error of material sense. Thus error began and will end the dream of   27

Fear comes
of error

matter. In the allegory the body had been
naked, and Adam knew it not; but now error
demands that *mind* shall see and feel through matter, the   30
five senses. The first impression material man had of

himself was one of nakedness and shame. Had he lost 1
man's rich inheritance and God's behest, dominion over
all the earth? No! This had never been bestowed on 3
Adam.

Genesis iii. 11, 12. And He said, Who told thee that
thou wast naked? Hast thou eaten of the tree, whereof I 6
commanded thee that thou shouldst not eat? And the man
said, The woman whom Thou gavest to be with me, she gave
me of the tree, and I did eat. 9

Here there is an attempt to trace all human errors
directly or indirectly to God, or good, as if He were the
creator of evil. The allegory shows that the 12
snake-talker utters the first voluble lie, which
beguiles the woman and demoralizes the man. Adam,
alias mortal error, charges God and woman with his own 15
dereliction, saying, "The woman, whom Thou gavest
me, is responsible." According to this belief, the rib taken
from Adam's side has grown into an evil mind, named 18
woman, who aids man to make sinners more rapidly than
he can alone. Is this an help meet for man?

Materiality, so obnoxious to God, is already found in the 21
rapid deterioration of the bone and flesh which came from
Adam to form Eve. The belief in material life and intelligence is growing worse at every step, but error has its 24
suppositional day and multiplies until the end thereof.

Truth, cross-questioning man as to his knowledge of
error, finds woman the first to confess her fault. She 27
says, "The serpent beguiled me, and I did
eat;" as much as to say in meek penitence,
"Neither man nor God shall father my fault." She has 30
already learned that corporeal sense is the serpent. Hence

The beguiling first lie

False womanhood

she is first to abandon the belief in the material origin of　1
man and to discern spiritual creation. This hereafter
enabled woman to be the mother of Jesus and to behold　3
at the sepulchre the risen Saviour, who was soon to manifest the deathless man of God's creating. This enabled
woman to be first to interpret the Scriptures in their true　6
sense, which reveals the spiritual origin of man.

Genesis iii. 14, 15. And the Lord God [Jehovah] said
unto the serpent, . . . I will put enmity between thee and　9
the woman, and between thy seed and her seed; it shall
bruise thy head, and thou shalt bruise his heel.

This prophecy has been fulfilled. The Son of the Virgin-　12
mother unfolded the remedy for Adam, or error; and the

Spirit and flesh

Apostle Paul explains this warfare between the
idea of divine power, which Jesus presented,　15
and mythological material intelligence called *energy* and
opposed to Spirit.

Paul says in his epistle to the Romans: "The carnal　18
mind is enmity against God; for it is not subject to the
law of God, neither indeed can be. So then they that
are in the flesh cannot please God. But ye are not in the　21
flesh, but in the Spirit, if so be that the spirit of God dwell
in you."

There will be greater mental opposition to the spirit-　24
ual, scientific meaning of the Scriptures than there has

Bruising sin's head

ever been since the Christian era began. The
serpent, material sense, will bite the heel of　27
the woman, — will struggle to destroy the spiritual idea
of Love; and the woman, this idea, will bruise the head
of lust. The spiritual idea has given the understanding　30

a foothold in Christian Science. The seed of Truth and $\quad$ 1
the seed of error, of belief and of understanding, — yea,
the seed of Spirit and the seed of matter, — are the wheat $\quad$ 3
and tares which time will separate, the one to be burned,
the other to be garnered into heavenly places.

Genesis iii. 16. Unto the woman He said, I will greatly $\quad$ 6
multiply thy sorrow and thy conception: in sorrow thou
shalt bring forth children; and thy desire shall be to thy
husband, and he shall rule over thee. $\quad$ 9

Judgment on error

Divine Science deals its chief blow at the supposed material foundations of life and intelligence. It dooms idolatry. A belief in other gods, other creators, $\quad$ 12
and other creations must go down before Christian Science. It unveils the results of sin as shown in
sickness and death. When will man pass through the $\quad$ 15
open gate of Christian Science into the heaven of Soul,
into the heritage of the first born among men? Truth is
indeed "the way." $\quad$ 18

Genesis iii. 17–19. And unto Adam He said, Because
thou hast hearkened unto the voice of thy wife, and hast
eaten of the tree of which I commanded thee, saying, Thou $\quad$ 21
shalt not eat of it: cursed is the ground for thy sake; in
sorrow shalt thou eat of it all the days of thy life: thorns
also and thistles shall it bring forth to thee; and thou shalt $\quad$ 24
eat the herb of the field: in the sweat of thy face shalt thou
eat bread, till thou return unto the ground; for out of it
wast thou taken: for dust thou art, and unto dust shalt $\quad$ 27
thou return.

In the first chapter of Genesis we read: "And God
called the dry land Earth; and the gathering together $\quad$ 30

of the waters called He Seas." In the Apocalypse it is   1
written: "And I saw a new heaven and a new earth: for

the first heaven and the first earth were passed   3
away; and there was no more sea." In St.
John's vision, heaven and earth stand for spir-
itual ideas, and the sea, as a symbol of tempest-tossed   6
human concepts advancing and receding, is represented
as having passed away. The divine understanding reigns,
is *all*, and there is no other consciousness.   9

The way of error is awful to contemplate. The illusion of sin is without hope or God. If man's spiritual

gravitation and attraction to one Father, in   12
whom we "live, and move, and have our be-
ing," should be lost, and if man should be governed by
corporeality instead of divine Principle, by body instead   15
of by Soul, man would be annihilated. Created by flesh
instead of by Spirit, starting from matter instead of from
God, mortal man would be governed by himself. The   18
blind leading the blind, both would fall.

Passions and appetites must end in pain. They are
"of few days, and full of trouble." Their supposed joys   21
are cheats. Their narrow limits belittle their gratifica-
tions, and hedge about their achievements with thorns.

Mortal mind accepts the erroneous, material concep-   24
tion of life and joy, but the true idea is gained from the

immortal side. Through toil, struggle, and sor-
row, what do mortals attain? They give up   27
their belief in perishable life and happiness; the mortal
and material return to dust, and the immortal is reached.

Genesis iii. 22–24. And the Lord God [Jehovah] said,   30
Behold, the man is become as one of us, to know good

and evil: and now, lest he put forth his hand, and take 1
also of the tree of life, and eat, and live forever; therefore
the Lord God [Jehovah] sent him forth from the garden 3
of Eden, to till the ground from whence he was taken.
So He drove out the man: and He placed at the east
of the garden of Eden Cherubims, and a flaming sword 6
which turned every way, to keep the way of the tree of
life.

A knowledge of evil was never the essence of divin- 9
ity or manhood. In the first chapter of Genesis, evil

Justice and recompense has no local habitation nor name. Creation is there represented as spiritual, entire, 12
and good. "Whatsoever a man soweth, that shall he
also reap." Error excludes itself from harmony. Sin
is its own punishment. Truth guards the gateway 15
to harmony. Error tills its own barren soil and buries
itself in the ground, since ground and dust stand for
nothingness. 18

No one can reasonably doubt that the purpose of this
allegory — this second account in Genesis — is to depict

Inspired interpretation the falsity of error and the effects of error. 21
Subsequent Bible revelation is coordinate
with the Science of creation recorded in the
first chapter of Genesis. Inspired writers interpret the 24
Word spiritually, while the ordinary historian interprets
it literally. Literally taken, the text is made to appear
contradictory in some places, and divine Love, which 27
blessed the earth and gave it to man for a possession, is
represented as changeable. The literal meaning would
imply that God withheld from man the opportunity to 30
reform, lest man should improve it and become better;
but this is not the nature of God, who is Love always, —

Love infinitely wise and altogether lovely, who "seeketh 1
not her own."

Truth should, and does, drive error out of all selfhood. 3
Truth is a two-edged sword, guarding and guiding.

Spiritual gateway Truth places the cherub wisdom at the gate
of understanding to note the proper guests. 6
Radiant with mercy and justice, the sword of Truth
gleams afar and indicates the infinite distance between
Truth and error, between the material and spiritual, — 9
the unreal and the real.

The sun, giving light and heat to the earth, is a figure
of divine Life and Love, enlightening and sustaining the 12
Contrasted testimony universe. The "tree of life" is significant of
eternal reality or being. The "tree of knowl-
edge" typifies unreality. The testimony of the serpent is 15
significant of the illusion of error, of the false claims that
misrepresent God, good. Sin, sickness, and death have
no record in the Elohistic introduction of Genesis, in which 18
God creates the heavens, earth, and man. Until that
which contradicts the truth of being enters into the arena,
evil has no history, and evil is brought into view only as 21
the unreal in contradistinction to the real and eternal.

Genesis iv. 1. And Adam knew Eve his wife; and she
conceived, and bare Cain, and said, I have gotten a man 24
from the Lord [Jehovah].

This account is given, not of immortal man, but of mortal man, and of sin which is temporal. As both mortal 27
Erroneous conception man and sin have a beginning, they must
consequently have an end, while the sinless,
real man is eternal. Eve's declaration, "I have gotten 30
a man from the Lord," supposes God to be the author

of sin and sin's progeny. This false sense of existence 1
is fratricidal. In the words of Jesus, it (evil, devil) is
"a murderer from the beginning." Error begins by 3
reckoning life as separate from Spirit, thus sapping the
foundations of immortality, as if life and immortality
were something which matter can both give and take 6
away.

What can be the standard of good, of Spirit, of Life,
or of Truth, if they produce their opposites, such as evil, 9
Only one
standard
matter, error, and death? God could never
impart an element of evil, and man possesses
nothing which he has not derived from God. How then 12
has man a basis for wrong-doing? Whence does he
obtain the propensity or power to do evil? Has Spirit
resigned to matter the government of the universe? 15

The Scriptures declare that God condemned this lie as
to man's origin and character by condemning its symbol,
A type of
falsehood
the serpent, to grovel beneath all the beasts 18
of the field. It is false to say that Truth and
error commingle in creation. In parable and argument,
this falsity is exposed by our Master as self-evidently 21
wrong. Disputing these points with the Pharisees and
arguing for the Science of creation, Jesus said: "Do men
gather grapes of thorns?" Paul asked: "What com- 24
munion hath light with darkness? And what concord
hath Christ with Belial?"

The divine origin of Jesus gave him more than human 27
power to expound the facts of creation, and demonstrate
Scientific
offspring
the one Mind which makes and governs man
and the universe. The Science of creation, 30
so conspicuous in the birth of Jesus, inspired his wisest
and least-understood sayings, and was the basis of his

marvellous demonstrations. Christ is the offspring of   1
Spirit, and spiritual existence shows that Spirit creates
neither a wicked nor a mortal man, lapsing into sin, sick-   3
ness, and death.

In Isaiah we read: "I make peace, and create evil. I
the Lord do all these things;" but the prophet referred to   6

Cleansing
upheaval

divine law as stirring up the belief in evil to its
utmost, when bringing it to the surface and re-
ducing it to its common denominator, nothingness. The   9
muddy river-bed must be stirred in order to purify the
stream. In moral chemicalization, when the symptoms
of evil, illusion, are aggravated, we may think in our igno-   12
rance that the Lord hath wrought an evil; but we ought
to know that God's law uncovers so-called sin and its
effects, only that Truth may annihilate all sense of evil   15
and all power to sin.

Science renders "unto Cæsar the things which are
Cæsar's; and unto God the things that are God's." It   18

Allegiance
to Spirit

saith to the human sense of sin, sickness, and
death, "God never made you, and you are a
false sense which hath no knowledge of God." The pur-   21
pose of the Hebrew allegory, representing error as assum-
ing a divine character, is to teach mortals never to believe
a lie.   24

Genesis iv. 3, 4. Cain brought of the fruit of the ground
an offering unto the Lord [Jehovah]. And Abel, he also
brought of the firstlings of his flock, and of the fat thereof.   27

Cain is the type of mortal and material man, conceived

Spiritual and
material

in sin and "shapen in iniquity;" he is not the
type of Truth and Love. Material in origin   30
and sense, he brings a material offering to God. Abel

takes his offering from the firstlings of the flock. A lamb 1
is a more animate form of existence, and more nearly resembles a mind-offering than does Cain's fruit. Jealous 3
of his brother's gift, Cain seeks Abel's life, instead of making his own gift a higher tribute to the Most High.

Genesis iv. 4, 5. And the Lord [Jehovah] had respect 6
unto Abel, and to his offering: but unto Cain, and to his
offering, He had not respect.

Had God more respect for the homage bestowed through 9
a gentle animal than for the worship expressed by Cain's
fruit? No; but the lamb was a more spiritual type of
even the human concept of Love than the herbs of the 12
ground could be.

Genesis iv. 8. Cain rose up against Abel his brother, and
slew him. 15

The erroneous belief that life, substance, and intelligence can be material ruptures the life and brotherhood
of man at the very outset. 18

Genesis iv. 9. And the Lord [Jehovah] said unto Cain,
Where is Abel thy brother? And he said, I know not: Am
I my brother's keeper? 21

Here the serpentine lie invents new forms. At first it
Brotherhood usurps divine power. It is supposed to say
repudiated in the first instance, "Ye shall be as gods." 24
Now it repudiates even the human duty of man towards
his brother.

Genesis iv. 10, 11. And He [Jehovah] said, ... The 27
voice of thy brother's blood crieth unto Me from the ground.
And now art thou cursed from the earth.

The belief of life in matter sins at every step. It in-   1
curs divine displeasure, and it would kill Jesus that it

Murder brings its curse   might be rid of troublesome Truth. Material   3
beliefs would slay the spiritual idea when-
ever and wherever it appears. Though error hides
behind a lie and excuses guilt, error cannot forever be   6
concealed. Truth, through her eternal laws, unveils
error. Truth causes sin to betray itself, and sets upon
error the mark of the beast. Even the disposition to   9
excuse guilt or to conceal it is punished. The avoidance
of justice and the denial of truth tend to perpetuate sin,
invoke crime, jeopardize self-control, and mock divine   12
mercy.

Genesis iv. 15. And the Lord [Jehovah] said unto him,
Therefore whosoever slayeth Cain, vengeance shall be taken   15
on him sevenfold. And the Lord [Jehovah] set a mark
upon Cain, lest any finding him should kill him.

"They that take the sword shall perish with the   18
sword." Let Truth uncover and destroy error in God's

Retribution and remorse   own way, and let human justice pattern the
divine. Sin will receive its full penalty, both   21
for what it is and for what it does. Justice marks
the sinner, and teaches mortals not to remove the
waymarks of God. To envy's own hell, justice con-   24
signs the lie which, to advance itself, breaks God's
commandments.

Genesis iv. 16. And Cain went out from the presence of   27
the Lord [Jehovah], and dwelt in the land of Nod.

The sinful misconception of Life as something less

SUN. The symbol of Soul governing man, — of   1
Truth, Life, and Love.

SWORD. The idea of Truth; justice. Revenge;   3
anger.

TARES. Mortality; error; sin; sickness; disease;
death.   6

TEMPLE. Body; the idea of Life, substance, and intelligence; the superstructure of Truth; the shrine of
Love; a material superstructure, where mortals congre-   9
gate for worship.

THUMMIM. Perfection; the eternal demand of divine
Science.   12
    The Urim and Thummim, which were to be on Aaron's
breast when he went before Jehovah, were holiness and
purification of thought and deed, which alone can fit us   15
for the office of spiritual teaching.

TIME. Mortal measurements; limits, in which are
summed up all human acts, thoughts, beliefs, opinions,   18
knowledge; matter; error; that which begins before,
and continues after, what is termed death, until the mortal
disappears and spiritual perfection appears.   21

TITHE. Contribution; tenth part; homage; gratitude.
A sacrifice to the gods.

UNCLEANLINESS. Impure thoughts; error; sin; dirt.   24

UNGODLINESS. Opposition to the divine Principle and
its spiritual idea.

UNKNOWN. That which spiritual sense alone compre- 1
hends, and which is unknown to the material senses.

Paganism and agnosticism may define Deity as "the 3
great unknowable;" but Christian Science brings God
much nearer to man, and makes Him better known as
the All-in-all, forever near. 6

Paul saw in Athens an altar dedicated "to the unknown
God." Referring to it, he said to the Athenians: "Whom
therefore ye ignorantly worship, Him declare I unto you." 9
(Acts xvii. 23.)

URIM. Light.

The rabbins believed that the stones in the breast- 12
plate of the high-priest had supernatural illumination,
but Christian Science reveals Spirit, not matter, as the
illuminator of all. The illuminations of Science give us 15
a sense of the nothingness of error, and they show the
spiritual inspiration of Love and Truth to be the only fit
preparation for admission to the presence and power of 18
the Most High.

VALLEY. Depression; meekness; darkness.

"Though I walk through the valley of the shadow of 21
death, I will fear no evil." (Psalm xxiii. 4.)

Though the way is dark in mortal sense, divine Life
and Love illumine it, destroy the unrest of mortal thought, 24
the fear of death, and the supposed reality of error. Christian Science, contradicting sense, maketh the valley to bud
and blossom as the rose. 27

VEIL. A cover; concealment; hiding; hypocrisy.

The Jewish women wore veils over their faces in token

of reverence and submission and in accordance with Pharisaical notions. 1

The Judaic religion consisted mostly of rites and cere- 3 monies. The motives and affections of a man were of little value, if only he appeared unto men to fast. The great Nazarene, as meek as he was mighty, rebuked the 6 hypocrisy, which offered long petitions for blessings upon material methods, but cloaked the crime, latent in thought, which was ready to spring into action and crucify God's 9 anointed. The martyrdom of Jesus was the culminating sin of Pharisaism. It rent the veil of the temple. It revealed the false foundations and superstructures of super- 12 ficial religion, tore from bigotry and superstition their coverings, and opened the sepulchre with divine Science, — immortality and Love. 15

WILDERNESS. Loneliness; doubt; darkness. Spontaneity of thought and idea; the vestibule in which a material sense of things disappears, and spiritual sense 18 unfolds the great facts of existence.

WILL. The motive-power of error; mortal belief; animal power. The might and wisdom of God. 21

"For this is the will of God." (I Thessalonians iv. 3.)

Will, as a quality of so-called mortal mind, is a wrong- 24 doer; hence it should not be confounded with the term as applied to Mind or to one of God's qualities.

WIND. That which indicates the might of omnipo- 27 tence and the movements of God's spiritual government, encompassing all things. Destruction; anger; mortal passions. 30

The Greek word for *wind* (*pneuma*) is used also for *spirit*, as in the passage in John's Gospel, the third chapter, where we read: "The wind [*pneuma*] bloweth where it listeth. . . . So is every one that is born of the Spirit [*pneuma*]." Here the original word is the same in both cases, yet it has received different translations, as in other passages in this same chapter and elsewhere in the New Testament. This shows how our Master had constantly to employ words of material significance in order to unfold spiritual thoughts. In the record of Jesus' supposed death, we read: "He bowed his head, and gave up the ghost;" but this word *ghost* is *pneuma*. It might be translated *wind* or *air*, and the phrase is equivalent to our common statement, "He breathed his last." What Jesus gave up was indeed air, an etherealized form of matter, for never did he give up Spirit, or Soul.

WINE. Inspiration; understanding. Error; fornication; temptation; passion.

YEAR. A solar measurement of time; mortality; space for repentance.

"One day is with the Lord as a thousand years." (II Peter iii. 8.)

One moment of divine consciousness, or the spiritual understanding of Life and Love, is a foretaste of eternity. This exalted view, obtained and retained when the Science of being is understood, would bridge over with life discerned spiritually the interval of death, and man would be in the full consciousness of his immortality and eternal harmony, where sin, sickness, and death are unknown. Time is a mortal thought, the divisor of which

is the solar year. Eternity is God's measurement of Soul-   1
filled years.

You. As applied to corporeality, a mortal; finity.   3

ZEAL. The reflected animation of Life, Truth, and
Love. Blind enthusiasm; mortal will.

ZION. Spiritual foundation and superstructure; in-   6
spiration; spiritual strength. Emptiness; unfaithful-
ness; desolation.

Chapter 18

Fruitage

Wherefore by their fruits ye shall know them. — JESUS.

That ye might walk worthy of the Lord unto all pleasing,
being fruitful in every good work,
and increasing in the knowledge of God. — PAUL.

Let us get up early to the vineyards;
let us see if the vine flourish, whether the tender grape appear,
and the pomegranates bud forth. — SOLOMON'S SONG.

T housands of letters could be presented in testimony of the healing efficacy of Christian Science and particularly concerning the vast number of people who have been reformed and healed through the perusal or study of this book.

For the assurance and encouragement of the reader, a few of these letters are here republished from THE CHRISTIAN SCIENCE JOURNAL and CHRISTIAN SCIENCE SENTINEL. The originals are in the possession of the Editor, who can authenticate the testimonials which follow.

RHEUMATISM HEALED

I was a great sufferer from a serious form of rheumatic trouble, my hands being affected to such an extent that it was impossible for me even to dress without assistance. The trouble finally reached the knees, and I became very lame and had to be assisted in and out of bed. I went to the different health resorts for the benefit I hoped to derive from the baths and waters that were prescribed by physicians, but found no permanent relief. I was placed under an X-ray examination, and was told that the joints were becoming ossified. I then consulted a celebrated specialist, who after a thorough examination said my condition would continue to grow worse and that I would become completely helpless.

At that time a copy of "Science and Health with Key to the Scriptures" by Mrs. Eddy was loaned me. I read it more from curiosity than with the thought of any physical benefit. As the truth was unfolded to me, I realized that the mental condition was what needed correcting, and that the Spirit of truth which inspired this book was my physician. My healing is complete, and the liberation in thought is manifest in a life of active usefulness rather than the bondage of helpless invalidism and suffering. I owe to our beloved Leader, Mrs. Eddy, gratitude which words cannot express. Her revelation of the practical rather than the merely theoretical application of Jesus' words, "Ye shall know the truth, and the truth shall make you free," proved to be my redeemer. I did not even have to apply to a practitioner, but am most grateful for the helpful words of loving friends. — E. B. B., Pasadena, Cal.

ASTIGMATISM AND HERNIA HEALED

It is nearly five years since I bought my first copy of Science and Health, the reading of which cured me of chronic constipation, nervous headache, astigmatism, and hernia, in less than four months.

Where would I be now, had not this blessed truth been brought to me by much persuasion of a very dear friend?

I certainly should have been deep in the slough of despond, if not in the grave. Am I truly thankful for all the good that has come to me and mine? I try to let my works testify of that; but to those whom I do not meet in person, I can truly say, Yes; I am indeed more thankful than words can express for the glorious healing that has come to me, both physical, mental, and moral, and I also convey herein, my song of gratitude to the dear Leader who has through her fidelity to Truth enabled me to touch at least the hem of Christ's garment. — B. S. J., Sioux City, Iowa.

SUBSTANCE OF LUNGS RESTORED

It was about fifteen years ago that Christian Science first came to my notice. At that time I had been a chronic invalid for a good many years. I had acute bowel trouble, bronchitis, and a number of other troubles. One physician had told me that my lungs were like wet paper, ready to tear at any time, and I was filled with fear, as my mother, two brothers, and a sister had been victims of consumption. I tried many physicians and every material remedy that promised help, but no help came until I found a copy of Mrs. Eddy's book, Science and Health. The book was placed in my hands by one who did not then appreciate it, and I was told that it would be hard for me to understand it. I commenced reading it with this thought, but I caught beautiful glimpses of Truth, which took away my fear and healed me of all those diseases, and they have never returned.

I would also like to tell how I was healed of a sprained

ankle. The accident occurred in the morning, and all
that day and during the night I gave myself Christian
Science treatment, as best I could. The next morning
it seemed to be no better, being very sore, badly swollen,
and much discolored. Feeling that I had done all I could,
I decided to stop thinking about it. I took my copy of
Science and Health and began reading. Very soon I
became so absorbed in the book that I forgot all about
my ankle; it went entirely out of my thought, for I had
a glimpse of all God's creation as spiritual, and for the
time being lost sight of my material selfhood. After two
hours I laid the book down and walked into another room.
When next I thought of my ankle, I found it was not hurt-
ing me. The swelling had gone down, the black and blue
appearance had nearly vanished, and it was perfectly well.
It was healed while I was "absent from the body" and
"present with the Lord." This experience was worth
a great deal to me, for it showed me how the healing is
done. — C. H., Portland, Ore.

FIBROID TUMOR HEALED IN A FEW DAYS

My gratitude for Christian Science is boundless. I
was afflicted with a fibroid tumor which weighed not
less than fifty pounds, attended by a continuous hemorrhage for eleven years. The tumor was a growth of
eighteen years.

I lived in Fort Worth, Tex., and I had never heard
of Christian Science before leaving there for Chicago
in the year 1887. I had tried to live near to God, and
I feel sure He guided me in all my steps to this healing and saving truth. After being there several weeks

I received letters from a Texas lady who had herself been healed, and who wrote urging me to try Christian Science.

Changing my boarding-place, I met a lady who owned a copy of Science and Health, and in speaking to her of having seen the book, she informed me she had one, and she got it and told me I could read it. The revelation was marvellous and brought a great spiritual awakening. This awakened sense never left me, and one day when walking alone it came to me very suddenly that I was healed, and I walked the faster declaring every step that I was healed. When I reached my boarding-place, I found my hostess and told her I was healed. She looked the picture of amazement. The tumor began to disappear at once, the hemorrhage ceased, and perfect strength was manifest.

There was no joy ever greater than mine for this Christ-cure, for I was very weary and heavy laden. I thought very little of either sleeping or eating, and my heart was filled with gratitude, since I knew I had touched the hem of his garment.

I must add that the reading of Science and Health, and that alone, healed me, and it was the second copy I ever saw. — S. L., Fort Worth, Tex.

SPINAL TROUBLE AND INDIGESTION HEALED

For many years I have relied wholly upon Christian Science for healing; and I am glad to acknowledge the spiritual help and many other benefits received from following its teachings. I have great cause to be grateful to God and to our revered Leader, Mrs. Eddy, for these blessings, which her discovery and love for humanity made possible. I had read but a few pages in our textbook, "Science and Health with Key to the Scriptures," when I saw that it was the truth, and that it contained something I had thought could never be found in this existence. Proofs of healing came immediately, and I was able to do much useful work without a sense of burden or fatigue.

As time went on I learned the nothingness of discouragement, and understood in a measure that God is my Life and that all action is in divine Mind. I was healed of spinal trouble; and nervousness and weakness faded away and were replaced by health and strength. A larger sense of joy and gratitude did much towards overcoming indigestion, which had caused suffering for a number of years. A sprained ankle was cured in a few hours by applying what I understood of Christian Science, and by holding steadfastly to the statement our Leader makes on page 384 of Science and Health, that "God never punishes man for doing right, for honest labor, or for deeds of kindness." The following day I walked two miles with no sense of discomfort. Beliefs of heredity and lack have been overcome, and self-will, self-love, and pride are less in evidence. — Miss G. W., Brookline, Mass.

A CASE OF MENTAL SURGERY

I have felt for some time I should give my experience in mental surgery. In May, 1902, going home for lunch, on a bicycle, and while riding down a hill at a rapid gait, I was thrown from the wheel, and falling on my left side with my arm under my head, the bone was broken about half-way between the shoulder and

elbow. While the pain was intense, I lay still in the dust,
declaring the truth and denying that there could
be a break or accident in the realm of divine Love,
until a gentleman came to assist me, saying, he
thought I had been stunned. I was only two and a
half blocks from home, so I mounted my wheel again
and managed to reach it. On arriving there I lay
down and asked my little boy to bring me our textbook. He immediately brought Science and Health,
which I read for about ten minutes, when all pain left.

I said nothing to my family of the accident, but attended to some duties and was about half an hour late
in returning to the office, this being my only loss of time
from work. My friends claimed that the arm had not
been broken, as it would have been impossible for me to
continue my work without having it set, and carrying it
in a sling until the bone knit together. Their insistence
almost persuaded me that I might have been mistaken,
until one of my friends invited me to visit a physician's
office where they were experimenting with an X-ray ma-
chine. The physician was asked to examine my left
arm to see if it differed from the ordinary. On looking through it, he said, "Yes, it has been broken, but
whoever set it made a perfect job of it, and you will
never have any further trouble from that break." My
friend then asked the doctor to show how he could
tell where the break had been. The doctor pointed
out the place as being slightly thicker at that part,
like a piece of steel that had been welded. This
was the first of several cases of mental surgery that
have come under my notice, and it made a deep
impression on me.

For the benefit of others who may have something similar to meet, I will say that I have overcome almost constant attacks of sick headaches, extending back to my earliest recollection. — L. C. S., Salt Lake City, Utah.

CATARACT QUICKLY CURED

I wish to add my testimony to those of others, and hope that it may be the means of bringing some poor sufferer to health, to happiness, and to God. I was healed through simply reading this wonderful book, Science and Health. I had been troubled periodically for many years with sore eyes, and had been to many doctors, who called the disease iritis and cataract. They told me that my eyes would always give me trouble, and that I would eventually lose my sight if I remained in an office, and advised me to go under an operation. Later on I had to wear glasses at my work, also out of doors as I could not bear the winds, and my eyes were gradually becoming worse. I could not read for longer than a few minutes at a time, otherwise they would smart severely. I had to rest my eyes each evening to enable me to use them the next day; in fact gas-light was getting unbearable because of the pain, and I made home miserable. A dear brother told me about Christian Science, and said that if I would read Science and Health it would help me. He procured for me the loan of the book. The first night I read it, it so interested me I quite forgot all about my eyes until my wife remarked that it was eleven o'clock. I found that I had been reading this book for nearly four hours, and I remarked immediately after, "I believe my eyes are cured," which was really the case. The next day, on looking at my eyes, my wife noticed that the cataract had disappeared. I put away my outdoor glasses, which I have not required since, and through the understanding gained by studying Christian Science I have been able to do away with my indoor glasses also, and have had no return of pain in my eyes since. This is now a year and a half ago. — G. F. S., Liverpool, England.

VALVULAR HEART DISEASE HEALED

Fourteen years ago my heart awoke to gratitude to God and the dear Leader at the same time. After a patient and persistent effort of three months' duration, to procure a copy of Science and Health (during which time I had visited every bookstore, and many of the second-hand bookstores in the city of St. Paul), and had failed to find it, I at last remembered that the stranger who told me I might be healed, had mentioned a name, and McVicker's Theatre Building in Chicago as being in some way connected with the work. I sent there for information regarding a book called Health and Science, and the return mail brought me the book, Science and Health, and in it I at once found sure promise of deliverance from valvular heart disease, with all the accompaniments, such as extreme nervousness, weakness, dyspepsia, and insomnia. I had suffered from these all my life, finding no permanent relief, even, in material remedies, and no hope of cure at any time. Only those who have been held in such bondage and have been liberated by the same means, can know the eager joy of the first perusal of that wonderful book.

Half a day's reading convinced me that I had found the way to holiness and health. I read on, thinking only of the spiritual enlightenment, content to wait until I should be led to some person who would heal me; but old things had passed away, and all things had become new. I was completely healed before I had met a Scientist, or one who knew anything about Christian Science, and before I had read a line of any other Christian Science literature except one leaf of a tract; so it is absolutely certain that the healing was entirely impersonal, as was also the teaching, which enabled me to begin at once demonstrating the power of Truth to destroy all forms of error. — E. J. W., North Yakima, Wash.

THE TRUE PHYSICIAN FOUND

It is with a deep sense of gratitude that I send the particulars of my healing through Christian Science. While visiting friends in the southwestern part of Ontario, about three years ago, my attention was called to Christian Science and the wonderful healing it was doing. I had lived in New York for twenty-five years, but had never heard of Christian Science before, to my recollection.

Up to that time, for seventeen years, I had suffered with indigestion and gastritis in the worst form, often being overcome from a seeming pressure against the heart. I had asthma for four years, also had worn glasses for four years. It seemed to me that I had swallowed every known medicine to relieve my indigestion, but they only gave me temporary benefit. I purchased a copy of Science and Health, and simply from the reading of that

grand book I was completely healed of all my physical
ailments in two weeks' time. I have used no medicine from that day to this, and with God's help, and
the wonderful light revealed to me through the reading
of Mrs. Eddy's book, I never expect to again. I used
to smoke eight or ten cigars a day, and also took an
occasional drink, but the desire for these has gone, — I
feel forever. I travel on the road, and am constantly
being invited to indulge, but it is no effort to abstain,
and in many instances I find that my refusal helps
others.

While I fully appreciate the release from my physical
troubles, this pales into insignificance in comparison with
the spiritual uplifting Christian Science has brought me.
I had not been inside a church for more than ten years,
to attend regular services, until I entered a Christian
Science church. What I saw and realized there, seemed
so genuine that I loved Christian Science from the very
start. I have never taken a treatment, — every inch
of the way has been through study and practical demonstration, and I know that all can do the same thing if they
will try.

Since I have been in Science I have overcome a case of
ulcerated tooth in one night through the reading of Science
and Health; also a severe attack of grip in thirty-six hours
by obeying the Scripture saying, "Physician, heal thyself." — B. H. N., New York, N. Y.

CANCER AND CONSUMPTION HEALED

I was a great sufferer for many years from internal
cancer and consumption. I was treated by the best of

I had long been a member of a Bible class in an orthodox Sabbath school, but I never felt satisfied with that which was taught; there was something lacking, I did not understand then what it was. I purchased a copy of Science and Health and began to study it. I wish I could express in words what that book brought me. It illumined the Bible with a glorious light and I began to understand some of the Master's sayings, and tried to apply them.

I had had a longing to live a better Christian life for many years, and often wondered why I failed so utterly to understand the Bible. Now I knew; it was lack of spiritual apprehension.

I did not know at first that people were healed of disease and sin by simply reading Science and Health, but found after a while that such was the case. At that time I had many physical troubles, and one after another of these ills simply disappeared and I found that I had no disease, — I was perfectly free. The spiritual uplifting was glorious, too, and as I go on in the study of this blessed Science, I find I am gaining surely an understanding that helps me to overcome both sin and disease in myself and in others. My faith in good is increased and I know I am losing my belief in evil as a power equal to good. The pathway is not wearisome, because each victory over self gives stronger faith and a more earnest desire to press on. — E. J. R., Toledo, Ohio.

GRATEFUL FOR MORAL AND SPIRITUAL AWAKENING

About four years ago, after I had tried different ways and means to be relieved from bodily suffering, a faithful friend called my attention to the teaching of Christian Science. After some opposition, I decided to investigate it, with the thought that if this teaching would be helpful, it was meant for me as well as for others; if it did not afford any help, I could put it aside again, but that I would find out and be convinced.

After I had read Mrs. Eddy's work, Science and Health, a few days, I found that my ailments had disappeared, and a rest had come to me which I had never before known. I had smoked almost incessantly, although I had often determined to use my will power and never smoke again, but had always failed. This desire as well as the desire for drink simply disappeared, and I wish to say here, that I received all these benefits before I had gained much understanding of what I was reading. Like a prisoner, who had been in chains for years, I was suddenly set free. I did not then know how the chain had been removed, but I had to acknowledge that it came through the reading of this book. I then felt an ardent desire to read more, and to know what this power was that had freed me in a few days of that which I had been trying for years to shake off and had failed. It then became clear to me that this was the truth which Jesus Christ taught and preached to free humanity almost two thousand years ago. It did not, however, occur to me to apply it in my business affairs; on the contrary, I first thought that if I continued in my study I would have to retire from business.

This did not happen, however, for I gradually found that the little understanding of this wonderful teaching which I had acquired became a great help to me in my business. I became more friendly, more honest, more loving to my fellow-men; and I also acquired better judgment and was able to do the right thing at the right time. As a natural result my business improved. Before I knew anything of Christian Science my business had often been a burden to me, fear and worry deprived me of my rest. How different it is now! Through the study of the Bible, which now possesses unmeasurable treasures for me, and of our textbook, Science and Health, and the other works of our Leader, I receive peace and confidence in God and that insight into character which is necessary for the correct management of any business. — W. H. H., Bloomfield, Neb.

HEREDITARY DISEASE OF THE LUNGS CURED

For a long time I have been impelled to contribute a testimony of the healing power of Truth. As I read other testimonies and rejoice in them, some one may rejoice in mine. I was healed by reading Science and Health. By applying it, I found it to be the truth that Jesus taught, — the truth that sets free.

From childhood I had never known a well day. I was healed of lung trouble of long standing. Consumption was hereditary in our family, my mother and three brothers having passed on with it. The law of *materia medica* said that in a short time I must follow them. I also had severe stomach trouble of over eight years' standing, during which time I always retired without supper, as the fear of suffering from my food was so great that I denied myself food when hungry. For over twenty years I had ovarian trouble, which was almost unbearable at times. It dated from

the birth of my first child, and at one time necessitated
an operation. I suffered with about all the ills that
flesh is heir to: I had trouble with my eyes from a child;
wore glasses for fourteen years, several oculists saying
I would go blind, one declaring I would be blind in less
than a year if I did not submit to an operation, which I
refused to do.

But thanks be to God whose Truth reached me through
the study of our textbook. Words fail to express what
Christian Science has done for me in various ways, for
my children, my home, my all. The physical healing
is but a small part; the spiritual unfolding and uplifting
is the "pearl of great price," the half that·has never been
told. — Mrs. J. P. M., Kansas City, Mo.

TEXTBOOK APPRECIATED

It has been my privilege to have interviews with
representatives of more than sixty per cent of the nations of this earth, under their own vine and fig-tree.
I had never heard a principle understandingly advanced that would enable mankind to obey the apostolic command, "prove all things," until Science and
Health with Key to the Scriptures was placed in my
hands. I believe that the honest study of this book
in connection with the Bible will enable one to "prove
all things."

I make this unqualified statement because of what
my eyes have seen and my ears heard from my fellow-
men of unquestioned integrity, and the positive proofs
I have gained by the study of these books. Many
supposed material laws that had been rooted and

grounded in my mentality from youth have been overcome. It required some time for me to wake up to our Leader's words in Miscellaneous Writings, p. 206: "The advancing stages of Christian Science are gained through growth, not accretion." I had many disappointments and falls before I was willing to do the scientific work required to prove this statement; yet notwithstanding the cost to ourselves, I am convinced that we cannot do much credit to the cause we profess to love until we place ourselves in a position to prove God as He really is to us individually, and our relation to Him, by scientific work.

I wish to express loving gratitude to our Leader for the new edition of Science and Health. In studying this new edition one cannot help seeing the wisdom, love, and careful and prayerful thought expressed in the revision. Often the changing of a single word in a sentence makes the scientific thought not only more lucid to him who is familiar with the book, but also to those just coming into the blessed light. All honor to that God-loving, God-fearing woman, Mary Baker G. Eddy, whose only work is the work of love in the helping of mankind to help themselves; who has placed before her fellow-men understandingly, what man's divine rights are, and what God really is. — H. W. B., Hartford, Conn.

RUPTURE AND OTHER SERIOUS ILLS HEALED

When I took up the study of Christian Science nearly three years ago, I was suffering from a very bad rupture of thirty-two years' standing. Sometimes the pain was so severe that it seemed as if I could not endure it. These spells would last four or five hours, and while everything was done for me that could be done, no permanent relief came to me until I commenced reading Science and Health with Key to the Scriptures. After I had once looked into it I wanted to read all the time. I was so absorbed in the study of the "little book" that I hardly realized when the healing came, but I was healed, not only of the rupture, but also of other troubles, — inflammatory rheumatism, catarrh, corns, and bunions.

I would never part with the book if I could not get another. I am seventy-seven years old, and am enjoying very good health. — Mrs. M. E. P., St. Johnsbury, Vt.

MOTHER AND DAUGHTER HEALED

When Christian Science came to me, I had been taking medicine every day for twenty years, on account of constipation. I had been treated by doctors and specialists; had taken magnetic treatments and osteopathy; had tried change of climate; had an operation in a hospital, and when I came out was worse than before. I was so discouraged, after I had tried everything I ever heard of, and was no better but rather grew worse, that it seemed as though I must give up trying to get well, when a friend suggested that I try Christian Science. I had heard that Christian Scientists healed by prayer, and I thought this must be the way Jesus had healed. I felt that this was all there was left for me to try. I sent for the book, Science and Health, and commenced to read it out of curiosity, not thinking or knowing that I could be helped by the reading, but thinking I must still take medicine and that I must also have treatment by a Scientist. I, however, dropped my medicine and read for three days; then a light began to shine in the darkness. I was healed of the trouble and have never had to take medicine since. I have studied Science and Health faithfully ever since, and other ailments have disappeared. My little daughter has also been healed and has learned to use this knowledge in her school work. — Mrs. O. R., Leadville, Col.

LIVER COMPLAINT HEALED

As my thoughts go back to the time when I believed I had nothing to live for, and when each morning's awaking from sleep brought a sense of disappointment to find myself still among the living (for I had hoped each night that I closed my eyes in sleep that it would be the last time), my heart overflows with love and gratitude to God for our dear Leader who discovered this blessed truth and to the dear ones who have helped me so lovingly and patiently over many rough places.

Twelve years ago, I consulted a physician because I had noticed some odd-looking spots on one of my arms. He said they were liver spots, but that it was not worth while prescribing for those few, that I should wait until I was covered with them. About three months later, with the exception of my face and hands, I was covered with them. Then I became alarmed and called on another physician who prescribed for me, but he finally said he could do no more for me. Other physicians were consulted with no better results. Six years ago, friends advised me to see their family physician, and when I called on him he said he was positive he could cure me, so I asked him to prescribe for me. At the

end of two years, after prescribing steadily, he said I
was so full of medicine that he was afraid to have me
take any more, and advised a rest. After having paid
out a small fortune, I was no better, and very much
discouraged.

Two years ago, having failed in business, I applied to
one of my patrons for a furnished room where I could
meet the few I still had left. This lady, who is a Christian
Scientist, loaned me Science and Health, and because
she asked me so often how I was getting on with the
book, I began reading it. I also attended the Wednesday evening meetings which I found very interesting.
After hearing the testimonies at the meetings, I decided
to speak to some practitioner about these spots, but
not until I had at least a hundred dollars on hand, because I thought I would require that amount for treatments, as I had been accustomed to paying high prices.
I had not inquired about prices, and in fact did not speak
to any one about my intentions, because I felt sensitive
on this subject. When I had read about half of Science
and Health, I missed the spots, and upon searching
could find no trace of them. They had entirely disappeared without treatment. In a few weeks the reading of that book had accomplished what *materia medica*
had failed to accomplish in ten years. It is impossible
to express the feeling of relief and happiness which came
over me then. — C. K., Astoria, N. Y.

A CONVINCING INVESTIGATION

While I have testified to those around me and in many
localities, of my healing in Christian Science, I feel that

it is high time I put the candle in the candlestick where all who will may see. My earliest recollection was a day of suffering, — a physical inheritance from my mother, which gave simple interest for a time until years advanced and compound interest was added. My father was a physician, and material remedies were used for my mother without avail, consequently his confidence in them for me was shaken, — in fact he often told me it was better to suffer without medicine than become a chronic doser, without pain.

I began teaching in early life and continued for more than twenty years, and during that time not a day passed without pain, or fear of pain, and only for my innate love of life it would have become an intolerable burden. For five years oatmeal was my chief food and I became almost as attached to it as Kaspar Hauser to his crust. I was early taught to have faith in God, and many times was relieved of pain only to have it appear again in an aggravated form.

At last my heart cried out for the living God, and the answer came by one of His messengers, who told me of Christian Science. I replied that I believed God could heal, but that I had no faith in the healing of Christian Science, but would like to investigate its theology, as it might aid in giving me some clue to the meaning of life. For three years I had searched the works of the most scientific writers to find the origin of life; many times I would think I had traced it to the beginning, but it would elude my grasp every time. One day in talking with my friend, she said she would like to loan me the textbook, Science and Health, which I very willingly accepted. Not long afterward I felt a severe attack of suffering. I opened the book for the first time and found a paragraph near the middle which attracted my attention. I read the same paragraph over and over for nearly two hours. When the tea bell rang I closed the book and I shall never forget my perception of the new heaven and the new earth, — everything in nature that I could see seemed to have been washed and made clean. The flowers that I have always loved so much, and that from childhood had told me such sweet stories, now spoke to me of the All-in-all, the hearts of my friends seemed kinder, — I had touched the hem of the garment of healing.

I ate my supper that evening forgetful of the preparations I had made for suffering, and when the next day began I was more zealous of good work than ever before. Since closing Science and Health at my first reading I have never been able to find the paragraph which I had read so many times over, the words seemed to have slipped away from me, but my joy knew no bounds at having found the pearl of great price. By the continued reading of the book I was entirely healed, and for fourteen years I have not seen a day of physical suffering. — Miss L. M., Rome, N. Y.

DEAFNESS AND DROPSY HEALED

I had been deaf from childhood. I suffered intensely after eating, and dropsy was another of my complaints. This, with consumption, caused one doctor to say, "It puzzles me; I have never seen such a case before as yours."

I met a friend who had been cured in Christian

Science, and she said, "Try Christian Science." I got
a copy of Science and Health and in three weeks I
was entirely cured. I felt uplifted. It seemed as if
God's arms were around and about me. I felt as if
heaven had come down to earth for me. After five
years of suffering can any one wonder at my unspeakable gratitude? — A. B., Pittsburgh, Pa.

GRATEFUL FOR MANY BLESSINGS

In 1894 I began the study of Christian Science. At
that time I was greatly in need of its healing truth.
For a number of years previous I had been a semi-
invalid with no hope of ever being well and strong
again. Several years before this time I had undergone
an operation which resulted in peritonitis. For three
years previous to my study of Science and Health
by Mrs. Eddy, I was scarcely ever free from headache
caused by the weakened and diseased condition of the
internal organs. At the time I began the study of
Christian Science I was taking five kinds of medicine.

I began to read Science and Health, and did not
take treatment, for I thought, "If this is truth, I shall
be healed; if it is not, I shall be able to detect it,
and will have nothing to do with it." I became a
devoted student and gradually my bodily diseases left
me, — I was free, and since that time, nearly ten
years ago, neither my two children nor myself have
taken any medicine; and our understanding of truth
has been able to meet and overcome any suggestion of
illness.

I was a devoted member of an orthodox church,

but as I grew older I began to question my beliefs, and to my questions I could find no satisfactory answer. I became dissatisfied and finally ceased attending church. I could not accept the idea of God taught there, and at last my friends looked sadly upon me as an atheist. There I stood until I learned to know God as revealed in Science and Health, and then all my questionings were answered. In my girlhood I had always prayed to the God I held in mind, and when the shadows of sickness, pain, and death came to my family, I prayed as only those can who know that if He helps not, there is none; but my prayers were unanswered. Then I closed my Bible, saying, "There is a mistake somewhere, perhaps some time I may know."

Only those who know the attitude of mind that I was in can understand the joy that came to me as I began to learn of God in Christian Science, and of my relation to Him.

Many proofs of the healing power of Truth and of His protecting care throng my thoughts. Seven years ago, when we were in a far distant country, where Christian Science was then unknown, my little daughter came in one morning from her school, saying, "Mother, I have measles; twenty of the girls are sick in bed and I am afraid they will put me there also." Her face, hands, and chest were covered with a deep red rash, throat sore, and eyes inflamed. We began immediately to do our work in Science and at night, when I left her at the door of the college, her face was clear, her eyes bright, and all fear destroyed. That was the end of the disease. — F. M. P., Boston, Mass.

A JOYFUL EXPERIENCE

In love and gratitude to God, and to Mrs. Eddy, the interpreter of Jesus' beautiful teachings, I wish to tell of some of the benefits which I have received from Christian Science. It is a little over a year since Science found me in a deplorable condition, physically as well as mentally. I had ailments of many years' standing, — chronic stomach trouble, severe eye trouble, made almost unbearable from the constant fear of losing my sight (a fate which had befallen my mother), also a painful rupture of twenty-five years' standing. These ailments, combined with unhappy conditions in my home, made me very despondent. I had entirely lost my belief in an all-merciful God, and I did not know where to turn for help. At that time Christian Science was brought to my notice, and I shall never forget the sublime moment when I perceived that an all-loving Father is always with me. Forgotten was all sorrow and worry, and after four weeks' reading in Science and Health all my ailments had disappeared. I am to-day a healthy, contented woman.

All this has come to pass in one short year, and my earnest desire is to be more and more worthy to be called a child of God. This is in loving gratitude for an understanding of this glorious truth. — Mrs. R. J., Chicago, Ill.

AN EVER-PRESENT HELP

It is a year since I began to read Science and Health, and I will now try to outline what a knowledge of its teachings has done for me.

My condition was then very trying; my eyes, which
had caused me much trouble since childhood, were
very painful. For these I had been treated by some
of the best specialists in my native land, and after
coming to the United States I had been doctored
much and had worn glasses for four years. I also had
catarrh, for which I had taken much medicine without
being relieved. In addition to this I was an excessive
smoker, using tobacco in some form almost constantly.
I had contracted a smoker's heart, and used liquors
freely.

The one who brought to me that which I now prize
so highly, was a book agent. I told him that I should
be forced to leave my trade on account of my eyes.
He then told me of having been healed of a cancer,
through Christian Science treatment. He showed me
a copy of Science and Health, which had the signs of
much use, and after being assured that if I did my part
I would be healed of all my diseases, I sent for a copy of
the book.

My recovery was very rapid, for after reading the
book only three weeks I was completely healed of the
tobacco habit. I will say, in regard to this healing,
that it did not require even as much as a resolution
on my part. I was smoking a cigar, while reading
Science and Health, when all the desire to continue
smoking left me, and I have never had a desire to use
tobacco in any form since then. My eyes were the
next to manifest the influence of the new knowledge
gained, and had soon so far recovered that I could go
about my work with ease, and I have had no more
use for glasses. To-day my heart is normal, the catarrh

has totally disappeared, and I am not addicted to the use of liquor.

Christian Science has proved to be an ever-present help, not only in overcoming physical ailments, but in business and daily life. It has also overcome a great sense of fear. The Bible, which I regarded with suspicion, has become my guide, and Christianity has become a sweet reality, because the Christian Science textbook has indeed been a "Key to the Scriptures" and has breathed through the Gospel pages a sweet sense of harmony. — A. F., Sioux City, Iowa.

SEVERE EYE TROUBLE OVERCOME

After hearing Christian Science lightly spoken of, from a Christian pulpit, I decided to go to one of the services and hear for myself. From infancy I had been devoted to my church, and as soon as I was old enough I was ever active in the work. Feeling it to be my duty to attend every service held in my own church, I took advantage of the Wednesday evening meetings. My first visit was not my last, I am thankful to say, for I saw immediately that these people not only preached Christianity, but practised and lived it. At that time I was wearing glasses and had worn them for sixteen years. At times I suffered the most intense pain, and for this phase of the trouble, one specialist after another had been consulted. All gave me very much the same advice; each one urged extreme carefulness and gave me glasses that seemed to relieve for a time. None of them held out any hope that my sight would ever be restored, saying that the

defect had existed since infancy, and that in time I should
be blind.

The thought of blindness was very distressing to me,
but I tried to bear it with Christian resignation, since
I thought that God had seen fit to afflict me; but since
I have learned that He is a loving Father, who gives
only good, I regret that I ever charged Him with my
affliction. I had no treatment, but I read Science and
Health, and my eyes were healed and glasses laid aside.
I can never find words to express my thanks to our dear
Leader, through whose teachings my sight has been regained. I can truthfully say that "whereas I was blind,
now I see" — through an understanding of Truth I
have found my sight perfect as God gave it. — Miss
B. S., Wilmington, N. C.

A TESTIMONY FROM IRELAND

It is with a heart full of love and gratitude to God,
and to our dear Leader, that I send this testimony to
the Field. I had never been a strong girl; had always
been subject to colds and chills, and suffered all my
life from a delicate throat. Seven years ago I had a
very severe attack of rheumatic fever and subsequently
two less severe ones. These left all sorts of evils behind them, — debility, chronic constipation, and several
others, so that with these ills my life was often a
burden to me and I used to think I never should receive relief or health. I had also lost all love for
God and faith in Him. I could not accept a God who,
as I then believed, visited sickness and sorrow upon
His children as a means for drawing them to Him.

I was in this state of mind and body when Christian Science found me. A dear friend, seeing my suffering, presented the truth to me, and though at first I did not believe that there could be healing for me, the Christian Scientists' God seemed to be the one I had been looking for all my life. I began to read Science and Health, and shall never forget my joy at finding that I could love and trust God. I took to studying the Bible, and read nothing but Science and Health and other Christian Science literature for a year. After studying the "little book" for about six weeks, I one day realized that I was a well woman, that I had taken no medicine for three weeks, and that my body was perfectly harmonious. The reading of Science and Health had healed me. The wonderful joy and spiritual uplifting which came to me then no words of mine can describe. I had also suffered from astigmatism and had for several years been obliged to use special glasses when reading or working, and could never use my eyes for more than half an hour; but from the first reading of Science and Health I found that I could read in any light and for any length of time without the slightest discomfort. I am not only grateful for the physical healing but for the mental regeneration. I rejoice that I am now able to help others who are sick and sorrowing. — E. E. L., Curragh Camp, County Kildare, Ireland.

THE TEXTBOOK MAKES OPERATION UNNECESSARY

In the early part of the year 1895 my physician said I must undergo a surgical operation in order ever to be well.

While in great fear, and dreading the operation, a kind neighbor called, and after telling me of Christian Science gave me a copy of Science and Health. She said I must put aside all medicine, and by reading faithfully she knew I could be healed. The book became my constant companion, and in a short time I was healed. Besides the relief from an operation, I was completely healed of severe headaches and stomach trouble. Physicians could give me no help for either of these ailments. For ten years I have not used medicine of any kind, and have not missed a Christian Science service on account of sickness during this period. I am perfectly well. To say that I am grateful to God for all this does not express my feelings. The physical healing was wonderful, but the understanding given me of God, and the ability to help others outweigh all else. I also love our dear Leader. — Mrs. V. I. B., Concord, N. H.

KIDNEY DISEASE AND EYE TROUBLE HEALED

Early in 1904 I was teaching in a private boarding-school. I was a very unhappy, discontented woman; I had kidney disease, besides sore eyes, and my general health was very bad. The doctor said that the climate did not suit me, and that I certainly should have a change. The best thing, he said, was to go back to France (my own country); but I did not like to leave the school, so I struggled on until July, when we went travelling for a month, but I came home worse than ever. I had a lot of worry, one disappointment after another, and I often thought that life was not worth living. In September, 1904, we heard for the first time of Christian Science through a girl who was attending our boarding-school, and who was healed through Christian Science treatment. We bought the textbook, "Science and Health with Key to the Scriptures" by Mrs. Eddy, and what a revelation it was and is to us; it is indeed the fountain of Truth. I had read Science and Health but a very short time when I took off my glasses, began to sleep well, and soon found myself well in mind and body. Besides this, it has brought harmony into our school, where there had been discord, and everything is changed for the better. I cannot describe the happiness that has come to me through Christian Science; I can only exclaim with the psalmist: "Bless the Lord, O my soul;" and may God bless Mrs. Eddy.

My one aim now is to live Christian Science, not in words only, but in deeds; loving God more and my neighbor as myself, and following meekly and obediently all our Leader's teachings. Words cannot express my gratitude to Mrs. Eddy for Christian Science. — S. A. K., Vancouver, B. C.

DISEASE OF BOWELS HEALED

When I first heard of Christian Science I had been afflicted for nine years with a very painful disease of the bowels, which four physicians failed even to diagnose, all giving different causes for the dreadful sufferings I endured. The last physician advised me to take no more medicine for these attacks, as drugs would not reach the cause, or do any good. About this time I heard of Christian Science, and had the opportunity of reading "Science and Health with Key to the Scriptures" by Mrs. Eddy, a few minutes every day for about a week, and I

was thereby healed. In looking back I found I had not
suffered in the least from the time I began reading this
book. It has been nearly seventeen years since this wonderful healing, and I have had no return of the disease.
My gratitude is endless and can be best expressed by
striving mightily to walk in the path our Leader has so
lovingly shown us in Science and Health. — Mrs.
J. W. C., Scranton, Pa.

HEALED BY READING THE TEXTBOOK

After doctoring about a year, I was obliged to give
up school and was under medical care for two years;
but grew worse instead of better. I was then taken to
specialists, who pronounced my case incurable, saying
I was in the last stages of kidney disease and could
live only a short time. Shortly afterward my uncle
gave me a copy of "Science and Health with Key to
the Scriptures," and asked me to study it. After studying a short time I was able to walk a distance of several
miles, which I had not been able to do for three years.
I also laid aside glasses which I had worn seven years,
having been told I would become blind if my eyes did
not receive proper care. It is over a year since I received God's blessing, and I am now enjoying perfect
health and happiness. I have never had my glasses on
since I first began reading Science and Health, and I have
not used any medicine. — L. R., Spring Valley, Minn.

A TESTIMONY FROM SCOTLAND

I came to Christian Science purely for physical healing.
I was very ill and unhappy; very cynical and disbeliev-
ing in regard to what I heard of God and religion.

I tried to live my life in my own way and put religion aside. I was a great believer in fate and in will-power, and thought to put them in the place of God, with the consequence that I was led to do many rash and foolish things. I am now thankful to say that my outlook on life is entirely changed; I have proved God's wisdom and goodness so often that I am willing and thankful to know my future is in His hands and that all things must work out for the best. I have found a God whom I can love and worship with my whole heart, and I now read my Bible with interest and understanding.

I was healed of very bad rheumatism simply by reading Science and Health. I had tried many medicines, also massage, with no result, and the doctors told me that I would always suffer from this disease, as it was inherited, and also because I had rheumatic fever when a child. I suffered day and night, and nothing relieved me until Science proved to me the falseness of this belief by removing it. I gave up all the medicines I was taking and have never touched any since, and that is more than two years ago. Before this I had often tried to do without a medicine that I had taken every day for ten years, but was always ill and had to return to it, until I found out that one Mind is the only medicine, and then I was freed from the suffering.

I had also suffered constantly from bilious attacks, colds, and a weak chest, and had been warned not to be out in wet weather, etc., but now, I am glad to say, I am quite free from all those material laws and go out in all sorts of weather. — R. D. F., Edinburgh, Scotland.

CURING BETTER THAN ENDURING

For eight years I was a great sufferer from weak lungs and after being treated by ten different physicians, in the States of Illinois, Missouri, and Colorado, I was told there was no hope of my recovery from what they pronounced tuberculosis, which was hereditary, my father having been afflicted with it. I was greatly emaciated and hardly able to be about. My general condition was aggravated by what the doctors said was paralysis of the bowels. Three physicians so diagnosed it at different times, and assured my husband that I could never get more than temporary relief. This indeed I found difficult to obtain, in spite of my almost frantic efforts. At times I was nearly insane from suffering, and after eight years of doctoring I found myself steadily growing worse. For four years I did not have a normal action of the bowels, and it was only by extreme effort and by resort to powerful drugs or mechanical means, with resultant suffering, that any action whatever could be brought about.

I had heard nothing of the curative power of Christian Science, and only to oblige a friend I went one night, about three years ago, to one of their mid-week testimonial meetings, in Boulder, Colorado. I was much impressed by what I heard there, and determined at once to investigate this strange religion, in the hope that it might have something good for me. I bought the text-book, Science and Health, and from the first I found myself growing stronger and better, both physically and mentally, as I acquired a better understanding and endeavored to put into practice what I learned. In one week

I was able to get along better without drugs than I had for years with them, and before three months had passed I was better than I had been any time in my life, for I had always suffered more or less from bowel trouble. Since that time I have taken no medicine whatever, and rely wholly upon Christian Science. My lungs are now sound, my bowels normally active, my general health excellent, and I am able to endure without fatigue tasks that before would have prostrated me. The study of our textbook was the sole means of my healing. — L. M. St. C., Matachin, Canal Zone, Panama.

SEVERE ECZEMA DESTROYED

It is only two years since I came from darkness into the light of Christian Science, and to me the spiritual uplifting has been wonderful, to say nothing of the physical healing. Words cannot express my gratitude for benefits I have received in that time. For five years I suffered with that dreaded disease, eczema, all over my body. Five doctors said there was no help for me. The suffering seemed as terrible as the hell fire that I had been taught to believe in. When Christian Science came to me two years ago through a dear friend, she gave me a copy of Science and Health and asked me to read it. I told her that I would, for I was like a drowning man grasping at a straw. I had been a Bible student for twenty-eight years, but when I commenced reading Science and Health with the Bible I was healed in less than a week. I never had a treatment. A case of measles was also destroyed in twenty-four hours after it appeared. — Mrs. M. B. G., Vermilion, Ohio.

SCIENCE AND HEALTH A PRICELESS BOON

I am a willing witness to the healing power of Christian Science, having had a lifetime's battle with disease and medical experiments. Various doctors finally admitted that they had exhausted their resources, and could only offer me palliatives, saying that a cure was impossible. I had paralysis of the bowels, frequent sick headaches with unutterable agony, and my mortal career was nearly brought to an end by a malignant type of yellow fever. Many were the attending evils of this physical inharmony, but God confounds the wisdom of men, for while studying Science and Health two years ago, the veil of ignorance was lifted and perfect health was shown to me to be my real condition, and to such there is no relapse. The constant use of glasses, which were apparently a necessity to me for years, was proven needless, and they were laid aside. Mrs. Eddy has made Scripture reading a neverfailing well of comfort to me. By her interpretation "the way of the Lord" is made straight to me and mine. It aids us in our daily overcoming of the tyranny of the flesh and its rebellion against the blessed leading of Christ, Truth. The daily study of the Bible and our textbook is bringing more and more into our consciousness the power of God unto salvation. — J. C., Manatee, Fla.

A CRITIC CONVINCED

With gratitude to God I acknowledge my lifelong debt to Christian Science. In 1895 I attended my first

Christian Science meeting, and was deeply impressed
with the earnestness of the people and the love reflected, but as for the spiritual healing of the physical
body, I did not believe such a thing to be possible.
I bought Science and Health and studied it to be
able to dispute intelligently with the supposedly deluded followers of Christian Science. I pursued the
study carefully and thoroughly, and I have had abun-
dant reason since to be glad that I did, for through this
study, and the resultant understanding of my relation to God, I was healed of a disease with which I
had been afflicted since childhood and for which there
was no known remedy. Surely my experience has
been the fulfilling in part of the Scripture: "He sent
His Word and healed them, and delivered them from
their destructions." I believe that Science and Health
reveals the Word referred to by David. — C. A. B. B.,
Kansas City, Mo.

BORN AGAIN

It was in April, 1904, that I first heard the "still,
small voice" of the Christ and received healing through
Christian Science; and the blessings have been so
many since, that it would take too much space to
name them. Reared from childhood in an intellectual
atmosphere, my paternal grandfather having been an
orthodox minister of the old school for forty years,
and my father a deep student, ever seeking for the
truth of all things, I began early to ponder and to
study into the meaning of life, and came to the conclusion before I was twenty that though God probably

existed in some remote place, still it was impossible to connect Him with my present living. My highest creed, therefore, became, "Do right because it *is* right and not for fear of being punished." Then began the suffering. Sorrow after sorrow followed each other in rapid succession; for ten long years there was no rest, the road was indeed long and hard and had no turning, until finally the one thing that had stood by me all through the trials, namely, my health, gave way, and with that went my last hope. But the last hour of the night had come, the dawn of day was at hand; a dear friend left Science and Health upon my piano one day, saying that I would gain much good by reading it.

Glad to get away from my own poor thoughts, I opened the "little book" and began to read. I had read only a short time when such a wonderful transformation took place! I was renewed; born again. Mere words cannot tell the story of the mighty uplifting that carried me to the very gates of heaven. When I began to read the book, life was a burden, but before I had finished reading it the first time, I was doing all my housework and doing it easily; and since that glorious day I have been a well woman. My health is splendid, and I am striving to let my light so shine that others may be led to the truth. There have been some mighty struggles with error, and I have learned that we cannot reach heaven with one long stride or easily drift inside the gate, but that the "asking" and the "seeking" and the "knocking" must be earnest and persistent.

For a long time I was always looking back to see if